TO THE BITTER END

The Final Battles of
Army Groups North Ukraine, A, and Center—
Eastern Front, 1944–45

Rolf Hinze

Translated with editing and minor revisions and additions by
Frederick P. Steinhardt, MS, PhD

CASEMATE
Philadelphia & Newbury

Dedicated to all the members of the Army and the *Volksturm* who gave their lives defending the German homeland from the enemy's grasp.

This edition of *To the Bitter End* is published in the United States of America in 2010 by
CASEMATE
908 Darby Road, Havertown, PA 19083

and in the United Kingdom by
CASEMATE
17 Cheap Street, Newbury, RG14 5DD

Published by arrangement with Helion & Company Limited.

This English edition © Helion & Company Limited, 2005.

Originally published as *Letztes Aufgebot zur Verteidigung des Reichsgebiets. Kampfe der Heeresgruppe Nordukraine/A/Mitte.*
German edition © Verlag Dr Rolf Hinze 1995. All rights reserved.

Translated with editing, minor revisions and additions by
Frederick P. Steinhardt, MS, PhD.

ISBN 978-1-935149-31-6

Cataloging-in-publication data is available from the Library of Congress and the British Library.

Printed and bound in the United States of America.

10 9 8 7 6 5 4 3 2 1

For a complete list of Casemate titles, please contact:

Casemate Publishers
Telephone (610) 853-9131 /, Fax (610) 853-9146
E-mail casemate@casematepublishing.com / Website www.casematepublishing.com

Casemate-UK
Telephone (01635) 231091 / Fax (01635) 41619
E-mail casemate-uk@casematepublishing.co.uk / Website www.casematepublishing.co.uk

Contents

Part A: 1944

Part B: The Great Soviet Winter Offensive

Part C: The Advance into Silesia

Part D: Final Battles

List of Maps

Publisher's Note

The English edition of this book would not have been possible to produce without the help of a number of people.

First and foremost, the publishers would respectfully like to dedicate this book to its translator, Mr Frederick Steinhardt. Fred went well beyond the call of duty in terms of the input and the effort he put into his translation work. He was always available to answer any questions we had. Unfortunately, very shortly before this book went to print, Hurricane Katrina hit New Orleans where Fred lived. Fred was safe. However, in the subsequent upheaval he was unable to carry out a final check of the text. Readers should therefore note that any mistakes or errors are the responsibility of Helion, and not the translator.

I would also like to thank Ian Baxter, at History in the Making, who responded at very short notice to our request for photographs. I think readers will agree that the selection he came up with adds a great deal to this book.

Finally, I would like to thank our copy editors, Richard and Gwyneth Fairbank, for their contribution.

Duncan Rogers
Helion & Company Ltd

Foreword

History consists of what has happened. One must not forget that the present is built upon the events of the past. It is acknowledged that unreserved recognition is not always given to negative events, since too many factors affect humanity. Only thus can an explanation be found for the fact that negative phenomena in the history of a people, or a state, are occasionally repeated. Nevertheless, such phenomena permit certain conclusions that are only possible if one has knowledge of the events. Thus, it is necessary to record what happened, so that a conclusion can later be drawn from past events.

The manner of presentation must permit the formation of logical conclusions. It seems obvious that events should be presented as they happened, and as they were perceived at the time. Indeed, one must see what knowledge those participants might have had, at the time, that served as a basis for their action, or their inaction.

As the decades have passed, people have constantly gained new knowledge and new viewpoints. Therefore it is clearly extremely difficult to present events objectively, without tinting them through a personally motivated world view, or by becoming judgmental. Those difficulties apply especially to World War II, since the victorious powers released a counter-wave of propaganda, specifically through their "re-education" programme in their efforts to erase the Nazis' propaganda. In turn, that was based on the necessarily subjective propaganda put out during the war. The various hostile sides in a war almost inevitably develop their own propaganda.

"Re-education" took place in all areas of education in Germany, particularly in the schools, the education of teachers, and in the media. It seemed as if the German people would have to wear hair-shirts for decades, even though the individual might bear no personal guilt. There was much talk of collective moral guilt.

If that were to be applied to all peoples, then today the citizens of the former USSR would have to bear the moral guilt for the destruction of millions of people in the forced labour camps of the Soviet Gulag. Guilt would be assigned in exactly the same way as for the mass killings in the German concentration camps, some might say much more so, because of their extent. The citizens of the former USSR knew what happened to their family members in the various Stalinist purges. It cannot be asserted to the same extent regarding what German citizens knew of the horrors of the concentration camps.

In addition came the many trials at the hands of the victors, such as the Nuremberg Trials. They were to provide the basis for future judgement, by international law, of measures occurring within and between states, even with retroactive effect. Such a basis could have had a positive effect for the future development of relationships between nations. Later, it could have been applied to all peoples, and all statesmen and military personnel. Consider, however, that since 1945 there have already been more than 150 wars, and never has anyone been held responsible for their origins.

Basic principles that are only applied to a very specifically defined group of people, but not to all, cannot provide the basis for fundamental principles of law, but necessarily give the impression of measures of revenge, taken by the victors, under the cloak of justice. The phrase *Vae victis*, i.e. woe to the vanquished, ruled the process of law in Europe after the Second World War. One has only to look at the camps in which German civilians were confined in the Soviet zone of occupation, and the forced labour camps in which German prisoners of war were confined after the surrender. The British and Americans delivered people to the Russians, with subsequent 10 or 11 year terms of forced labour, and massive loss of life. Further back, one thinks of the time of the Russian Revolution, and the serial shootings of former emigrants, of members of the Vlassov Army, of Cossacks, Turkestanis and other peoples of the USSR who were "repatriated" to Russia by the British.

For decades, nothing was said of the atrocities perpetrated by the Red Army and Soviet partisans, upon German wounded especially, and workers in the rear areas. The highest courts and authorities of Britain, including Churchill and Eden, took the position that one had to maintain good relations with the Soviet Union because of the terms of the future peace. After the First World War, in contrast with their previous motivation of commitment of invasion forces to fight against the Red Army, they then professed to see the USSR as a constitutional state, and Stalin turning into a democrat.

Yet at the same time, there were reports of British officers being present when people were turned over to the Soviets. The reports indicated that some people were selected and shot by members of the Red Army or KGB. Regardless, the British delivered large numbers of former citizens of the USSR to the Red Army. Soviet prisoners of war, who had previously been in German hands, included those who had fought on the German side, or had worked in the *Organisation Todt*, even those of the *Ostarbeiter*, i.e. residents of conquered eastern territory who had been conscripted for labour.

Those people greatly feared penal action upon repatriation to their former homeland. Regardless of that, British officials allowed into the camp Soviet repatriation commissions that registered all persons unwilling to be repatriated. In accordance with the demands of the Soviet officers, the British immediately transferred all such people to separate camps. They were the first to be turned over to the Russians. Their fate was known from the reports of British officers regarding delivery of former Soviet citizens in Murmansk and Odessa. That did not prevent the British from sending many other former Soviet citizens, who did not wish to be repatriated, to the same fate.

Among the actions that were prosecuted, and subsequently resulted in convictions at the Nuremberg proceedings, were not only the conduct of a war of aggression, but also the delivery of peoples to forced labour. After 1945, the British in particular returned many thousands of former citizens to the USSR, for which they were never called to account.

Nor did anyone speak of the carpet-bombing of German cities that was directed against non-combatants. The provisions of the Hague Convention for the Conduct of Land Warfare expressly protected non-combatants. The silence regarding such operations that are contrary to international law, i.e. war crimes by the Western Powers, results in a totally distorted picture of the norms of behaviour in war.

1 Position of *Heeresgruppe Mitte*, 20 June 1944

This is particularly true with regard to the strict internal discipline of the *Wehrmacht*, which hardly anyone doubts. However, that has been overshadowed by the destruction of humanity in the concentration camps. That did not involve international measures. They were to be judged by the principles of international law, particularly those of the Hague Convention for the Conduct of Land Warfare.

The purpose of "re-education" was mainly to justify the compulsory measures taken against the German people. Those were the confiscation of areas of German territory, reparations, and the general trainloads of plunder in the form of dismantled factories. There was the punishment of those who resisted such dismantling by restriction of their necessities of life. There were countless other restrictions. A large part of the media, and many writers, followed up those restrictions.

Today, it is difficult to gain an objective picture of events, and conduct of the members of the various armies involved in the war. In any case, the endeavour for objective presentation of events can only move on to a time when the generation of the participants is smaller in number, and they no longer play a part in presenting an account of what actually happened. In addition, it is inescapable that members of later generations will naturally find it difficult to put themselves into the minds of those who actually took part in such historic events. Yet, without such a way of imagining, it seems that it will not be possible to write objective history.

Germany's prospects for victory collapsed with the fall of Stalingrad, and with them, the nimbus, i.e. the aura, of the invincibility of the *Wehrmacht*. That collapse strengthened the self-confidence of the soldiers of the Red Army. In addition, the combat theatres multiplied. It was not just a matter of combating the partisans in White Russia who seriously affected the removal of wounded, and the supply of personnel and materiel. There was then the battle against partisans in Yugoslavia, who were supported by Britain, the African Front, and later the Italian Front, and subsequently the Invasion Front.

The German homeland could not meet the demands of supplying personnel and materiel to all those fronts. In all sectors the troops felt that they were inadequately supported. There were shortages of medical supplies, weapons, ammunition and above all, fuel. It was necessary to be economical with everything. The Eastern Front especially, suffered from that enforced economy. The Red soldiers, on the other hand, had no concerns about fuel supplies and were, in addition, constantly reinforced. The USSR had an apparently inexhaustible reservoir of manpower. There were also Stalin's hobby-horses, i.e. the armoured forces and the artillery. Both of those received great support from the Western Powers, particularly by provision of tanks, shells and trucks. With such mobility and equipment the Red Army continued to forge ahead, following the horse-drawn German infantry.

Germany attempted to make good the shortage of combat formations by activating new formations, such as the Galician 14th *Waffen-Grenadier-Division der SS (ukrainische Nr. 1)*. It consisted of young Ukrainians from eastern Poland who came of military age during the German occupation. With totally inadequate military training, they were thrown into the battle near Brody, where they could not meet the expectations demanded of them. Hitler refused to employ other units based on foreign peoples, even though, in the meantime, a Vlassov-Army came into being with several fully equipped divisions. On the other hand a Cossack division and a Turkomen division fought well on the German side, the latter initially in Yugoslavia, and later on the Italian front. The Galician division was used in Slovakia, later in the South Ukraine and then in the Steiermark.

At the start of the Soviet summer offensive, *Heeresgruppe Nordukraine* had to give up formations to *Heeresgruppe Mitte*. They were then lacking in adequate defence when, some time later, the Soviet offensive started against the *Heeresgruppe*. *Heeresgruppe Mitte* then had to attempt to prepare for the Soviet assault by painstaking construction of positions, careful reconnaissance and the movement of troops. The shortage of formations became repeatedly evident in the later defensive fighting, where their lack of mobility was particularly critical. In addition, there were shortages in the supply of fuel, weapons and ammunition. Again and again individual elements were separated from their divisions and committed in other locations to fill the gaps. Finally, *Heeresgruppe Nordukraine* was forced to restrict its activities to preventing the Soviets from advancing too far to the west, into the *Generalgouvernement*. The *Generalgouvernement* was the administrative region established in the occupied section of Poland in 1939. The German effort was to build bridgeheads, employing the joint action of armour available from various *Panzer-Divisionen*, and the concentrated fire of the Divisions' artillery batteries.

The Soviet offensive against *Heeresgruppe Südukraine* finally necessitated the transfer of additional formations from *Heeresgruppe Nordukraine*. They were needed for the fighting in Siebenbürgen and in the Debrecen area, as well as in Slovakia. All of that complicated the mission of *Heeresgruppe Nordukraine*, namely in preventing the further advance of the Soviets to the west.

In July and August 1944, the Soviets withdrew a series of formations that had faced the central front of *Heeresgruppe Nordukraine*. Later that became their right wing. In fact the Soviets no longer concerned themselves with the planned breakthrough to the west towards Krakow, merely focusing on improving their jump-off positions for a planned future offensive.

PART A

1944

I

Soviet Offensive Operations against *Heeresgruppe Nordukraine* Summer 1944

Heeresgruppe Nordukraine

German prospects for success vanished after the loss of the Battle of Stalingrad. Too many battle-worthy formations were missing when it later came to occupying the positions of the front lines. Therefore, during and after that battle, it demanded major efforts to build one line of defence after another. The last outpouring of strength was in the battle between Bjelgorod and Orel, i.e. the Battle of Kursk. Every detail of the German troop strengths and armament had been passed on to the Red Army, well in advance, by the *"Rote Kapelle"* i.e. the 'Red Orchestra'. Hitler turned it into a failure! He responded to the landing of the United States forces on the Italian mainland, from Sicily, by suddenly pulling out the 2nd *SS-Panzer-Korps* just after the successful armoured battle of Prochorowka. The Soviets immediately advanced through the resulting gap, gaining substantial ground to the west.

In the ensuing battles, at first with small, but later with total success, the Soviets employed the German tactics of breakthroughs, and subsequent pursuit resulting in a envelopment. Based on surprise, those tactics had been used in various campaigns. The Red Army had set as its objective the forcing back of the German forces, to be followed by the liberation of the greater part of the German occupied lands of the Soviet Union. The Battle of Kursk soon brought about the liberation of major areas of the Ukraine. From 22 June 1944, the offensive against *Heeresgruppe Mitte* then smashed through the major eastward stretching salient in the German front that stretched east of Witebsk, Mogilew and Bobruisk. That brought Soviet forces almost to the *Reichs* border in East Prussia, and further south to the Vistula.

For their "Bagramjan" offensive, the Soviets deceived the German command regarding its *Schwerpunkt*[1] and direction. The German supreme command, i.e. Hitler, deduced that the Soviets would advance from Kowel to the north. Therefore the *OKW* i.e. *Oberkommando der Wehrmacht*, pulled troops and weapons from the entire *Heeresgruppe Mitte* sector, and concentrated them in the Kowel sector. However, the offensive against *Heeresgruppe Mitte* then led to the withdrawal of formations from that sector. Those formations were then lost for days, due to partisans delaying the German rail transport. Unavailable for any combat use, the *Heeresgruppe Nordukraine* front was thus seriously weakened. In turn, that offered the Soviets a favourable opportunity to also launch an offensive against *Heeresgruppe Nordukraine* with the concentrated units of their 1st Ukrainian Front.

---

1   Focal point

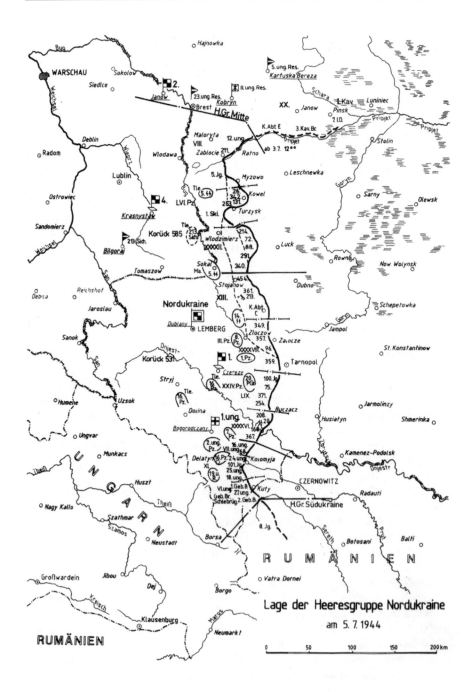

2 Position of *Heeresgruppe Nordukraine*, 5 July 1944

The description of the enemy situation makes it clear that the German formations in the front had no available reserves. It was also evident that, thanks to the lend-lease American trucks, the Red Army benefited from an advantage in mobility over the German formations. German infantry had no transport and their weapons were horse-drawn. That encouraged the Soviets to launch a similar thrust in the *Heeresgruppe Nordukraine* sector, at the precise time that the entire *Heeresgruppe Mitte* front collapsed. Following the first breakthroughs, the Russians advanced recklessly into the depths of the German defensive sectors.

They used what was by then a well established tactic, of pulling in air forces for short periods from other sectors, and engaging German troop movements, particularly reinforcements, on their way forward. The attack on the Germans opened with an astonishing mass of armour, and above all, artillery. Soviet accounts are inconsistent, to the point of being unusable, in stating the amounts of heavy weapons and ammunition used. The Soviets began to level the German positions, and to soften them up for the assault with artillery barrages that used vast amounts of ammunition, and lasted for hours.

The Soviet Strategic Concentration

According to Soviet records, the 1st Ukrainian Front had over 1.2 million men, 13,900 mortars and guns with a calibre greater than 76mm, 2,200 tanks and self-propelled guns, and 2,806 aircraft. The same Soviet records also stated that the opposing German formations comprised 40 divisions with 600,000 men, 900 tanks and self-propelled guns, 6,300 guns and mortars, and 700 aircraft. Thus, according to Soviet sources and reconnaissance, their forces greatly exceeded the German forces facing them. In addition they had excellent supplies of ammunition for mortars and guns, i.e. Stalin's hobby-horses. Within a few hours, all that would succeed in preparing for an attack to soften up the German positions.

Gradually, it led the Germans to pull back out of the foremost position, even before the start of the attack. They would leave only a few observers, thus sparing the main body of their forces from the effects of the enemy artillery preparation. However, the excellent Soviet reconnaissance, at that period of the war, soon recognised the German tactical plans, with the result that their infantry followed close behind the rolling barrage and kept a forward advance.

Based on the results of their reconnaissance, the Soviets paid particular attention to the moving up of German armoured formations. Those formations were not to go into action in the front lines but were initially to remain in reserve. The German front proved very uneven with regard to the combat experience of individual formations. The 14th *Waffen-Grenadier-Division der SS*, i.e. *1. ukrainische Division*, was made up of Ukrainian volunteers from eastern Poland. They had reported for duty in the German *Wehrmacht*. Thus the 14th was committed to action when its men were still totally lacking in adequate training.

The Soviets selected the Kowel area for their continuing advance. It was assigned great importance because of the various westward leading road and rail connections. The state of such transportation routes frequently influenced the location of the *Schwerpunkte* of Soviet attacks. Thus, it came about that a *Schwerpunkt* in the Kowel sector offered the Soviets the possibility of separating *Heeresgruppe*

Nordukraine from *Heeresgruppe Mitte*. On the southern flank, the Soviets attempted to drive the predominantly Hungarian formations back against the Carpathians. They wanted to prevent German formations moving past the northern face of the Carpathian and Beskides Mountains to the other *Heeresgruppe*. The objective was to win the Carpathian Passes. German *Sperrkomandos*, i.e. blocking parties, later blocked those passes in the Hungarian held sectors for some time.

Start of the Attack

In the first attacks, it was evident that the Soviet command had studied the co-operation of their different armed groups, resulting in co-ordination between infantry, artillery, and ground attack aircraft. As they had done in action against the 3rd *Panzerarmee* and 9th *Armee* of *Heeresgruppe Mitte*, the primary targets of the ground attack planes were the artillery positions. Using bombs and strafing, such attacks prepared the way for the infantry. There was heavy fighting. German Stukas knocked out 56 enemy tanks, some at close range.

On 1 March 1944, during a quiet interlude, while both sides were recuperating and rebuilding battered formations, the main line of resistance was shortened around Witebsk, on the northern wing of *Heeresgruppe Mitte*. The 131st *Infanterie-Division* was therefore free for other assignments. That was over two months before the massive Soviet attack that forced the collapse of *Heeresgruppe Mitte*. The division was withdrawn from the main line of resistance for movement by rail to the Leonowo area, on the Duna River. There the 131st *Infanterie-Division* was involved in actions against partisans until 16 March 1944. Orders then arrived for the Division to proceed towards Kowel.

A battery of German Wespe self-propelled light howitzers. The Wespe was issued to *Panzerartillerie* regiments in *Panzer* and *Panzergrenadier* divisions

Advancing Russian troops surrounded the city of Kowel. The encircled city garrison was commanded by *SS-Obergruppenführer* Gille, the commander of the 5th *SS-Panzer-Division "Wiking"*, who was separated from his division. The garrison consisted of soldiers of the *Waffen-SS*, police, field-railway personnel, other troop elements, and logistical units. From the beginning of March, the garrison of the city held that important railway and highway hub against the Russians, until German troops were able to break the ring of encirclement at the end of April.

On 17 March, units of the 131st *Infanterie-Division* marched to the Obel railway station, then proceeded by rail via Polosk–Molodetschno–Minsk–Baranowitsche–Brest–Lublin, to Luboml.

Armee-Oberkommando 2 attempted to use *General* Hoßbach's 56th *Panzer-Korps* to build a thin security line. It consisted of strongpoints further to the west, until German troops could be brought in, and the attack to relieve Kowel could begin. The onset of the thaw resulted in deepening mud throughout the pathless region of the Pripet River and its marshes. The thaw complicated the advance towards Kowel.

Russian resistance increased daily. On 19 March, the 131st *Infanterie-Division* arrived in Luboml at about 17.00 hours. They immediately started detraining, moving out the following morning. By order of the commander-in-chief of the troops around Kowel, *General der Infanterie* Hoßbach, the attack was to be launched immediately along the Luboml–Kowel railway line.

Advance elements of the 131st *Infanterie-Division* reached Maziajowo on 23 March, and using trucks, proceeded to join the *III.(gep.)/ SS-Panzer-Grenadier-Regiment 9 "Germania"*, that had newly arrived from France. On 25 March, a strong *Kampfgruppe*, led by the commander of the 131st *Infanterie-Division*, started towards Kowel. Russian resistance rapidly stiffened. Days and weeks of hard fighting and heavy losses ensued, as the relief forces battled their way along the railway line, and through the adjoining countryside.

On 6 April, first contact was established with the encircled forces in Kowel. However, it was not until the end of April that the enemy forces were pushed back. Defensive positions then pushed forward approximately 10 kilometres past Kowel, finally ending the city's close encirclement.

Soviet Advance

The Soviets gradually gained significant ground in the other sectors of the central front of *Heeresgruppe Nordukraine*. They forced the German formations to fall back to the "Tiger Position", and later to the Bug River line. The advance towards Chelm and Lublin, in the gap between *Heeresgruppe Mitte* and *Heeresgruppe Nordukraine*, offered them the opportunity for unhindered advance into the depth of the German positions. They took repeated chances to turn in behind the left wing of *Heeresgruppe Nordukraine*. Individual divisions were engaged in extremely hard fighting. Thus the 342nd *Infanterie-Division* shot down 3 aircraft and destroyed 88 Russian tanks in a single day. Some of them were knocked out by artillery, others in close-quarters combat. Despite enemy bombs, and strafing attacks that hit the division command post, the division held fast. At the end of the Soviet penetrations in the centre of the 26th *Infanterie-Division* sector of Pary duby-

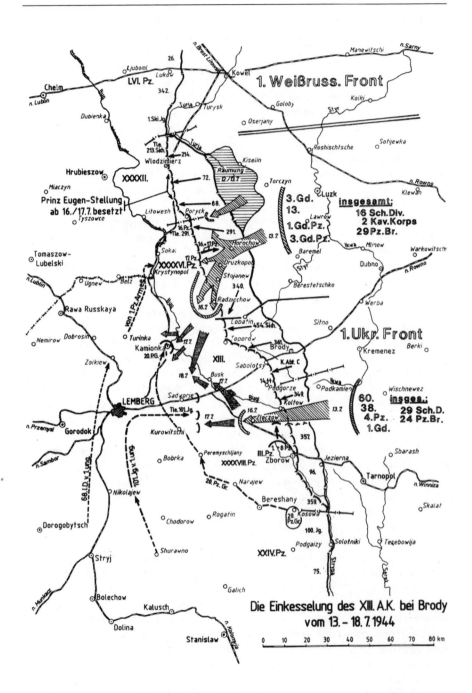

3 The encirclement of 13th *Armee-Korps* at Brody, 13–18 July 1944

Krubel, particularly the Smydyn bridgehead, the Soviets continued to attack *III.(gep.)/ SS-Panzer-Grenadier-Regiment 9 "Germania"* and a company of the *II./ SS-Panzer-Regiment 5*.

Massive armoured attacks were launched along the *Rollbahn*, a major highway designated for military transport, and a railway line. Each attack was supported by 40–50 ground attack aircraft that preceded the armoured spearheads by bombing the critical Maciejow–Buda railway overpass. Individual tanks travelled as far as 8 kilometres along the railway into the hinterland. 84 Russian tanks were knocked out that day by *SS-Panzer-Regiment 5* and the artillery, resulting in the failure of the intended Soviet breakthrough. German infantry had allowed the Soviet armour to roll over them. But then they beat back the waves of Soviet infantry that were advancing behind the tanks. Further Soviet attacks in the evening also foundered.

The German command wanted to eliminate the only success of the previous day's Russian attack, namely the penetration near Dolsk. After successful preparation by an effective Stuka bombing attack, the northern attack group fought its way to the road crossing over the stream, 2.5 kilometres south of point 194.4. They cleared the old main line of resistance. To the south, the Soviets also launched a counter-attack with armoured support, denying success to the German attack. The Soviets changed their troops facing the 342nd *Infanterie-Division*. At about midnight of 14 July, the 342nd *Infanterie-Division* regained German possession of the site of the penetration near Dolsk.

New Wave of Attacks

On 18 July, after a series of lesser attacks, the Soviets launched a new major attack, preceded by an hour and a half of bombardment. 14 rifle divisions, with strong armoured support, advanced between Dolsk and Smydyn, with the *Schwerpunkt* on both sides of Targowiszcze and Maciejow. The 342nd *Infanterie-Division* essentially held its position. The 26th *Infanterie-Division* suffered several deep penetrations in its foremost line. However, the entire corps had to conduct a withdrawal as rapidly as possible. There was no longer any guarantee that the "Tiger" position could be held. The German command specified two lines of resistance for a phased withdrawal to the Bug River. On the evening of 19 July, the position of the northern wing in front of the Bug proved no longer tenable. Enemy armour was already in Luboml, threatening the 253rd *Infanterie-Division* with a double envelopment, and also threatening the northern flank of the 342nd *Infanterie-Division*. The 1st *Ski-Jäger-Division* fell back, fighting, to the Bug. Battles in the preceding days had so exhausted the troops' strength that they could no longer carry out the planned improvement of the Bug position.

The flat riverbed of the Bug, with its numerous fords and bridge locations, barred it from consideration as a serious hindrance. The enemy was especially ruthless in keeping his masses of soldiers hot on the heels of withdrawing troops. On 20 July, the Soviets penetrated south of Kladniow, to the Skryniczyn area in the sector of the 1st *Ski-Jäger-Division*. A German counter-attack failed, leaving the Soviets holding their bridgehead.

On 20 July, it became apparent that the Bug position was no longer tenable in the sectors of the 253rd and 26th *Infanterie-Divisionen*. At 10.00 hours, 6 enemy tanks with infantry riding on them, stood on the west bank of the Bug south of Opalin. Infantry and armour moved south and west from the Hniszow area. Enemy armoured spearheads reached the railway line from Siedlizsce. They also achieved a penetration of the 5th *Jäger-Division* positions with the same direction of advance to the west and south west, against the deep flank of the 26th *Infanterie-Division*.

Further Loss of Land

Again and again, as the defensive battles continued, terrain had to be given up becuse it lacked sufficient possibilities for the establishment of an adequate defensive position. There was also an inadequate amount of weaponry. During the night of 21 July the Soviets took Chelm in a *coup de main*. By the afternoon of 22 July, they were already at the edge of Lublin and continued across the Wieprz River.

Where the German forces stood on the defensive, they knocked out a series of Soviet tanks. The troops waited for the arrival of the 17th *Panzer-Division*. They had been ordered to cover the north flank in the Piaski area, and further to support the north flank by holding open the area around Krasnystaw. The 17th *Panzer-Division* received a series of missions that it could fulfil at the same time. Above all, there was a serious shortage of fuel that led to the draining of fuel tanks, and the destruction of many vehicles, in order to maintain the mobility of the armour.

In the coming days, the 56th *Panzer-Korps* and the 42nd *Armee-Korps* coordinated their withdrawal movements. The 42nd *Armee-Korps* was also in a difficult position because initially the Soviets attacked the 291st *Infanterie-Division* and the left wing of the 340th *Infanterie-Division*. There the Soviets achieved deep penetrations until the 16th and 17th *Panzer-Divisionen* counter-attacked on 13 and 14 July. They restored contact with the open left flank of the 340th *Infanterie-Division*. However, the attacks did not attain the assigned objectives.

Retreat to the Vistula

On 14 July, the 340th *Infanterie-Division* was in grave danger of being rolled up from the rear. Fighting on the left wing of the *Heeresgruppe* repeatedly weakened the defensive forces. Retreat ensued from the Wieprz. Finally came the fighting retreat to the Vistula. The Soviets thereby managed to cut off the entire 13th *Armee-Korps*, which attempted to break out in several waves. However, only isolated elements succeeded. To put it simply, the German formations were missing that were needed to hold a coherent defensive position. Time after time, troops could not be committed in the *Heeresgruppe Nordukraine* sector because of the great gap between it and *Heeresgruppe Mitte*. The defensive fighting, far on the left wing to prevent outflanking, then forced the retreat to the Wieprz and finally, to the Vistula.

At all costs, the *OKW* wanted to hold the line at the Vistula as a defendable winter position. On the other hand, the Soviets had to win ground across the Vistula for the future advance towards Berlin and Krakow. Accordingly, they strove to build the requisite bridgeheads with adequate depth for the required concentration of artillery and armoured forces. Heavy fighting developed around Lemberg, which the Soviets eventually bypassed to the north and finally, to the south. In light of the strain on individual formations, in the sectors of the other *Heeresgruppen, Heeresgruppe Nordukraine* could not expect significant help from elsewhere.

At the end of August, the German forces attempted a counter-attack against the Soviets, concentrating all the armoured and artillery forces available at that time. But they attained only limited success. The new Soviet tactic of establishing a *Pak*, i.e. an anti-tank gun front, echeloned in depth, immediately after capturing a section of terrain, proved itself, with the help of the 7.62 cm *'Ratschbum'* anti-tank guns. They were so named for the sound of their high-velocity, their flat trajectory, and the noise of its discharge and impact coming practically at the same moment. Their low profile allowed them to be easily camouflaged in the front lines. Against them, attacks by German tanks working alone achieved only limited local success. The desired use of the German *Luftwaffe* against such positions, and against the advancing enemy armour, generally failed due to shortage of fuel. At the end of August, motorised forces for the attacks were, in part, immobilised or only received enough fuel at the last moment to make their vehicles mobile.

At that point, the German command observed that the Soviets were building defensive positions in the Vistula sector. That suggested a planned pause, or at the very least, the abandonment of further aggressive intentions in the autumn of 1944. The German command concluded that the Soviet offensive towards Krakow and Berlin had come to a halt for the time being. Reconnaissance results indicated that the Soviets were initially filling out their badly battered formations and re-supplying them with ammunition. In addition, they had to improve their logistical system, converting the railways to their broader gauge and building new supply bases. That activity offered the Germans a chance to organise their formations, to fit in the returning convalescents, and integrate recruits into individual combat groups. Above all, it was necessary to build an array of multiple lines of defence, so that even the weak forces that were available would be able to stand fast. A new, strong Soviet attack was expected that would be especially notable for the accompanying massively superior artillery. The Germans had to hold firm.

For the time being, hostilities in the centre and on the left wing of *Heeresgruppe Nordukraine* were limited to reconnaissance. Both sides based their hopes on patrols and assault detachments, the latter bringing back prisoners. In those two sectors of *Heeresgruppe Nordukraine* at least, a calm period with almost no combat activity set in.

II

Soviet Offensive in the Beskides

Change of Soviet Plans

The construction of defensive positions in the Vistula bridgehead front was soon explained when the Soviets pulled troops out of those sectors for commitment to the south. In co-operation with their forces thrusting north through Siebenbürgen, they focused on cutting off the German Carpathian salient that jutted far to the east. That required a major reorientation for the Soviet forces with regard to plans, combat tactics and equipment of the troops. With amazing speed, instructions reached the troops for teaching them the peculiarities of fighting in the mountains. When attacking on such a front, the broken terrain would prevent the Soviets from employing their usual great masses of infantry.

Artillery would have to fire at high angles of elevation. Tanks with their flat trajectory guns could not accomplish much in high mountains, to say nothing of the problems that the road conditions would present to heavy vehicles. The few roads, and even fewer railway lines that were available, would have to be reserved for the heavy weapons and armoured vehicles. All other formations would be restricted to byways, with their locally wet and swampy underpinnings.

According to Soviet sources, they had 74 rifle divisions and 6 cavalry divisions, 10 tank and mechanised corps, along with 13,900 guns, and mortars of 76mm or greater calibre, as well as 1,614 tanks and self-propelled guns. The 1st Czech Army Corps also belonged to that Soviet front. Supported by 2 air armies, the 2nd Ukrainian Front had a total of 843,000 men.

Soviet sources stated that the forces of the German *Heeresgruppe Nordukraine* consisted of 34 infantry and 5 armoured divisions. They had 1 motorised infantry division and 2 infantry brigades, with a total of over 600,000 men. In fact they totalled 900,000 including rear-area troops, 900 tanks and assault guns, 6,300 guns and mortars, supported by 700 aircraft of *Luftflotte* 4.

The Soviets activated a new Command, the Independent 4th Ukrainian Front, commanded by Petrow, for the action against the Beskides and the Carpathian front.[1] At the beginning of August, that front launched its first move-

---

1 Translator's note – Early in October 1943 *Stavka* underscored recent victories and the start of a new phase in the war by renaming the front commands. The former South Front became 4th Ukrainian Front. As Erickson (*The Road to Berlin*, pp 199 and 293) makes clear, between April and May 1944, in a drastic alteration in its distribution of strategic armies, the Soviet command moved commanders around and transferred the armies of the old 4th Ukrainian Front from the Crimea to the 2nd and 3rd Ukrainian Fronts. The 4th Ukrainian Front then reappeared some time later when, at the end of July 1944, "*Stavka* decided to create a new Front command. Following Marshal Koniev's recommendation the 4th Ukrainian Front

A Soviet mortar team in action.

ments towards the southwest against the foothills of the Carpathians. They cleaned up the Drogobytsch industrial region. Sambor fell to the enemy. There was increasing German opposition, and the Soviet troops were exhausted. There were also complicated combat conditions in the hill and forest terrain of the Carpathian foothills. All of that, for the time being, caused the command of the 4th Ukrainian Front to go over to the defensive, and to carefully prepare for the conquest of the Carpathians.

On 29 August 1944, Stalin's directive finally ordered all the westward facing Vistula bridgeheads, in all sectors, to shift to the defensive. They were to build deeply echeloned defences along the front, with at least three lines of defence, to a depth totalling 30 to 40 kilometres. Strong corps and army front reserves were to be held in readiness. For the time being that put an end to the Lemberg and Sandomierz offensive operations.

Preparations of the newly activated 4th Ukrainian Front then ran in high gear. An advance into the Hungarian plains was intended, cutting off the *Armeegruppe* of *Generaloberst* Heinrici i.e. *Panzer-Armeeoberkommando* 1, with the 1st Hungarian Army and various German formations. The formations cut off would also include the German *49th Gebirgs-Korps* and its 100th and 101st *Jäger-Divisionen*, and the 13th Hungarian Infantry Division. An *Armeegruppe* usually consisted of a single army and miscellaneous units, whereas a *Heeresgruppe* consisted of several armies. Heinrici's 1st *Panzer-Armeeoberkommando* had tactical control over the 1st

was formed from Koniev's left flank ... The commander of the 4th Ukrainian Front, Petrov, received a preliminary directive to prepare an offensive operation, designed to seize the eastern Carpathians ...".

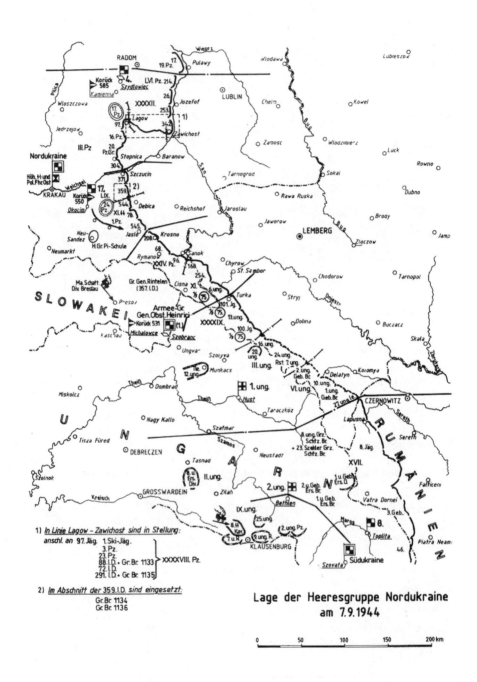

4 Position of *Heeresgruppe Nordukraine*, 7 September 1944

Hungarian Army, so it was referred to as *"Armeegruppe Heinrici"*. It was, however, subordinate to *Heeresgruppe A,* and later, when the 1st Hungarian Army was withdrawn, it reverted to its former designation of 1st *Panzer-Armee.* It would also be necessary to attack the left adjoining 11th *Armee-Korps,* with the 75th, 254th and 168th *Infanterie-Divisionen* and 6th Hungarian Infantry Division, as well as the 24th *Panzer-Korps,* with the 96th, 68th and 208th *Infanterie-Divisionen.*

The first attack preparations were essentially directed against the Beskides front. However, the German forces there were considered to be too strong, requiring that additional Soviet forces be brought up. The Germans, too, brought up additional forces to reinforce the southern wing of *Heeresgruppe Nordukraine* i.e. *Armeegruppe Heinrici,* as a result of their own reconnaissance of the enemy situation. The 1st *Panzer-Armee* was reinforced with the 68th and 75th *Infanterie-Divisionen,* the 24th *Panzer-Division,* 1st *Ski-Jäger-Division,* 357th *Infanterie-Division,* and later, the 45th and 253rd *Infanterie-Divisionen.*

There was a change in objectives for the Soviets, from an attack to the west to one directed towards the southwest and south. It resulted in the sudden reorganisation of the Soviet formations of the 4th Ukrainian Front. That also led to the redesignation of the German *Heeresgruppe Nordukraine* to *Heeresgruppe A.* There had to be a shift in the sector boundaries between the German 1st *Panzer-Armee,* (24th *Panzer-Korps*) and the 17th *Armee* (11th *SS-Armee-Korps*). Thereby the 96th and 208th *Infanterie-Divisionen,* 545th *Grenadier-Division,* and 78th *Sturm-Division* came under the command of the 11th *SS-Armee-Korps,* and the 68th *Infanterie-Division* under the 24th *Panzer-Korps.* The level of German troops remained almost constant. However, they were continually weakened through losses in the heavy fighting. The 96th *Infanterie-Division,* in particular, was in the *Schwerpunkt* of the fighting and was later pulled out for reconstitution.

At the beginning of September 1944, the 4th Ukrainian Front faced the German 1st *Panzer-Armee* under Heinrici, and the Hungarian 1st Army, with a total of 160,000 men, 1,790 guns and mortars, and 25 tanks and assault guns. Those German strengths accorded to Soviet sources.

The left sector of the German Front that faced the wing of the Soviet 1st Guards Army was the most densely manned. Included were the 96th, 168th and 254th *Infanterie-Divisionen,* as well as the 101st *Jäger-Division* and the Hungarian 1st and 13th Infantry-Divisions. The 100th *Jäger-Division* was facing Uzgorod Chutz and reinforced the Hungarian formations. All those formations had suffered heavy losses in past fighting and were greatly weakened. At the end of August and the beginning of September, the German formations filled their ranks again by incorporating returning convalescents. According to Soviet sources, that brought the divisions to 70% of their table-of-organisation strengths. However, they had no significant operational reserves.

Start of the Attack – Readiness for the Attack – 28 August in the Beskides Foothills

If the plans for cutting off the German Carpathian salient led to changes in the Soviet preparations, so too did reports arriving from Slovakia about the state of the movement for an uprising. The operations plan foresaw an advance to the Slovak

Germans inspect a captured Soviet machine-gun position. The weapon is a Maxim
water-cooled 7.62mm Model 1910

border and conjunction with the Slovak troops and partisans. In order to develop
the attack, and after breaking through the German defensive zone, the 1st Czechoslovakian Corps, the 1st Cavalry Corps and two tank brigades were to enter the
battle. The 1st Czechoslovakian Airborne Brigade would either jump into the area
north of Stropkov, over the positions of the main body of the Slovak divisions, or
would be landed on an airfield. 50 Douglas aircraft would be needed for three
waves of planes. On the third day of the operation, the 1st and 2nd Slovak Divisions would advance in an attack from the area north of Stropkov. [2]

To force their breakthrough of the German defences, the Soviet command
planned a density of 140 tubes of artillery and mortars, including 82mm mortars,
for every kilometre of front, with 2 units of fire each. The Supreme Soviet command regulated the commitment of its formations in detail, with objectives stated
for each day of the attack. Readiness to fire was to be established by 18.00 hours on
7 September, and the artillery preparation was to last 50 minutes. In the meantime,
the Soviets prepared their troops for fighting in the mountains.

---

2   Translator's note – The Czechoslovakia that was created by the Treaty of Versailles at
the end of the First World War included Moravia and Bohemia, where the majority of
the population was Czech, and Slovakia, which was predominately Slovak. The Slovaks
had deep resentments against the politically dominant Czechs, who discriminated
against the Slovaks and treated them as 'dumb yokels'. The substantial German
population was an additional complication. When, after first annexing the
Sudetenland, Germany invaded the rest of Czechoslovakia, Moravia and Bohemia were
occupied, while Slovakia was left independent, under the clerical-fascist Tiso regime.
Slovakia enjoyed a charmed life for most of the war, apparently exempt from the chaos
around it. It was only as Germany's collapse approached its borders that a movement
developed, primarily in the Slovak army, that planned the uprising here referred to.

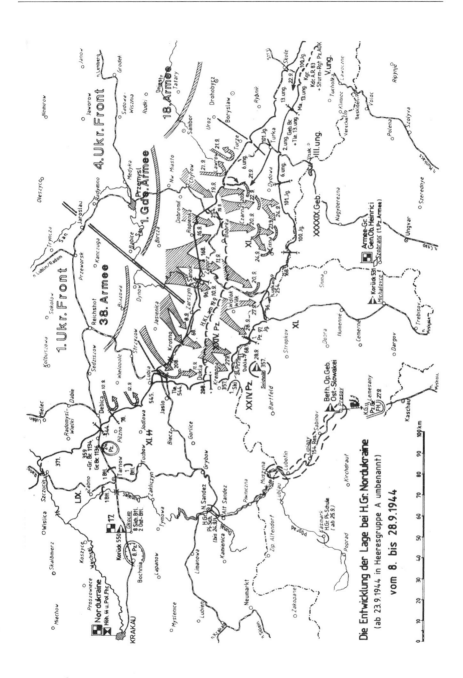

5 Development of the position of *Heeresgruppe Nordukraine*, 8–28 September 1944

On the morning of 7 September, the Soviet 1st Guards Army was to begin with an armed reconnaissance. They would reconnoitre the foremost German lines of defence, find out their manning, system of fire, and the peculiarities of their obstacles. The Soviets gained 80 kilometres of ground with their first attacks before running out of steam. Unfavourable weather conditions complicated any further advance. The mountain roads and paths proved to be softened by rain. Poor visibility hindered the use of aircraft. The Red Air Force flew 38 sorties. However, reports reached the Germans that some Slovak divisions and partisan groups were endangering the Carpathian passes. Thus the Germans gained the chance to reinforce their positions in the sectors under attack by the Soviet troops, and also brought in formations from adjoining sectors.

German formations then launched counter-attacks from the southwest and southeast towards Sanok. German artillery fire was also greatly intensified. The 96th *Infanterie-Division* and elements of the 254th *Infanterie-Division*, along with elements of the 168th *Infanterie-Division*, launched up to 15 attacks daily in several directions. The infantry were accompanied by 7 to 10 tanks and assault guns. Thereupon the Soviet 1st Guards Army attacked south of Sanok and in the Zagorz area, achieving penetrations into the German positions and broadening the front of their attack to 18 kilometres. German formations successfully blocked further advance.

The foundering of the Soviet attack led to orders from the highest levels, on the Soviet side, that commanders of regiments had to remain no more than 1 kilometre from the first line. Division commanders had to stay within 2 kilometres of the foremost line. Artillery was to be positioned directly at the combat outposts and, on the march, 300 to 1,500 metres behind the first line of infantry.

On 14 September, German formations cut off the Soviet 1st Guards Cavalry Corps from the main body of the Soviet 38th Army, with a counter-assault in the Gloisce–Lysa Gora area. It was only on 24 September that it was possible to free the corps from the encirclement. The Soviet forces that were committed, particularly the 38th Army, did not carry out their assigned missions. Nevertheless, the Soviet command felt that they had drawn strong German forces against them with their attacks, thereby easing the situation for the Slovak uprising on its eastern front.

The terrain added to the difficulties for the Soviets by enforcing separation of the commitment of their major formations. Eight passes in the eastern Beskides were at stake, including four passes above the Jasiolka River valley, with a paved road and a main road that linked the Jasiolka valley with the valleys of the Ondava and Laborec rivers. The pass with the Jasiolka–Humenné road reached an elevation of a mere 600 metres and a minimal grade. Further to the east were the two Kalinov passes, both with unpaved roads that linked the valleys of the Wisloka and Jasiolka with the valley of the Laborec. The Sana–Humenné road led over the Radoszyce pass and the divide between the East Beskides and Ukrainian Carpathians to the Lupkow Pass, over which ran the Sanok–Humenné railway line.

A column of German vehicles fords a river in the Beskides.

Continuation of the Attack

From 8 September to 8 October 1944, the Soviets' main focus was on the northern flank of the Beskides from Sanok, back into the Beskides Mountains. The first preparations scouted the German positions and defences. Then followed the artillery preparation on 8 September. It was aimed particularly at the right hand sector of the 96th *Infanterie-Division*, where the Soviets achieved penetrations, but no more. On 9 September, at 06.30 hours, they therefore repeated their attack with an unusually intense hour and a half of artillery preparation. The German artillery, especially that of *Artillerie-Regiment* 196, mainly targeted the concentration areas of the Soviet infantry. Nevertheless, the Soviet bombardment gradually thinned the ranks of the German grenadiers. The Soviets could then thrust forward into the gaps. The picture was the same for *Grenadier-Regiment* 417 of the 168th *Infanterie-Division*, on the right of the 96th *Infanterie-Division*.

Soon a yawning gap opened between *Grenadier-Regimenter* 287 and 284. There were no available reserves worth mentioning. Bicycle and *Pionier* platoons had to be thrown in, to close the first great gaps. The newly activated *Feld-Ersatz-Bataillon* 196, i.e. a field replacement battalion, was committed immediately as *"Eingreifgruppe Schlegel"* but was unable to secure a lasting contact between the two adjoining regiments. Therefore a hastily formed *"Kampfgruppe 82"*, under *Oberstleutnant* Förster, had to work with *Grenadier-Regiment* 287 to clean up a penetration north of Poraz. But that too, failed to achieve complete success. The Soviets attacked *Grenadier-Regiment* 287 with armour, forcing the German command to pull the front line back to Poraz, whilst the left wing of *Grenadier-Regi-*

ment 283 remained on the hill north of Wolica. To support their ground troops, the Red Army sent strong air forces that dominated the sky over the weak German air defence. Soviet planes strafed and bombed the main dressing station in Plonna.

Despite isolated counter-attacks, it was impossible to re-establish a continuous line of defence. The troops thus had to settle for contesting every foot of the Soviet advance. *Grenadier-Regiment* 283 held its positions for a long time. The artillery especially, needed vast amounts of ammunition. On 11 September, *Grenadier-Regiment* 442 of the 168th *Infanterie-Division* was attached to the 96th *Infanterie-Division*, intending by attacking, to close the gap between *Grenadier-Regimenter* 287 and 284. That attack by *Grenadier-Regiment* 442 was not fully effective against numerically superior Soviet forces. It could only hold off a Soviet breakthrough and occupy the second position. The next day, the Soviets launched a strong attack, with armour, against the Tukarnia Hill 777. The 16 September *Wehrmacht* report mentioned the hard fighting of the 96th *Infanterie-Division*.

The Soviets committed their Czech Legion, with 6 tanks, against the Tukarnia Hills 777 and 713, exacting serious losses from the German forces. But there were simply too few combatants remaining in action, to man a continuous line. In that broken hill country they could not secure, let alone hold the broad sector, over 20 kilometres as the crow flies.

To the right and left, *"Kampfgruppe Schlegel"* was formed from *Grenadier-Regiment* 287, *Feld-Ersatz-Bataillon* 196, I./ *Jäger-Regiment* 228 of the 101st *Jäger-Division* , and *Grenzwacht,* i.e. border guard, *Bataillon* 9. The latter was attached to *Grenadier-Regiment* 287. There were also the *Grenadier-Regiment* 283 and battalions of *Grenadier-Regiment* 284, with remnants of *Füsilier-Bataillon* 96. A battery of *Artillerie-Regiment* 196 fired from the main line of resistance, until overrun in hand-to-hand fighting. The division called up all the rear area services into action, but Przpyszow remained in enemy hands.

Hampered by the terrain, the troops could only fight in isolated *Kampfgruppen,* thereby being exposed to envelopment by the Soviets. The 96th *Infanterie-Division* was broken up into three physically separated combat sectors, with no contact between them. In the constricted, pathless, mountainous, forest terrain construction of a main line of resistance was extraordinarily difficult. Several successful attacks brought in prisoners and stopped the Soviet advance. Nevertheless, the formations along the railway line had to fall back to the south, to hills north of Oslawica, and finally, to Lupkow. However, it still remained possible to control the formations. A regiment of the 254th *Infanterie-Division* relieved *Kampfgruppe Lorenz* of the 96th *Infanterie-Division* in its positions. The I./*Jäger-Regiment* 228 and *Grenzwacht-Bataillon* 9 returned to their parent formations. *Grenadier-Regiment* 287 and *Feld-Ersatz-Bataillon* 196 returned to the 96th *Infanterie-Division*. Remnants of *Grenadier-Regiment 287* were left to defend the forested heights between Jasiel and Habura.

The 1st *Panzer-Division* is brought up

However, all that troop movement fell far short of building an adequate line of defence against the strength of the Soviet attacks. Accordingly, the *Heeresgruppe* had to bring in the 1st *Panzer-Division,* from the central sector of *Heeresgruppe*

Norkdukraine/A. The division moved by forced marches from the great bend of the Vistula to the foothills, arriving in the area northwest of Sanok by 10 September. By then the battle was already at its high point, so the 1st *Panzer-Division* had to continue its march, without stopping, towards Zmigrad.

Employment of armour was limited in such hilly terrain. Nevertheless, elements of the 1st *Panzer-Division* saw abundant and varied action. Despite strong support by *Panzer-Artillerie-Regiment* 73, the attempt to take the commanding Hill 526, near Zmigrod, along with elements of *Grenadier-Regiment* 1083 of the 544th *Grenadier-Division*, did not succeed. Therefore the emphasis moved to an advance towards Lysa-Gora. They would try to contain the enemy forces that had already broken deep into the front of *Heeresgruppe Nordukraine*, and were advancing towards the Dukla Pass. On 13 September, the 1st *Panzer-Division* took Lysa-Gora in their line of march, and forced the enemy forces further back into the foothills of the mountains.

III

Uprising in Slovakia

Apparently, the Soviets assigned a greater importance to the attack from the north towards Dukla Pass, than to the advance from Nyrigehaza northward, i.e. the forces fighting their way northward from the plains of Hungary, judging by the poor condition of the formations engaged there. The attack from the north was to be assisted by the commitment of the two Slovak divisions in eastern Slovakia. They were stationed in the eastern point of Slovakia. The Slovak army officers, who would later lead the uprising, had the apparent intent, on receipt of the appropriate signal from the Red Army, of going into action and attacking.

At any rate, the Soviets concerned themselves with stirring up unrest in the occupied area west of their main line of resistance. The objective was to achieve an uprising or rebellion. To that end, they had parachuted groups of agitators into the *Generalgouvernement* of Poland, into the Protectorate of Bohemia and Moravia, into Slovakia and also into Hungary. All of those were to form resistance groups. At that point Slovakia was a peaceful oasis, not directly affected by the events of the war.

During the use of Slovak troops in the Crimea, elements of those formations had already defected to the Red Army, especially from the 1st Slovak Infantry Division, on 31 October 1943. The Division had abandoned its vehicle park, and most of its guns. Of the original 10,500 men comprising the Slovak 'mobile division',

Two members of the Waffen SS

5,000 remained. The Red Army immediately consolidated into corresponding formations the Slovaks who had gone over to them, forming the Czechoslovakian Brigade. In the course of 1944, that brigade in turn was expanded into the 1st Czechoslovakian Army Corps, with almost 60% Slovaks.

800 men of a Slovak security division deserted, as a group, to the Ukrainian partisans. The remnants of the seriously weakened formations were converted into construction brigades. They were used for labour in the rear areas of the frontal zone, initially in Rumania, and later in Italy. In any case, by the end of 1943 there were no longer Slovak troop elements in action on the German side. The exception was of a Slovak *Jagdfliegerstaffel* i.e. fighter squadron, with German Me 109 aircraft.

Czechoslovakian soldiers also fought in the ranks of the Western Allies, but were no longer separated as Slovak or Czech. There was a total of 9,225 men in the 2nd Czechoslovakian Middle-Eastern Battalion, in the 200th Czechoslovakian Light Fliers' Regiment, *Fliegerregiment*, as well as in various flying units. From the start of the Russian campaign, Slovak losses amounted to 8,720 men, including 1,800 killed, 2,970 wounded, and the remainder missing or deserted.

Preparations for the Uprising

Although Slovakia was, in effect, a peaceful oasis, lacking in nothing,[1] there was a somewhat confused intention among the Slovak officers. They hoped to go over to the Soviet Union, thereby attaining advantages in the case of a Soviet victory. There was no intention of losing the existing national organisation of Slovakia, particularly its independence from the Czechs. All that was desired was to remove the Tiso regime and introduce democracy.

However, the deliberations of various military commanders developed independently over the course of time. At least initially, for reasons of concealment, they attempted to maintain a willingness to co-operate with German officialdom. At that time, there were no German formations in Slovakia. That afforded opportunities for the various commanders of the Slovak Army to make organisational preparations, particularly in stockpiling weapons at the places intended for mobilisation of the uprising. However, one difficulty arose in that the resistance movement, or uprising, was not controlled by a single hand, and had no unified setting of objectives. Some wanted independence for Slovakia and wanted to preserve its existence as an independent state. That was contrary to the intentions of the London based Beneš regime. Some strove for the reunification of Slovakia with the Czechs, in Bohemia and Moravia, to form a Czechoslovakian state. An important distinction must be drawn, between those who desired restoration of the previous Czech dominated Czechoslovakia, and those who desired a federation of two equal and independent states, one Czech, the other Slovak. In addition, there were resistance and partisan groups, formed by agents dropped in by the Soviets. Through illegal radio transmissions, the communist led groups called for acts of disruption, and incited the population to partisan action in the interests of the Red Army,

---

1   Translator's note – Items of food and clothing and consumer goods that were strictly rationed or downright unavailable in Germany were readily available in Slovakia.

The Slovak communists, Šmidke and Bacilek, were dropped by parachute near Warsaw, on the night of 22 July. Karel Bacilek, whose mission was to maintain radio contact with Moscow, dropped out of the picture. The result was that radio contact was not established with Moscow, the Soviet regime, nor with the Red Army. Šmidke was brilliantly successful. He had been commissioned, by the Gottwald-group of emigrant Slovak communists in Moscow, to put the damaged Slovak communist party back on its feet, and to organise a new 5th Illegal Central Committee of the Slovak Communist Party. Lack of direct radio contact remained problematical.

General Svoboda was commander of the 1st Czechoslovakian Brigade, and later became the Czechoslovakian national president. He ordered the Soviets to establish contact with the Slovak army, by parachuting in a party of two officers and a corporal, to the area of the Slovak infantry divisions Grün, Blazicek and Lakota. They needed to establish contact with "anti-fascist" thinking officers and soldiers, with the message in a letter from General Svoboda.[2]

Organisation of the Uprising

The three major resistance and uprising groups in Slovakia teamed up to form national committees. They consisted of five representatives of the middle-class parties, five Social Democrats and five Communists, without consideration of the Tiso People's Party. The chairman was to be elected by a majority. However, agreement in the common interest presented difficulties. The middle-class parties and Social Democrats were for maintaining the appearance of co-operation with the Tiso regime and the Germans. That seemed to offer the best possibility for preparation of an uprising. Above all, it would give the German authorities no reason to call for the occupation of Slovakia. The Soviet supported partisans, however, did not hold to those guidelines. Therefore the regular Slovak troops and police had to conduct punishment actions against the partisan groups. Some of those however, were without serious intent.

Partisan bands were formed around, and led by, the trained groups parachuted in by the Soviets. Importantly, there was the realisation that they were not controlled by the 5th Illegal Central Committee of the Slovak Communist Party in Slovakia but, through their links, to the Soviet Red Army. The 5th Illegal Central Committee of the Slovak Communist Party, organised by Šmidke, reined in, and maintained control over, the partisan groups that were formed and led by Slovak communists. The groups that had been infiltrated in, or dropped in by the Soviets, were led by Soviet officers, or by carefully vetted Slovak officers selected from Soviet POW camps.

---

2   Translator's note – Grün, Blazicek and Lakota were selected by General Svoboda from his 1st Czechoslovakian Brigade specifically to persuade, with the help of papers and a personal letters from Svoboda to the commanding officer of the Slovak division, officers of Slovak army units in Eastern Czechoslovakia to defect with their troops to the Soviets. Although they did not make it to General Jureck, they did get to Lieutenant Colonel Lichner, who defected with his regiment. This party is not to be confused with the trained and organized groups dropped by the Soviets to form and lead partisan bands.

A column of German StuG III assault guns rolls through a village. This photograph affords an excellent view of the side skirts (*Schürzen*) fitted to the vehicles as protection against Soviet anti-tank rifles.

They had their own direct radio communications with, and took their orders from the Ukrainian Communist Party, led by Nikita Kruschev. The more or less unified Slovak resistance, and the military planners of the uprising, had a vital interest in avoiding premature actions. Such actions could provoke German occupation of Slovakia, before the Soviet forces were close enough to link up with the Slovak troops of the uprising. However, at the end of June 1944, Kruschev undertook a programme of actively stirring up resistance movements that would take immediate and violent action. Those acts of the Soviet controlled resistance groups seriously jeopardised the success of the uprising.

Start of Partisan Activity

In illegal radio broadcasts, the parachuted emissaries of the Red Army called for the formation of partisan groups, and for them to attack railway lines and rail transport. However, that was not initially on a large scale. Accordingly, Slovakia remained an oasis of peace. In the summer of 1944, without causing anyone any concern, more than 7,000 children from the German homeland even spent their vacations in Slovakia. It was part of the programme to evacuate children from the intensely bombed cities of the *Reich*.

During the period from 26 July to 10 August, the situation changed. The Red Army air force dropped a series of partisan detachments of nearly 500 men over Poland, Moravia, Hungary and Rumania. Each detachment was completely equipped with radios and medical supplies. Their leaders were militarily experienced, politically examined Soviet partisans, or captured officers. One third of the partisan detachments consisted of Soviet citizens as cadre personnel, instructors, radio operators and doctors. Radio contact of the partisan bands was with Kiev, and thus, with Nikita Kruschev as chief of the Ukrainian Communist Party.

Intensification of Partisan Activity

On 10 August, a partisan brigade of about 40 men in Slovak uniforms, armed with rifles and machine-pistols, attacked railway bridge Nr. 3 near Kostolani, and damaged the bridge. They blew up a railway bridge between Bijrstrabie and Lubutin, and also the west end of the Kysak-Margecany railway bridge. Later, another detachment of 50 chosen and trained partisans, commanded by Welitschkow, landed on the strongpoint. On 20 August, the overall number was about 750 men. They raided police stations, disarmed bridge guards, destroyed cables and electrical wires, and shot down dispersed German soldiers. In addition, they let loose a reign of terror against the populace, particularly against the resident *Volksdeutsche*, while protecting the Slovaks.[3]

Led by a French company commander, French soldiers and escaped German prisoners of war also joined the partisan bands, and went armed into action. They gained legitimisation through radio contact with the London based Czech-Slovak exile regime.

The Slovak Army

In the meantime, the Slovak Chief of General Staff, Lieutenant Colonel Golian, built up the army's organisation with the two mobile divisions stationed in the east of Slovakia. Lieutenant Colonel Golian was appointed Chief of Staff of the Command of Land Combat Forces under General Turanec. He was in an ideal position to manipulate and control troop dispositions. Indeed, he knew every detail regarding the Slovak armed forces, except troops at the front and the Slovak Air Force. On a specified signal, to come from the Red Army, they were to work in conjunction with the attack of the Soviet formations, specifically the 1st Czechoslovakian Army Corps. Jointly they would open the passes through the Beskides, and open the way for free entry into Slovakia. The Red Army hoped it would result in an unopposed advance, particularly to the west. Then they would move towards Krakow, to relieve the Soviet formations fighting *Heeresgruppe A*, and also to the Vienna basin. The 1st Slovak Army Corps in eastern Slovakia consisted of the 1st and 2nd Infantry Divisions, with several active infantry regiments, and a total strength of about 24,000 men. It was equipped with 15,000 carbines, 1,000 light and 250 heavy machine-guns, 150 mortars and 70 guns supplied by the Germans.

---

3   Translator's note – *Volksdeutsche* were ethnic Germans whose forebears had emigrated while retaining their culture.

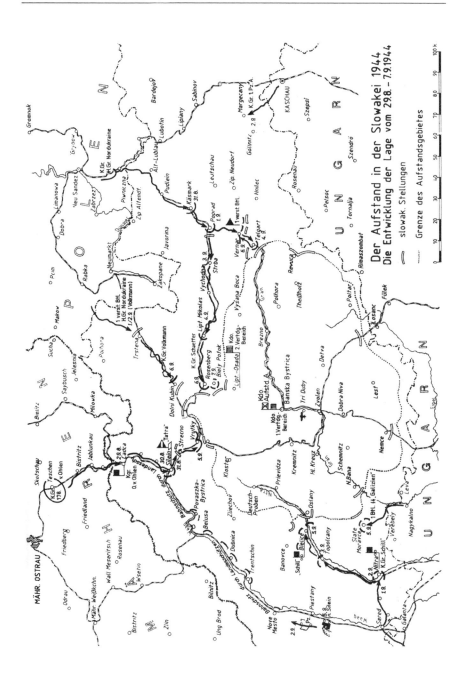

6 The uprising in Slovakia 1944: development of the situation
29 August–7 September 1944

The Slovak General Ingr maintained radio contact with the Soviets and requested weapons for the uprising. General Ingr was the head of the Czechoslovakian Ministry of Defence in the exiled government in London. But there was a lack
of direct radio communication between the officers' conspiracy, the unified resistance groups of the National Council, and the 5th Illegal Central Committee of
the Slovak Communist Party, and with Moscow, the Soviet Regime or the Red
Army. Therefore communications from those groups, and even from the Slovak
Communist Party, followed the circuitous path of going through the Beneš exiled
government in London, and then being passed on by them to Moscow.

Thus at one point General Ingr, in London, requested the British Government to supply the partisans with the weapons mentioned below. Then, from
London, he requested the Soviets to supply communist partisan groups with
weapons. The exiled regime in London was in competition with the communists, as to which side would be recognised as the legitimate post-war government of Czechoslovakia. The choice was between the western sponsored Beneš
regime, or the Soviet sponsored, emigrant Slovak communist party in Moscow,
Gottwald's group. So there were infinite possibilities for complications and
cross-purposes. General Ingr turned to the British with the request for 500 pistols, 500 machine-pistols, 100 anti-tank rifles and requisite ammunition, and
500 kg of explosives.

Radio contact with the Czech exiled regime in London was nearly uninter-
rupted, while contact with Moscow remained an ongoing problem. Contact with
the Central in Moscow, represented by Gottwald and Dimitrow, was repeatedly
interrupted. Gottwald led the Central in Moscow, the emigrant command of the
Communist Party of Czechoslovakia. Dimitroff was in charge of the Executive of
the Communist International, in Moscow. Gottwald's group selected Šmidke and
Bacilek to be dropped by parachute. Bacilek was to provide radio contact, but apparently was a failure from the start, the reason unexplained. Lack of radio contact
remained a problem for the communist party in Slovakia with the result that Moscow was simply not informed of Šmidke's eminent success. Šmidke was sent in by
Gottwald's group to put the Slovak Communist party back on a solid footing, re-
organise it, establish a 5th Illegal Central Committee of the Slovak Communist
Party and organise national committees throughout Slovakia on a broad basis.
They would include representatives of the middle-class parties, the Social Democrats and the Communists. However, the partisan bands were entirely separate,
were organised and led by agents dropped by and responsible to the Red Army.
They had their own radio contacts, and paid little or no heed to efforts to control
their acts by the military conspiracy planning the uprising, i.e. the Slovak 5th Illegal Central Committee or the national committee. The independent acts of the
partisan bands triggered German occupation before the planned uprising was
ready. During the subsequent fighting, the partisan bands repeatedly failed to fulfil
missions assigned to them, frequently vanishing from the battlefield, and leaving
military units with exposed flanks.

Due to the total lack of radio communication between the Slovak Communist Party in Slovakia and Moscow, Šmidke finally, was flown secretly into Russia from Slovakia. That mission was complicated by intrigue both in Slovakia
and in Moscow, with the result that two separate planes flew in a mix of dele-

gates. The Soviets and the emigrant Slovak Communist Party in Moscow detained Šmidke and the others, incommunicado, during the critical chain of events that precipitated the German occupation of Slovakia and the insurrection. Thus, when he most needed information, Golian was unable to communicate with Šmidke. He waited in vain to learn the plans of the Soviet Army, and for the signal that was supposed to come from the Red Army when they were close enough to support the uprising.

The Trigger

Regarding tactical progress, the partisan bands concerned themselves little about co-ordination with the two Slovak uprising movements. So they carried out a series of ambushes of *Volksdeutche* and isolated German vehicles. But, in addition, there came an event with grave consequences. On 27 August, a train from Zvolen, its German name Altsohl, arrived at the St. Martin station. (Turèiansky Svatý Martin).[4] In it rode the German military mission to Rumania, and 22 officers under *Oberst* Ott, returning from Bucharest to Germany. Elements of Slovak formations, led by the partisans who had denied the authority of the Tiso regime in Preßburg, i.e. Bratislava, stopped and searched the train. They interned the passengers, brought them to a barracks and shot the entire military mission, apparently by orders originating from the Soviet partisan leader Welitschkow.

The uprising was supposed to start in mid-September, as soon as German troops crossed the Waag River line in the west, the Polish border to the north, or the Hungarian border to the south. There was also the far less desirable second alternative. That would be in the event of the movement of German occupation forces into Slovakia. Lieutenant-Colonel Golian, with his headquarters in Neusohl (Banská-Bystrica), issued corresponding preparatory orders to 43 garrison staffs and garrison administrations. They had to establish intensified readiness for combat, and the organisation of the garrisons for all round defence.

Contrary to expectations, the incident of the disarming and shooting of the German military delegation did not constitute the signal for the uprising in Slovakia. It did not, however, remain hidden from the observation of German officialdom. Completely lacking were the German formations needed to immediately occupy Slovakia. All German formations were already fully committed on all fronts. Nevertheless, by order of Reichs foreign minister von Ribbentrop, the German ambassador Ludin sought and obtained permission from State President Tiso for German troops to move into the country.

---

4   Translator's note – In the long and complex history of Slovakia most of the cities and towns were actually founded by immigrant Germans, thus, having well-established German names. Until recently, most of the cities and towns in Slovakia have been shown in atlases with their German names. Since WWII, however, the Slovak names have generally been used. Therefore, where the author used the German name, the Slovak name will normally be given in parentheses.

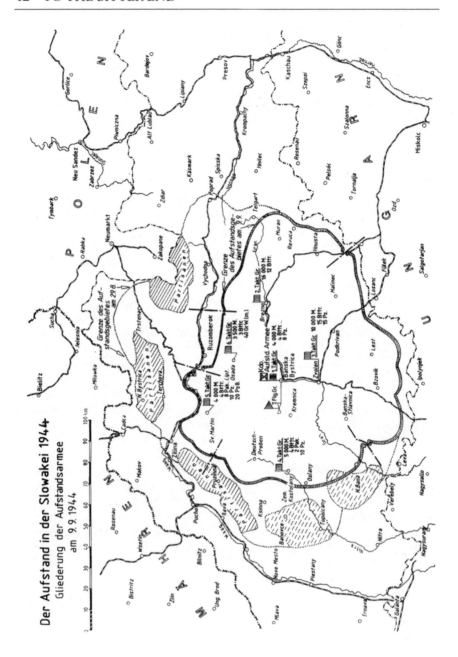

7 The uprising in Slovakia 1944: organisation of the army of the uprising,
9 September 1944

A German assault gun liberally endowed with additional camouflage

German Troops march in

On 19 August, the *Kampfgruppe* of *Oberst* von Ohlen, i.e. 178th *Panzer-Division*, moved into Slovakia towards Sillein (Žilina).[5] The *Reichsprotektor Böhmen und Mähren*[6] and *Heeresgruppe Nordukraine* were ordered to put together *Kampfgruppen* in regimental strength. They were to advance into the industrialised area of Slovakia from the southwest via Preßburg (Bratislava), and from the northeast via Poprad (Deutschendorf). The Germans viewed that action against the military uprising as a police action. Accordingly, *SS-Obergruppenführer* Berger was placed in command, as the *Oberbefehlshaber in Slovakie*, but without a specified mission. *Oberstleutnant* Uechtritz, the chief of staff to the *Oberbefehlshaber* was the person who was, in effect, the actual source of military command that directed the German actions. The *Kampfgruppen* moved into Slovakia from the west almost

---

5   Translator's note – The 178th *Panzer-Division* was a replacement and training division. Although designated a *Panzer-Division*, in truth, it amounted to no more than a weak infantry brigade. Venohr describes it as consisting of one infantry regiment with three weak battalions of 600 men each, one motorised battery of heavy 15 cm field howitzers and one *Panzer-Kompanie* with about 15 combat vehicles. In early September (?) *Kampfgruppe* von Ohlen was redesignated "Division Tatra" and *Generalleutnant* Loeper assumed command.

6   Translator's note – Bohemia & Moravia.

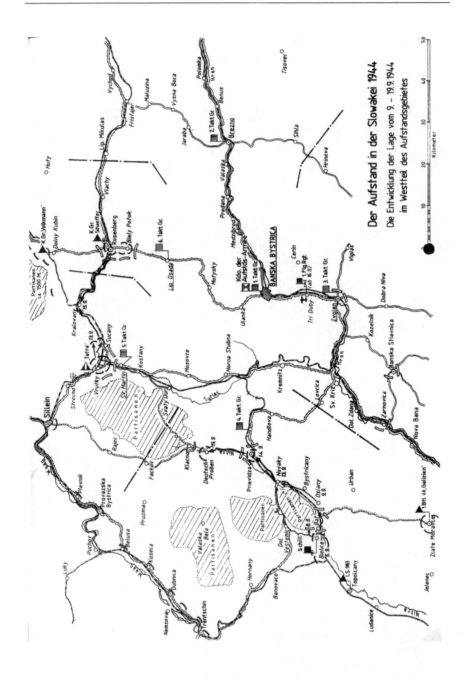

8 The uprising in Slovakia 1944: development of the situation in the western area of
operations, 9–19 September 1944

without objectives. Elements of German divisions from the Kosice (Kaschau) area followed the 178th *Panzer-Division*.[7]

While that was happening, the Slovak troops stationed in eastern Slovakia awaited orders to attack towards the east, taking from the rear the German troops defending the Carpathians. The Red Army had not yet achieved the prerequisites specified for triggering the uprising. The chief of staff of the Slovak 1st Army Corps stationed in the east, General Talsky, defected to the Soviets with his staff, taking 38 military aircraft, including several German Me 109s. The Germans then disarmed and imprisoned the now leaderless Slovak elite troops. From a total of 24,000 men, only 2,000 escaped capture by the Wehrmacht and made their way through to the insurgents in central Slovakia. *Oberstleutnant* Uechtritz, formerly liaison officer with the Slovak 'Mobile Division', as Chief of Staff to the *Befehlshaber Tschechoslovakie*, led the operation against the Slovak army of the uprising in eastern Slovakia.

With that, the danger of an uprising was averted in western and eastern Slovakia, but not in central Slovakia. After initially gaining ground, the German forces advancing from the west ran into opposition.

Activation of an Army of the Uprising

Lieutenant Colonel Golian directed the preparations, and from his command post in Neusohl (Banská Bystrica), the activation of a Slovak army of the uprising in the Brznow (German-Brezno)–Zvolen (German-Altsohl)–Banská-Bystrica (Neusohl) triangle. To that end he called up all those liable to military obligation of the 1939 and 1940 classes. The Slovak Air Force at that time had 57 aircraft. Only seven of those were Messerschmitt fighters, the rest being medical and commercial machines.

The first step, in the organisation of the forces of the uprising, was assignment of infantry and artillery to the individual defence areas, and the stabilisation of their lines. That halted the German advance from the west, on or about 7 September. Golian encountered significant difficulties in incorporating the partisans into the defensive front, as they essentially took orders from Moscow and did not place themselves under Golian's command.

Golian was well aware of the fact that the forces of the uprising at his disposal lacked the combat effectiveness of German forces. Furthermore, German soldiers were highly regarded by the Slovaks. In addition to the superiority in numbers of the forces on hand, i.e. 15,000 men, the mobilisation call brought in an additional 15,000 men. 40% of them were incorporated into the combat formations in the following two weeks, though with an inadequate supply of weapons. Golian departed from the previous practice of assignment of division and defensive sectors. He was in favour of so-called "tactical groups", each in brigade strength, with an independent air group. That was more appropriate to the operative requirements

---

7   Translator's note – The group that advanced from the northeast, capturing Kežmarok on 31 August and Poprad on 1 September consisted of a reinforced battalion of the *Waffen-SS* named *Kampfgruppe Schäfer* and a reinforced battalion of the 86th *Infanterie-Division*, a grand total of 2,400 men. (Venohr, p. 191.)

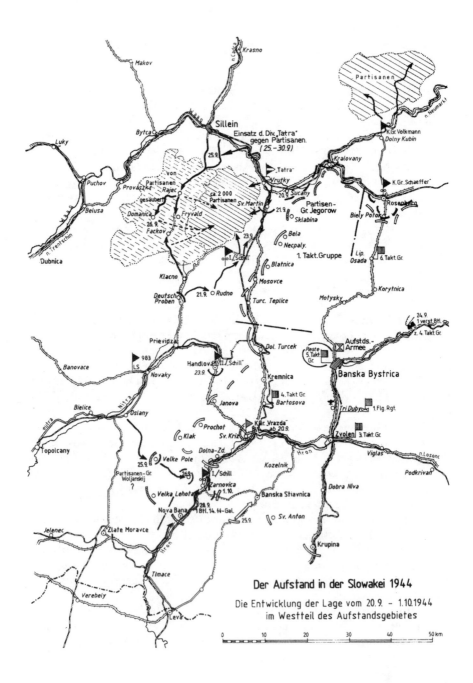

9 The uprising in Slovakia 1944: development of the situation in the western area of
operations, 20 September–1 October 1944

and geographical situation. The Germans were thus faced with 6 mixed *Kampfgruppen* of assorted arms.

The armament of the forces of the Slovak uprising at that time included 43 pre-war Czech tanks. The forces of the uprising had 40 mortars and 162 guns, including a dozen 7.5 cm anti-tank guns on self-propelled mounts, and several 2cm anti-aircraft guns. They also had 300 Czech type 37 heavy machine-guns, and 1500 Czech type 24 light machine-guns. Both of those were said to be nearly equal in performance to the famed and feared German type 34 and 42 machine-guns. The insurgents thus outgunned the German forces in artillery. Although their armour was more numerous than that of the Germans, their 43 pre-war Czech type 38 light tanks were gravely inferior in armament, and protection, to the German force's 18 *Panzer* IV, two Tiger tanks and 16 *Sturmgeschütze*. The balance of armament swung fundamentally against the Slovaks on 19 October, when the 18th *SS-Freiwilligen-Panzergrenadier-Division "Horst Wessel"* and *Sonderregiment* (special regiment) *Dirlewanger*, joined the fighting.

Until then, the German formations had consisted of one infantry regiment, with five weak battalions of 600 men each, one motorised battery of heavy field 15cm howitzers, and about 15 combat vehicles of the 178th *Panzer-Division* under command of *Oberst* von Ohlen. All other formations first had to be formed. To that end, the combat training school in Bohemia had to give up personnel and form individual combat units, such as *Kampfgruppe "Schill"*. In addition, *Kampfgruppe* Wittesnmeier came from *Heeresgruppe Nordukraine*. Finally came the totally inadequately trained elements of the 18th *Freiwilligen-Panzergrenadier-Division "Horst Wessel"* from Hungary.

First Slovak Defensive Fighting

The forces of the uprising were able to hold their positions on the three sectors of the front on 18 and 19 September. The 178th *Panzer-Division*, whose mission was to advance to the south, had been held up in the Vrutky area from 7 September by tough Slovak resistance. The Slovak 5th Tactical Group attacked the division from all sides, repeatedly getting around its flank security. That particular Slovak formation shone with its strong aggressive spirit. At last it received 20 anti-tank rifles from the Red Army, flown in to the Tri-Duby airfield, and other materiel, in response to Brigadier General Golian's pleas for help.[8]

On 9 September, the Slovaks attacked the Vrutky position from the rear with armour support, thereby suffering heavy losses. Nevertheless, the next day they renewed the attack, the final attack coming on 12 September. The 178th *Panzer-Division* did, indeed, repulse those attacks. But it did not consider it had the strength

---

8   Translator's note – The following passage from Wolfgang Venohr, *Aufstand in der Tatra*, p. 190, clarifies Golian's position after the start of the uprising: "Lieutenant Colonel Jan Golian commanded the '1st Czechoslovakian Army in Slovakia" – the official designation of the army of the uprising since 31 August 1944 – as temporary commander in chief until the arrival of Division-General Viest [from London]. Golian was promoted to full colonel at the start of September, shortly afterward to brigadier general."

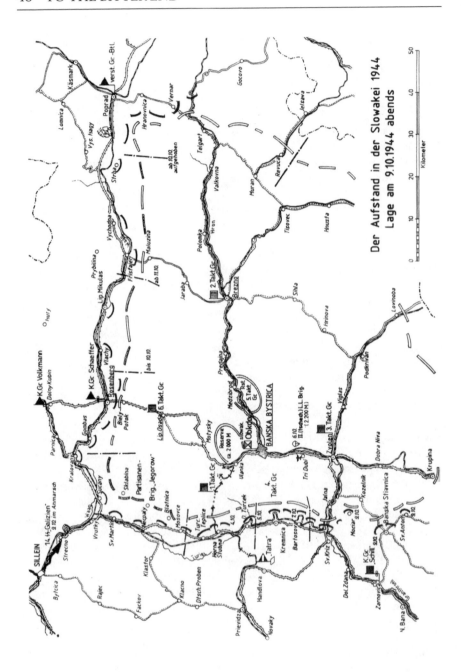

10 The uprising in Slovakia 1944: the situation on the evening of 9 October 1944

to carry out the intended advance into the territory of the uprising, to link up with *Kampfgruppe Schäfer*, which had captured Rosenberg on 6 September. It was only on 15 September that contact was established with *Kampfgruppe Schäfer*, with a bridgehead over the Waag River.

In the southwestern part of Slovakia *Kampfgruppe Schill* advanced along the Nitra or Neutra River valley, until the entire valley was in German hands. The Kampfgruppe gained the rear of the 5th Slovak Tactical Group, thus improving the combat situation for the German formations.

Slovak flyers with German Me 109 fighters did not amount to a serious danger, though they did manage to shoot down one Ju 88. Help from the Red Army finally arrived at the end of October, in the form of attacks by the 1st Czechoslovakian Fighter Plane Regiment with 22 Soviet machines, after their landing at Tri-Duby. The crews were extremely well trained and attacked the German air-strip at Piestany, destroying 7 machines there. On 18 September, they shot down one Ju 88 and three *Fieseler Störche*.

Dwindling Defensive Strength of the Uprising

The mobilisation did little good for General Golian for the simple reason that he could not provide arms for the recruits. Everything was lacking. Again and again, calls went out to the Red Army, and to the Czechoslovakian exile regime in London for support. Every type of equipment was lacking. They did not want to share the fate of the Warsaw uprising which had been left completely in the lurch. It would have been an easy matter for the Western air forces to have flown in massive amounts of weapons, ammunition, rations, uniforms and equipment to the Slovak uprising. In contrast with Warsaw, there was even an airfield available on which planes could land and take off, without interference from the German Luftwaffe.

Deliveries from the Red Army also amounted to no more than a drop in the ocean. However, later authors in the USSR spoke of supposed masses of captured German weapons being provided. General Golian had expected that the Soviets would fly in the two brigades of the Czechoslovakian Army Corps, instead of bleeding them white in the fighting for the Beskides passes. The Red Air Force could not provide significant assistance, since it was already stretched to the limit in the fighting on the Beskides front. Apparently it could not then be made available for the transport of heavy weapons and other supplies. Therefore, in the event, promises of troops amounted merely to the delivery of the 2nd Airborne Brigade when it was too late.

From the middle to the end of September the Slovaks stood entirely alone. The army of the uprising disposed of 15,000 men in the fighting units. In addition there were 7,000 partisans. The Germans faced them with 12,000 men, some of whom were questionable in their suitability for use at the front. In addition, the Germans had about 10,000 men in *Landwehr* (35–45 year-old reserves) and *Landesschütz* (regional-defence) units for guarding objectives in western Slovakia.

In effect, at that time Slovakia was torn in three parts. East and west Slovakia were occupied by the Germans, and used as rear areas for staging and support of their troops. Central Slovakia was the theatre of war. However, within the area, the command of the uprising had difficulty in asserting its authority, as the partisan groups refused to accept General Golian's authority. That affected not only organised

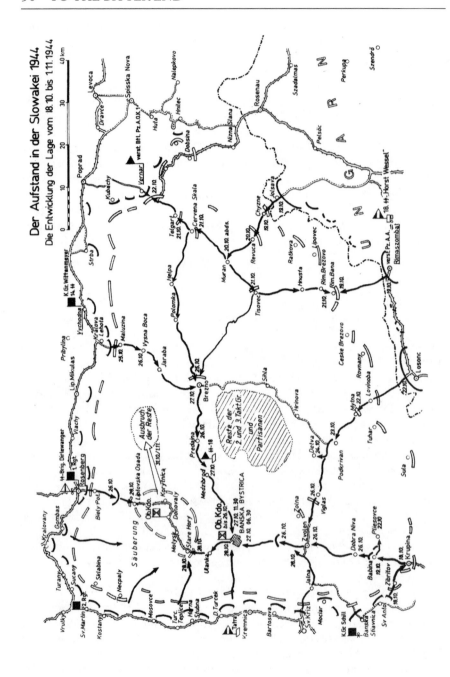

11 The uprising in Slovakia 1944: development of the situation, 18 October–1 November 1944

commitment to action, but also troop discipline, especially in the rear area. Neverthe-less, the forces of the uprising undertook an advance with the 2nd Tactical Group to the east and gained 15 kilometres to build a new main line of resistance.

Another tactical group, the 5th Tactical Group, held back the German attacks in the north, while the 4th Tactical Group lost the city of Handlova to the 2nd Bataillon of *Kampfgruppe "Schill"*. The German formations only gained ground slowly. *Panzer-Division "Tatra"*, formerly 178th *Panzer-Division, Kampfgruppe von Ohlen*, took the high ground between Sucany and Turèiansky Svatý Martin from the 5th Tactical Group. Their fighting power slipped at the moment when the 1st *"Schill" Bataillon* emerged in its rear, and a portion of the uprising's troops fled west into the mountainous terrain behind the German lines.

Further Fighting

The German formations did not develop the strength to break through the defensive lines of the Slovak tactical groups, and limited themselves to mopping up the terrain. In addition, there was no unified German command. The *Heeres* Army rear area in eastern Slovakia came under *Wehrmacht* command of *Oberstleutnant Uechtritz*. West Slovakia, on the other hand, was treated as a police action, under the Waffen-SS.

Defence became increasingly difficult for the uprising because of the shortage of weapons and ammunition. From one day to the next, hopes rested on a Soviet breakthrough on the Beskides front, from which the uprising would receive sup-port. In the meantime, *Bataillon "Schill"* forced its way on through the valley of the Gran (Hron) River. *Bataillon "Schill"* and *Panzer-Division "Tatra"* both received support from the *14th Waffen-Grenadier-Division-der SS (ukrainische Nr. 1)*[9]. On 28 September, the bridges over the Gran east of Zarnovica were in German hands. German spearheads were within 25 kilometres of the centres of the uprising in Zvolen (Altsohl) and Banská Bystrica (Neusohl).

On 4 October, *Panzer-Division "Tatra"* stormed the heights of *Obersturen* and captured several enemy guns. On 6 October, the division again assaulted Kremnica (Kremniz), with support from Stukas and ground-attack aircraft. The 1st *Bataillon "Schill"* also advanced and took Pitelova. In light of those developments, General Golian saw the uprising already following the fate of the Warsaw uprising. General Viest had been waiting in Moscow to be flown into Slovakia by the Russians. He took over command of the forces of the uprising, by order of the Czechoslovakian exile regime in London.[10] By means of immediate counter-attacks his forces recap-

---

9   Translator's note – According to Michael Logusz, Galicia Division – *The Waffen-SS 14th Grenadier Division 1943-1945*, (pp. 290 ff.). *Kampfgruppe* Wildner, a reinforced battalion, was committed separately from the main body of the division. Venohr (p. 246) records that the reinforced battalion was attached to *Kampfgruppe* "Schill" on 28 September. The main body of the division was committed separately in the Žilina (Sillein) area, the area in which *Panzer-Division* "Tatra" operated.

10 Translator's note – After 40 days of commanding the "1st Czechoslovakian Army in Slovakia" Brigadier General Golian handed over command to Division-General Rudolf Viest who had, by chance, arrived at the same time as the 2nd Czechoslovakian Airborne Brigade late in the evening of 6 October.

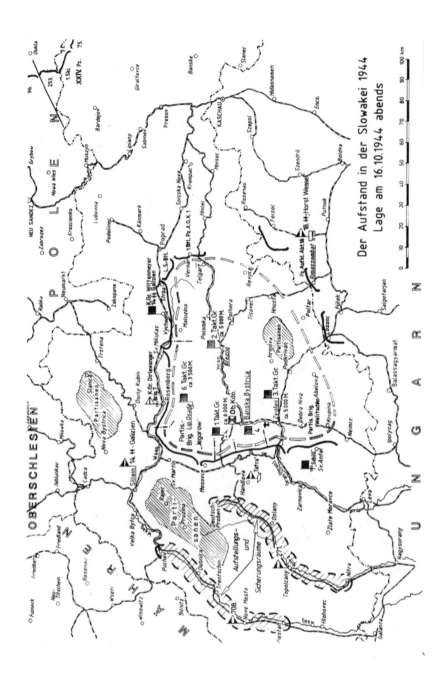

12 The uprising in Slovakia 1944: the situation on the evening of 16 October 1944

tured several localities. However, General Viest did not gain command of the partisans. They were under the control of the partisan leaders Jegerow and Welitschko, and of Colonel Molow who had been flown in from the Soviet Union. When the Red Army finally reached the Slovak border on the Beskides front, that brought no relief to the forces of the uprising, for the German lines of defence still held firm.

During the uprising, the Red Army provided 2,082 machine-pistols, 630 rifles, 256 anti-tank rifles, 467 light machine-guns, 90 heavy machine-guns, 23 anti-aircraft machine-guns, five mortars and 1,000 kg of explosives. The Western Allies delivered 80 machine-guns, 100 bazookas, 5,000 doses of anti-tetanus serum, and 20,000 wound-dressing packets. The 1st Czechoslovakian Fighter-plane Regiment that had flown in was supplied with fuel and bombs from the Soviet Union.

German Reinforcements

During that time, the German occupation troops in west Slovakia gained strength. Along with three railway companies, 7 *Flak-Abteilungen* i.e. anti-aircraft battalions arrived. 4 of them defended the Waag River valley from Nove Mesto to Poprad and 1 protected the Preßburg (Bratislava) area. An improvised regimental formation with 6 battalions served to defend against partisan attacks. The 271st *Volks-Grenadier-Division* with 7,200 men held the Nitra or Neutra River valley as far as Deutsch-Proben (Nitrianska Pravno). The 708th *Volks-Grenadier-Division* occupied the western part of the Waag River valley, from Nove Mesto to Puchov, with 6,000 men. The Galician 14th *Waffen-Grenadier-Division der SS (ukrainische Nr. 1)* with 14,300 men, extended continuous coverage through the northern Waag valley from Puchov to Štrba. A Landesschützen battalion and an armoured train from *Heeresgruppe Heinrici* closed the gap between Štrba and Poprad.

The forces of the uprising increased to 48,000 men, three to four times the number available to the German *Polizeibefehlshaber* (police commander), Höfle. In addition, only a small fraction of the German forces were fit for action at the front. Some consisted of older, untrained men. The officers were mostly wounded or reactivated older officers. At that point *Panzer-Division "Tatra"* and *Kampfgruppe "Schill"* had about 6,000 men. By order of the *Heeresgruppe, Panzer-Division "Tatra"* had to turn over Grenadier-Bataillon 1009 to the 1st *Panzer-Division.*[11] It was incorporated into the regiment, restoring it to a battle ready condition. *SS-*

---

11 Translator's note – According to Venohr (p. 253), although Höfle received orders from *Heeresgruppe* Nordukraine on 1 October to immediately pull the *Offizieranwarter* (officer candidates) of *Bataillone* 1008 and 1009 out and set them in march back to the combat training school, Höfle was not the man to let his attack plans go by the board, so he simply ignored the order and postponed compliance until he was able to spare those critically important units from the hard fighting. On 10 October, as soon as the fighting near Kremnica was over, *Bataillon* 1009 was entrained and dispatched to join the 1st *Panzer-Division.* Rolf Stoves, in his history of the 1st *Panzer-Division* (p. 671) records that, among the events of 20 October, *Sicherungs-Ausbildung Bataillon* 1009 , with about 700 men, was attached in those days to *Panzer-Grenadier-Regiment* 1, which had been in action with only a single weak battalion.

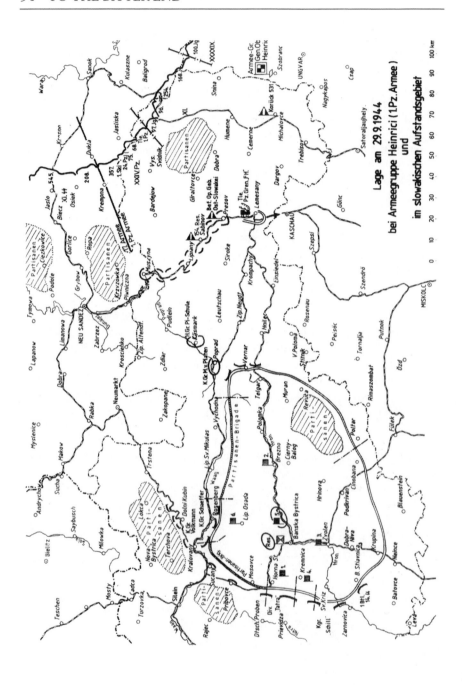

13 Situation on 29 September 1944: *Armeegruppe Heinrici* (1st *Panzer-Armee*) and the
uprising in Slovakia

Sonderregiment Dirlewanger, with 4,000 men and three batteries of artillery, took over the sector of *Kampfgruppe Schäfer*. A battalion of Luftkrieg students, with two batteries of artillery, took over maintaining contact with *Panzer-Division "Tatra"*.

The German command planned to close in on the army of the uprising from all sides, advancing from the northeast of Liptovsk Hrádok with three reinforced battalions of the Galician *14th Waffen-Grenadier-Division der SS (ukrainische Nr. 1)* (Kampfgruppe Wittenmeier), After a short period of training near the front the battalion advanced with 4,000 men via Kralova Lehota towards Brznow i.e. Bresno. It had to attack Brznow from the north and east. *Polizeibefehlshaber* Höfle planned the decisive thrust as coming from the southeast from the 18th *SS-Freiwilligen-Panzer-Grenadier-Division "Horst Wessel"* with 8,000 men, but with a frontal breadth of 70 km. The formation had to advance northward over the Hungarian-Slovak border and take the Slovak defenders in the rear.

The *"Horst Wessel" Division* had been formed from *Volksdeutsch* in Hungary. The thrust was delayed, because there was not enough rolling stock on the railway to transport the Division to the Slovak border in time. Some of its soldiers did not even have complete uniforms, let alone equipment. The division lacked infantry, gun and anti-tank companies, as well as the reconnaissance *Abteilung*. Only one third of the artillery had been assembled.

Resistance of the Uprising Crumbles

In mid-October, the leadership of the uprising recognised that there was no longer any realistic hope of action by the Red Army. Serious tension developed between the Slovak army command, which wanted to continue the regular military resistance, and the partisan supreme staff. They exerted pressure to have the army disband, scatter into the mountains, and go over to partisan tactics. In light of the failed hopes for relief by the Red Army, the resistance of the Slovak soldiers became exhausted. Nevertheless, orders to hold out continued to arrive from the exile regime in London.

General Viest saw the greatest danger from the *Kampfgruppe "Schill"* battalions in the southwest. He accordingly committed there the elite Czechoslovakian 2nd Airborne Brigade that had been flown in from the Ukraine. That brigade first protected the approaches by mining them with Soviet wooden cased mines, and barriers of felled trees. Nevertheless, *Kampfgruppe "Schill"* continued to advance. They captured two localities, and then made a change in direction that caught the Slovak command unprepared.

German formations attacked from all sides. *Panzer-Division "Tatra"* advanced from the west and *SS-Sonderregiment Dirlewanger* from the north. *Kampfgruppe "Schill"* and the 18th *SS-Freiwilligen-Panzer-Grenadier-Division "Horst Wessel"* achieved the only decisive successes. They seemed to take the Slovak forces of the uprising totally by surprise, having avoided the Slovak reconnaissance. On 20 October, the right wing of the 18th *SS-Freiwilligen-Panzer-Grenadier-Division "Horst Wessel"* thrust forward, and broke through the Slovak line of defence. Meanwhile the other eastern Slovak fronts held firm in the east, north and west. At that time, General Viest planned to abandon the resistance, break up the formations into small groups, and then go into action as partisans in the mountains. The London exile regime, however, forbade such a course.

On 25 October, the German formations, especially *Kampfgruppe "Schill"* and the 18th *SS-Freiwilligen-Panzer-Grenadier-Division "Horst Wessel"* continued their advance and captured the city of Brezno. The partisan commanders withdrew their brigades from the pocket, in order to wage guerilla war from the mountains with their 3,000 men. Only Jegorow's 'Stalin' Brigade remained on the front with the army of the uprising. On 26 October, the resistance of the forces of the uprising and the 1st Czechoslovakian Army in Slovakia collapsed. On the night of 26 October, *Kampfgruppe "Schill"* occupied Neusohl (Banská Bystrica), the former central base of the uprising.

Members of the 1st Tactical Group, west of Neusohl, continued to put up resistance against *Panzer-Division "Tatra"* and to the north, against *SS-Sonderregiment Dirlewanger.* Even though the exile regime in London continued to issue orders to hold on, the loss of all hopes for relief by the Red Army enervated the soldiers of the Slovak army. General Viest issued orders from Donnovaly, north of Neusohl, for the remaining formations to act exclusively as partisans. That marked the start of what General Golian had already feared after the outcome of the Warsaw uprising. The defensive fighting had cost the lives of about 5,000 Slovak soldiers. Over 15,000 were taken prisoner. The main body of the 2nd Airborne Brigade went into the mountains, joining the partisans.

IV

Schwerpunkt Shifts from the Beskides
to the Carpathians

The Soviet plan of attack had allotted five days to establish contact with the Slovaks, a distance of about 100 km. That assumed an average advance of 20 kilometres per day to Presov. As the Soviet 38th Army could not make effective use of its armour in the mountains, the Soviet command had used a massive amount of artillery. On 8 September, 1,000 Soviet guns of all calibres struck the first blow, on a 10 kilometre front, with a barrage that lasted 2½ hours, with 150 guns per kilometre, as against two to three tubes on the German side. Initially, the *Schwerpunkt* was on the right wing in the Krosno area. Later, the offensive broadened to a width of 80 kilometres. The Soviet attacks foundered on the resistance of the 68th *Brandenburgische Infanterie-Division*. The 2nd Czechoslovakian Army Corps with the 25th Tank Corps, 1st Guards Cavalry Corps and the 52nd, 67th and 101st Rifle Corps attacked the lines of the German 68th, 46th and 253rd *Infanterie-Divisionen*, with a superiority in infantry of 4:1 and in artillery of 10:1.

Strong German resistance caused the Soviets to shift the attack to other sectors. Accordingly the 17th Guards Rifle Corps initially was to hold the former lines and then close up to the movement using by-roads. It consisted of over 23,200 men, 495 guns and mortars, including anti-tank guns and 920 machine-guns. Facing it were the Hungarian 1st and 2nd *Gebirgsbrigaden*, the Hungarian 10th *Infanterie-Division*, 27th *Jäger-Division*, one border detachment and about two independent infantry battalions with a total of 33,000 men, 452 guns and mortars and about 1,170 machine-guns. The figures came later from Soviet sources.

The Soviets hoped that those attacks on the broader Carpathian front would provide relief to the Beskides front. In light of the fact that the roads were locally only usable for heavy vehicles in dry weather, the Soviets depended on infantry attacks, via unimproved roads and footpaths, with the concern to improve routes for bringing up medium and light artillery. The southern outliers of the Carpathians, however, offered only limited possibilities of advance. There were a restricted number of valleys running in the desired direction of advance, as well as steep slopes and dense forest. As a result of such conditions underfoot, the Carpathians could only be crossed by relatively small troop formations. They had to work with the tactical co-operation of companies, battalions and occasionally regiments. Their movement and direction depended on the unevenness of the terrain. On the other hand, the tall, dense forests provided good opportunities for concealment, but made for complicated orientation.

The further the Soviet advance detachments moved into the foothills of the Carpathians, the stiffer proved the resistance of the German and Hungarian formations. The terrain favoured construction of strong defences on the route of the advance.

On the other hand, the advance towards the Carpathians from the east and northeast, offered the possibility of relieving the formations fighting on the

German field artillery preparing to fire

Beskides front, and in that way, to hasten the advance into the Hungarian plains. Everywhere, however, the paths and routes of advance were seriously disrupted by German pioneers with mines and bridge demolitions, so that every advance could be relatively easily held back by small German units. All of that repeatedly forced the Soviets to seek detours that were difficult of access. Unfavourable weather caused the Soviets additional difficulties. Downpours rendered the mountain paths nearly impassable. Thick fog over the peaks and in the valleys interfered with artillery support, and prevented the use of aircraft. Uzgorod and Muacevo remained the objective.

Further Fighting on the Carpathian Front

The heavy fighting in the month of September had not brought the Soviets the desired success, regardless of the personnel and logistical difficulties on the German side. The Germans had made skilful use of the opportunities offered by the terrain, thereby contributing to the limited accomplishments of the Soviet troops, despite their self-sacrificing commitment. The defenders appeared to depend mainly on heights that provided good observation of approaches, passes and roads, as well as built-up areas. The areas between the strongpoints, valleys, roads and approaches to the peaks, were secured with interlocking fields of machine-gun fire. Dead angles were guarded by squads with machine pistols. The German troops had constructed a variety of obstacles, and had mined the outpost area and advanced positions, roads and valleys. Trees had been felled as barriers, margins of woods secured with barbed wire, valleys and roads secured with anti-tank ditches and

Such muddy and waterlogged conditions were typical during the combats fought during the autumn of 1944

'dragon's teeth' i.e. concrete pyramids. In addition, German formations had blown all the bridges. Not only had they mined the roads and their hedge-tops, on which they retreated, but also pullouts and areas suitable for rest, such as woods, meadows, gardens and springs.

According to Soviet reports, when forced to evacuate hills or ridge lines the German troops clung fast to the next heights, which had been provided with prepared firing positions for guns and mortars. Timely fortification, mainly on hills commanding the roads, turned them into powerful strongpoints and nests of resistance, surrounded with trenches, wire entanglements and mine fields. The Germans did not pull forces back from sectors under attack, unless Soviet troops in a sector had penetrated the entire tactical depth of the German defence. In such cases, the retreat of the main forces was covered by special detachments held in readiness for that purpose. Groups of 15 to 30 men with three to five light, or two or three heavy machine-guns were dug in on the hills and put up stiff resistance. It was only when they were in danger of imminent encirclement or envelopment that they fell back to the next hill. Because of the difficult underfoot conditions of the mountainous terrain, the German troops were seldom able to bring reinforcements to the heights that were under attack. Instead, they launched counter-attacks with armoured vehicles, delivered sudden, strong artillery barrages from two or more sides simultaneously, and then consolidated anew for defence in the next sector.

October Fighting

According to the results of Soviet reconnaissance, the number of German formations had increased since the early days of September. The overall numbers, however, had substantially declined, as a result of heavy losses in the approaches to the high mountain chains of the Carpathians. On 1 October, the 4th Ukrainian Front was faced by the German 1st *Panzer-Division*, the 96th, 168th and 254th *Infanterie-Divisionen*, the 97th and 101st *Jäger-Divisionen*, elements of the 357th *Infanterie-Division*, Hungarian 6th, 7th, 10th, 13th, 16th and 24th *Infanterie-Divisionen*, as well as the Hungarian 1st and 2nd *Gebirgsbrigaden* i.e. mountain brigades. In addition, there were 15 independent battalions and reinforcing elements, with 500 heavy and medium guns, 390 anti-tank guns, 451 mortars and 2,725 machine-guns, as well as 103 tanks and assault guns, according to Soviet sources.

Furthermore, the Soviets had to make painstaking preparations for each attack. Without such preparations they could gain no ground from the German and Hungarian formations. The September fighting cost the Soviets about 80,000 men, 25% of them killed. The 1st Czechoslovakian Army Corps under General Svoboda, which incorporated Slovaks who had earlier defected to the Soviets, lost 8,000 men, of whom about 30% were killed. Each day cost about 1,000 men lost, with about 250 killed and 750 wounded. In the first three weeks, the Soviets lost 442 tanks and assault guns for a total ground gain of 20 kilometres.

On 30 September and 1 October, the Soviets reorganised their formations and prepared for a general attack. 49 Soviet divisions and 3 Czechoslovakian brigades then faced 14 German and 7 Hungarian divisions who were defending a 360 kilometre front. The Soviets had a 2:1 superiority in infantry, 3:1 in artillery and mortars, and superiority in the air. The Soviets still hoped to bring help to the Slovak uprising. When the 2 Slovak divisions, positioned in eastern Slovakia, dropped out of consideration for such action, the resistance movement in Central Slovakia fought on for some time.

Soviet expectations of better success against the Hungarian forces on the Carpathian front, than against German formations, appeared confirmed by the 240 kilometre ground gained by the end of November. In sharp contrast was the mere 7.5 to 50 kilometre gain against the purely German forces holding the Beskides front.

V

Positional Fighting at the End of 1944 and Soviet Preparations for the 1945 Offensive

During the fighting in the Beskides and Carpathians, the situation in the central and left portions of the *Heeresgruppe Nordukraine* sector had quietened down. In fact the Soviets repeatedly delivered sudden artillery barrages on a broad front, but without launching any attacks on the sectors thus prepared. In fact they limited themselves each time to smaller sectors and used stationary troops, not attack troops. That fact, and the identified activity in fortifying positions, led to unmistakable conclusions regarding Soviet intentions. It seemed that they did not plan any immediate attack, but were planning to withdraw their formations for use in other sectors, probably on the Beskides and Carpathian fronts. According to the results of reconnaissance, one or another formation would be relieved for replenishment and refreshment.

The Germans, too, thinned out their manning of the front. They withdrew various formations, such as pulling out the 1st *Panzer-Division* at the beginning of September, to support the Beskides front. Some of the formations remaining had little combat experience, such as the *Kampfgruppe* of the 18th *SS-Freiwilligen-Panzer-Grenadier-Division "Horst Wessel"*. The 8th and 24th *Panzer-Divisionen* were also pulled out of the front line. Thus the remaining formations did not even consider themselves able to complete the planned improvement of the positions. Such scant manning of the front emphasised the urgent need to form reserves.

As the formations of *Heeresgruppe Nordukraine* had by then left the Ukraine, a change in the *Heeresgruppe* designation seemed appropriate. Henceforth, it was to be known as *Heeresgruppe A*. However, that re-designation was certainly unrelated to the relocation of the Soviet frontal boundaries.

From time to time, after long periods of Soviet artillery fire on a broad front, infantry operations were carried out in a single sector, with the support of individual tanks. They were possibly only to irritate German formations, to cause unrest, and to take prisoners for intelligence purposes. Such intentions were also the basis for similar actions by German elements.

Soviet Preparations for Attack

Unfortunately, the results of reconnaissance were not limited to encouraging evidence regarding fortification of positions on the Soviet side. At about the end of November and beginning of December, there also came indications of work in preparation for an offensive.

The map must have helped the Soviet command in making their plans. Bridgeheads of the type, width and depth of the Vistula bridgeheads, that enabled the concentration of major formations of all arms, seemed made for a continued advance to the west. German air reconnaissance brought reports of the construction of a series of bridges over the Vistula, and the preparation of firing positions, ammunition dumps, tanks and dummy guns. Everything led to the conclusion, that upon completion of their massive preparations, the Soviets planned a continued offensive to the west. The number of Soviet formations increasingly continued to fill the combat maps, which did not exactly encourage the German troops. Judging by previous experience, they could expect massive employment of artillery, followed by waves of armour. Such tactics had brought success to the previous Soviet offensive. However, the situation suggested that the Red Army would prepare for, and launch an offensive towards Berlin.

The Germans planned the construction of positions, including multiple positions with combat positions backing each other up in depth. At the start of preparatory artillery fire, the intention was to withdraw to the rear the troops manning the foremost trenches, according to the principle of the main defensive area or *Hauptkampffeld*. However, everywhere there was a lack of units that could concentrate on constructing positions to the planned and the desired extent. Aside from that, mere construction of positions could not secure a defensive success. Far more vital would be provision of the requisite combat formations to man them. At the very least, they would be needed in reserve. Up to the start of the Soviet offensive on the enemy side, preparations were carried out in the knowledge of the complete inferiority of the German forces, to those of the Soviets, in personnel and materiel. Among other aspects, the situation was true for both air forces and armour, and also with respect to the German shortage of fuel. The Germans had to be very economical with everything.

The Germans moved individual formations according to the results of reconnaissance. Due to the fuel situation, such movements were generally made on foot or by rail, with the result that they could hardly be concealed, or be rapid. The Soviets endeavoured to mislead German reconnaissance with dummy tanks and guns. In addition, sounds of vehicles and track noises in sub-sectors of the Baranow bridgehead were intended to feign the *Schwerpunkt* of the attack. Strong enemy air reconnaissance was an unmistakable indicator of Soviet preparations, as was registration of the artillery with high bursting points.

Diversionary Attacks

Diversionary tactics in other sectors of the front supported the intended delusion. The Soviets continued to advance against the right wing of the Carpathian front. Their apparent intent was to prevent the movement of additional German formations to the central front of the *Heeresgruppe*. Even more importantly, they wanted to cause more forces to be moved to the right wing. In the sector of the German 3rd *Gebirgs-Division* of the 7th *SS-Armee-Korps*, Batka was lost after hard fighting. The *Kampfgruppe* 4th *Gebirgs-Division*[1] repulsed weak enemy attacks. The Soviets also launched diversionary attacks against the 1st *Panzer-Armee* and 5th Hungarian Army Corps, *Korpsgruppe Le Suire*, penetrating into Tora. The 1st *Ski-Jäger-Division* of the 49th *Gebirgs-Korps* and 97th *Jäger-Division* repulsed strong attacks that were preceded by artillery fire on both sides of the Miskolc–Kaschau road, and at Hernad. Counter-attacks successfully closed the gap in the front, on the bound-

---

1   Translator's note – When a division was so reduced by casualties and other losses that it could no longer be considered a division, it was referred to as a *Kampfgruppe*.

A captured Soviet 76.2mm ZiS-3 gun pressed into action against its former owners.

ary between the 254th *Infanterie-Division* and 1st *Ski-Jäger-Division* on 20 December. The next day an attack ensued against the 3rd and 4th *Gebirgs-Division* with the 1st Hungarian *Armee* of *Armeegruppe Heinrici*. It then had to clean up the resulting penetration, as did *Kampfgruppe Le Suire* in the sector of *Gruppe Schulz* of the 5th Hungarian *Armee-Korps*. The 97th *Jäger-Division* repulsed attacks supported by armour, as did the 254th *Infanterie-Division* and the 101st *Jäger-Division*.

On 23 December, an enemy penetration occurred west of Steffelsdorf, on the far side of the *Heeresgruppe* boundary. It had to be cleaned up in co-operation with the front, from Steffelsdorf to the area southeast of Rosenau, in part with hasty counter-attacks. In *Armeegruppe Heinrici* the 1st Hungarian *Armee* repulsed enemy attacks. They forced back enemy forces that had penetrated on both sides of Wosgyan, as well as north of Steffelsdorf, and near Beje. Southeast of Pelsöc, a hill changed hands three times before ending up in enemy hands. The Soviets broadened their penetration south of Schmöllnitz. The 208th *Infanterie-Division* pushed forward an attack on Groß-Steffelsdorf, as far as the next fork in the road. Meanwhile, the Soviets achieved two penetrations after heavy artillery fire. The fighting cost both sides heavy losses on their sides of the Großmichel–Kaschau road, in the sector of the 254th *Infanterie-Division*.

On 25 December, the Soviets continued to attack Osgyan–Steffelsdorf in the Beje sector, and southwest of Pelsöc. *Korpsgruppe Le Suire* engaged in costly fighting without succeeding in closing a gap achieved by the Soviets. At that time, negative effects of the renewed partisan movement became apparent. They benefited from supply by air in the area of Rosenberg, Novo Bystrica, Sillein and north of Briesen.

On 5 January a counter-attack followed an enemy penetration in the sector of the 168th *Infanterie-Division*. A penetration south of Rakow by the 48th *Panzer-Korps*, was cleaned up with similar success. A counter-attack resulted in the capture of 45 prisoners, 5 anti-tank guns and 21 machine-guns. In the 9th *Armee* sector, the Soviets penetrated the lines of the 251st *Infanterie-Division* of the 8th *Armee-Korps*, using air and armoured support, but they were repulsed. The Soviet air force, favoured by good weather, showed heightened activity with 950 incursions on 5 January.

On 6 January, the Soviets also launched local attacks elsewhere in the sectors of the 4th *Armee* i.e. 48th *Panzer-Korps*, 68th *Infanterie-Division*, of the 9th *Armee* i.e. 251st *Infanterie-Division* of the 8th *Armee-Korps*, and also that of the 56th *Panzer-Korps* on both sides of the Zwolen – Pulawy road. Similar enemy assaults continued in the days that followed, among others against the 17th *Infanterie-Division* i.e. 56th *Panzer-Korps*, and the 357th *Volks-Grenadier-Division*.

Soviet Preparations

From Soviet sources it is apparent that by the end of November 1944, planning for the new offensive towards Berlin was already in progress. Berlin, however, was not the only objective. Also targeted were Breslau, and especially the Upper Silesian industrial region, which Stalin wanted to gain in undamaged condition. In fact the Red Army was still locked in fighting in Hungary and Slovakia. However, it had replenished personnel and material so that most of its formations could then take part in new attack operations.

The existing bridgeheads provided ideal bases for attack. The Sandomierz, also known as the Baranow bridgehead over the Vistula, had a front extending for 125 kilometres and a depth of 60 kilometres, allowing the concentration of comprehensive forces. The Soviet plan was to break out of that Vistula bridgehead on a 40 kilometre front, initially in the general direction of Breslau. The German troops were to be cut off in the Kielce–Radom area, and destroyed. Then, after the German formations had been driven off, the Oder was to be crossed. According to Soviet sources the Red Army had available for that purpose 3,660 tanks and self-propelled guns, over 17,000 guns and mortars, and 2,580 aircraft. The 1st Ukrainian Front alone included over 8 general armies:

5th Guards Army
21st Army
52nd Army
60th Army
13th Army
59th Army
3rd Guards Army
6th Army
3rd Guards Tank Army
4th Tank Army
4th, 7th, 31st and 25th Independent Tank or Mechanised Corps
1st Cavalry Corps
1st Cavalry Corps
Artillery Breakthrough Corps

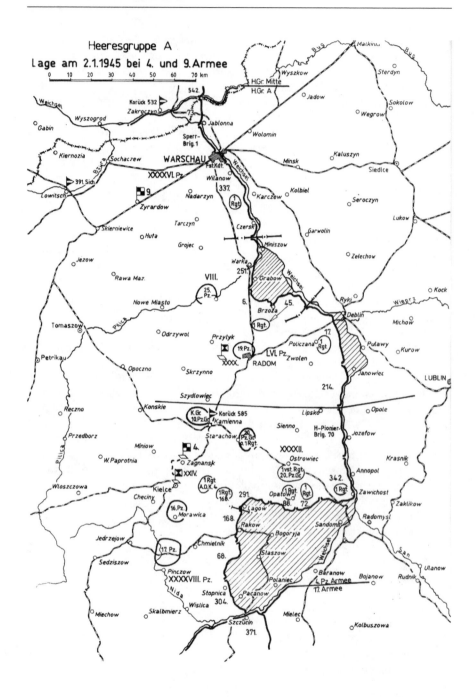

14   *Heeresgruppe A*: 4th *Panzer-Armee* and 9th *Armee*, 2 January 1945

plus several Artillery Breakthrough Divisions.

The last few were similar to a German artillery division i.e. a formation made up exclusively of artillery forces to support specified frontal *Schwerpunkte.* Such concentration of fire seemed necessary to the Soviet command, as previous experience suggested that losses were due to the slow tempo of the attack. Great masses of artillery would help the troops achieve the fastest possible breakthrough.

Initially, the command required, as preparation for a possible German counter-attack, the digging of approximately 1,500 kilometres of rifle and communications trenches, and 1,160 combat positions and observation posts. All of that was to be in readiness for the artillery blow. For the attack from the Vistula bridge-heads, the Soviets constructed 11,000 artillery and mortar positions, 10,000 bunkers for various cover, and over 2,000 kilometres of motor roads. Each division and each tank brigade was provided with 2 supply roads, to avoid traffic jams. 30 bridges were built over the Vistula and 3 ferries with great carrying capacity were established, according to Soviet sources. In addition, they set up 400 dummy tanks, 500 dummy motor vehicles and a 1,000 dummy guns. Soviet air reconnaissance photographed the German positions, and provided every front commander with maps annotated with the German positions.

On the German side, the Soviet reconnaissance identified provision of reserves behind the front of the Sandomierz Vistula bridgehead, consisting of the 16th and 17th *Panzer-Divisionen,* and the 10th and 20th *Infanterie-Divisionen.*

That movement of German armoured forces to directly behind the front line was the result of Hitler's express intervention, and contrary to the plans of his military commanders. In the event of a Soviet attack that was driven forward with motorised forces, with the objective of a rapid breakthrough, sufficient time had to be gained for the necessary combat reconnaissance to ensure that the German armoured forces would be committed at the tactically correct place. However, that would be impossible if those tactical reserve forces were positioned directly behind the front. In some circumstances, they would be subject to the Soviet artillery preparation. The Soviets refer to that decision of Hitler's as a "mistaken decision". The Germans made the same judgement. The preparation by the Soviet artillery was to cover the German positions to a minimum depth of 10 kilometres, so that there would be no further infantry resistance to be expected from there. Over and above that, it was to prepare an even greater depth of up to 20 kilometres.

Situation on the German side

The map showed what was a depressing situation on the German Eastern Front. Indented by the enemy Vistula bridgeheads, especially depressing was the limited array of troops. A peaceful resolution of the war no longer seemed possible at that stage. Earlier diplomatic feelers in Stockholm, in 1944, remained fruitless. Hitler made any negotiations, especially those of a peace based on compromise and abdication, dependent on the achievement of a favourable negotiating position that he envisioned as a result of his military successes. An additional hindrance was the demand by the Western Powers for "unconditional surrender". Churchill's behaviour made it doubtful that the Western Powers would lay down their weapons in the event of a possible armistice with Russia. A particular concern was what would

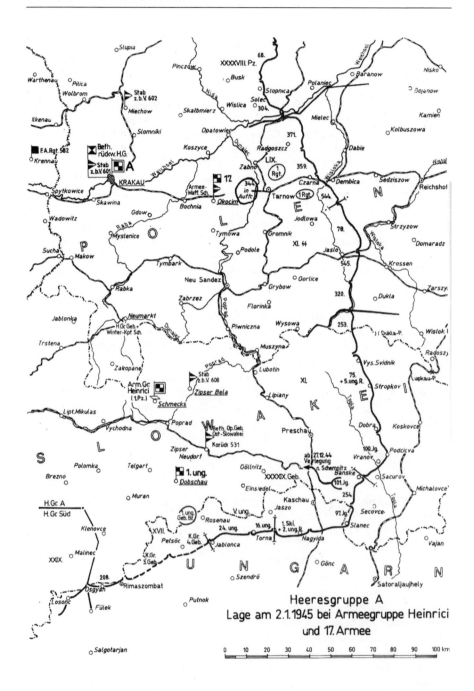

15   *Heeresgruppe A*: *Armeegruppe Heinrici* and 17th *Armee*, 2 January 1945

happen to the occupied lands. The German troops would have to fall back immediately, with the consequent danger that all the liberated lands of Europe would then turn against Germany. Goebbels encouraged that peace initiative, but failed to convince Hitler. It appears uncertain whether or not the Soviet Union's feelers were seriously extended in Stockholm, but at least they could have been investigated. During the second half of the war, the *Reichs* regime made no further effort on the diplomatic scene. Hitler hoped that the partners in the Western Alliance would fall out among themselves. He convinced himself that the Ardennes offensive against the Western Powers would be a total success, with the possible development of readiness for negotiation on their part. However, it assumed that the Soviets would not take advantage of a hoped for German advance in the west, in order to launch a simultaneous relief offensive.

In the meantime, in the costly fighting in various sectors of the Eastern Front, the German army had lost too many formations that lacked combat experience. In all sectors of the front, German forces were substantially inferior in personnel and materiel. The homeland proved incapable of replacing the losses in manpower, let alone doing so with battle experienced soldiers. Also, despite a great surge in production at the end of 1944, the armaments industry could not produce the requisite supply of weapons and ammunition. Particularly troubling was the reduction in petrol production. That was a result of the loss of vital oil production regions in Rumania and Hungary, and of western air attacks on synthetic petroleum plants. In March 1944, the synthetic oil plants still produced 180,000 tons of aviation fuel. In September 1944, that figure had dropped to a mere 5,300 tons. Petrol production for motor vehicles dropped, from 134,000 tons to 48,000 tons. In addition, air attacks on railway centres impacted on the bringing together of parts for firearms, fire-control equipment, motor vehicles and other military equipment, as well as supplies.

Command Conflicts over Assignment of Forces

Responsibility, for assignment of troops on the Eastern Front rested with Chief of the General Staff Guderian. He attributed the highest priority to that front, but was unable to convince Hitler of its importance. While Guderian wanted to retain the maximum possible forces on the Eastern Front, he had to give up one formation after another to the Western Front. Above all else, Guderian fought against the belief expressed by the commanders, that the available forces should be assigned to all the fronts in proportion to their current needs. That would have resulted in total tactical passivity. Meanwhile, Hitler hoped to change the situation with an offensive blow threatening other sectors of the front. However, that would leave the German front stripped of troops or, at the very least, inadequately supplied. The signs of an impending major offensive should have provided the utmost stimulus to transferring, as reserves, combat capable formations up behind the lines of the Eastern Front. Hitler described the reports of the enemy situation as "the greatest bluff since Genghis Khan." In his planning, he obviously relied on the end of the western offensive to provide opportunity to shift formations to the east.

However, the Ardennes offensive was postponed until December, after the armour committed there was brought to a halt by a shortage of fuel. Thus, the offensive could not be continued. But Hitler still refused to give in to Guderian's urging for the most rapid possible transfer of the combat formations standing in the west, to turn to face the Eastern Front. Hitler later ordered those formations to Hungary. Possibly, he had the thought in the back of his mind of protecting his nearby, and at one time his Austrian homeland. However, with that move, those forces were badly missed on the actual main Eastern Front of *Heeresgruppe Mitte* and *Heeresgruppe A*.

The Soviets were in no hurry to start their great offensive. Even if the German forces in the west were to achieve success, they would still be tied up in action for some time. In addition, it would take a certain amount of time for their transportation, so there was no pressure for the start of the Soviet attack. In the event that the German troops were successful in the west, Stalin would be able to make political capital out of that against the Western Powers.

Heeresgruppe Nord did not expect any decisive attack by the Red Army. That particular *Heeresgruppe* was well equipped, and remained in the Baltic region simply to tie down enemy forces, and for other political reasons. Those 30 Divisions that were stationed on the Kurland front could have provided substantial reinforcement for *Heeresgruppe Mitte* and *Heeresgruppe A*. But decisive political considerations played a role, as did concerns of the naval high command. If the Kurland front was evacuated, they foresaw serious danger to the shipment of ore transport from northern Sweden, and also to the training of U-boat crews. The final German attempt to restore land communications with *Heeresgruppe Kurland* ended on 13 October 1944. On 26 October, Hitler ordered the transfer of three infantry divisions i.e. 11th, 61st and 121st *Infanterie-Divisionen*, and one *Panzer-Division* i.e. 4th *Panzer-Division*, to *Heeresgruppe Mitte,* and for each to be at the disposal of *OKH. Heeresgruppe A* received nothing at all from that troop movement.

The High Command considered the sector of *Heeresgruppe Mitte* to be in greater danger than that of *Heeresgruppe A*. That may well have been because they assigned the highest probability to an advance on Berlin, possibly past the northern side of Warsaw, and also from the Pulawy bridgehead. Their assumption was of a parallel weak advance along the Beskides towards the Silesian industrial district. The Command saw the Soviet Pulawy and Warka bridgeheads as particularly threatening. Thereby they underestimated the significance of the broader and deeper Baranow bridgehead, in the great bend of the Vistula, and ignored reconnaissance results giving evidence of the concentration there of the Red Army. The Warka bridgehead was also frequently referred to as the Magnuszew bridgehead.

Despite repeated energetic warnings by the highest *Wehrmacht* Commanders, particularly Guderian, Hitler had the *Führer-Begleitbrigade* and the *Füher-Grenadierbrigade* transferred to the west. Furthermore, he had the 3rd, 6th and 8th *Panzer-Divisionen* along with the 3rd *SS-Panzer-Division "Totenkopf"* and the 5th *SS-Panzer-Division "Wiking"* pulled out of the main Eastern Front. They were sent to the Hungarian combat theatre, thus withdrawing those urgently needed divisions, along with their Eastern Front experience. In order to come up with forces to occupy the rear defensive positions, Guderian arranged for the activation of 100 *Festungs-Infanterie-Bataillone,* i.e. fortress infantry battalions, with corresponding batteries, which would man the rearward defence lines. However, 78 of those, almost 80%, were sent to the west rather than to the east. Captured guns were sup-

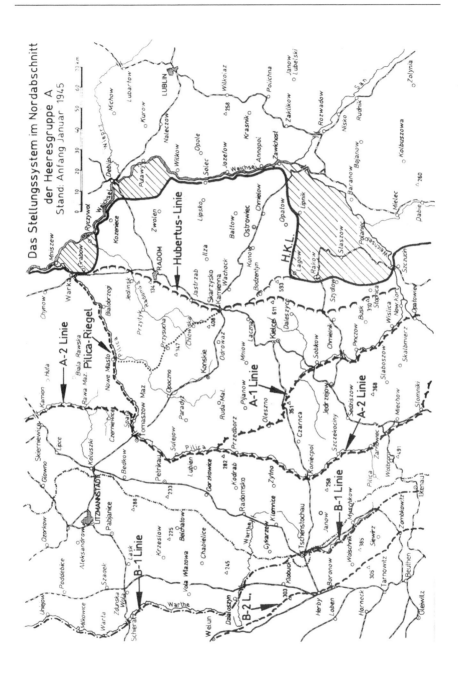

16 Defensive systems in the northern sector of *Heeresgruppe A*, early January 1945

posed to be built into the planned lines of defence. In the event, most of the captured guns, of 75mm or greater calibre, were sent to the Western Front. Only some 2,000 lesser calibre guns, with limited ammunition supplies, were sent to the East. It may well be that the creation of the *Landsturm*, later called *Volkssturm*, was a result of the realisation that the fortress troops, created by Guderian, were not used where he had planned. An additional problem for the *Volkssturm* was that its armament and equipment was the responsibility of the political *Gauleiter*, which introduced ambivalence into the chain of command.

Tactical Preparations

Thus, *Heeresgruppe A* found itself with a 700 kilometre front, completely inadequately equipped, and facing a major Soviet offensive. Moreover, Hitler influenced the formation of the reserves. The military commanders foresaw the placement of reserves further back behind the front. Their first commitment, after the *Schwerpunkt* of the enemy attack, was evident. It would determine the location of their commitment, once the direction of the enemy objectives and his tactics of attack were clear. Hitler, on the other hand, required that the *Panzer* divisions be positioned directly behind the main line of resistance, which subjected them to the extended artillery preparation of the Soviets' second wave. But most importantly, the reserve formations would become involved in the initial assault of the enemy movements. That would lead to a lack of clarity, regarding the development of the situation, needed at such a time, and in such battles. As a matter of necessity, great risks had to be taken. The troops defending the positions had to be supported with the requisite reserves, meaning they had to serve as tactical or operational reserves. With their help, the enemy armoured and motorised formations that broke through, would be attacked and destroyed.

The previously worked out missions assigned to the armies, foresaw the transfer of *Panzer-* divisions from one army to another, depending on the various developing situations. Thus, *Armeeoberkommando* 17, i.e. the 17th *Armee* Command, was to replace the valuable 8th *Panzer-Division* in the Tarnow area with the 208th *Infanterie-Division*. The 8th *Panzer-Division* would then be sent to the 4th *Panzer-Armee*. The 24th *Panzer-Korps* was supposed to position the 8th, 16th and 17th *Panzer-Divisionen* and the 20th *Panzer-Grenadier-Division* in two operational groups. They were to be located northeast and south of Kielce, to intercept the expected main Soviet advance in that area. The *Heeresgruppe* instructions foresaw several alternatives for the counter-attack. There was also the possibility of sending the 8th *Panzer-Division* and 20th *Panzer-Grenadier-Division* north to the 9th *Armee*, where it was thought that the greatest danger would originate from the Pulawy bridgehead.

Within the framework of the 9th *Armee*, the 40th *Panzer-Korps*, with the 19th and 25th *Panzer-Divisionen,* was positioned west and southwest of the Warka bridgehead. Its primary assignment was to deal with the probable hasty counter-attacks from the Warka bridgehead towards the west, as well as advances from the Pulawy bridgehead. Additionally, it was to prepare for a possible shift of the corps towards Warsaw, and also the possible movement of the 19th *Panzer-Division* in the direction of the Baranow bridgehead.

As part of the establishment of a main defensive area, i.e. *Hauptkampffeld*, the 4th *Armee* ordered construction of a so-called *Großkampf–HKL*, a major main line of battle resistance. Depending on the conformation of terrain and tactical requirements, it would run at a distance of a half to 4 kilometres behind the main line of resistance. Immediately before the start of the massive offensive, most of the troops manning the front line would move back to the *Großkampf-HKL* to avoid being wiped out by the massive artillery preparation. Between the main line of resistance and the *Großkampf-HKL* ran an intermediate position, so that the attacker would have to overcome a total of three lines, in order to penetrate the *Großkampffeld*, the major defensive battle area.

The primary purpose of occupying the *Großkampf-HKL* was to remove the troops from the known, and feared, massive enemy artillery fire. Defence against the infantry and armoured attacks would ensue in the first and second positions, before the fighting began in the *Großkampf-HKL*, as the third position. According to how far the enemy broke into that position, the tactical reserves would intervene and seal off the penetration. The operational reserves would only become involved after a complete breakthrough of the *Großkampfzone*, but in expectation of certain attrition by the attacking troops.

The location of the main line of defence, *Großkampf-HKL*, was within a distance of only 2 to 10 kilometres behind the main line of resistance. That placed it within the area covered by the Soviet artillery preparation, which reached a depth of 10 kilometres. Thus troops positioned within that depth would not have been withdrawn from the effects of the enemy artillery preparation[2].

As a rule, the armies pulled a battalion, sometimes a regiment, out of the front line and held them in readiness 2 to 10 kilometres behind the front, in exposed sectors. Thus, the German troops were committed to a rigid line of defence. But they were then lacking for a war of movement. They particularly lacked the necessary mobility to deal with a deep penetration of enemy forces. In light of the weakness of the troops, it was to be expected that the Soviets would achieve breakthroughs after completion of their usual artillery preparation. Therefore, the command had to prepare a defence in greater depth, as in the Hubertus Line. Only then would there be a possibility for the mobile formations to contain the enemy in the rear area. In such a case, the German troops would then regain the initiative. However, the fact that by Hitler's express orders, the reserves were held so close behind the foremost line, eliminated all such possibilities even before the actual start of the fighting.

A version of the plans also came out whereby the entire army front would be pulled back 20 to 30 kilometres behind the existing line. That was to take place just

---

2   Translator's note – In his memoirs (p. 342) Guderian describes how he intended that the *Großkampflinie* be constructed 20 kilometres behind the main line of resistance. It was to be painstakingly camouflaged and kept manned with security forces. Instructions were to be given that, before the start of the enemy artillery preparation, the main body of the troops manning the main line of resistance was to fall back to the *Großkampflinie*, thus avoiding the effects of the Soviet artillery preparation. Hitler, however, became greatly upset and insisted that the *Großkampflinie* be established between two and four kilometres behind the main line of resistance.

before the Soviet attack so as to allow the attack to fall on thin air, and render the months of preparation pointless. The Soviets then would have had to move their heavy weapons forward and organise a new attack. More comprehensive plans emerged under the code-name *"Schlittenfahrt"*, i.e. sleigh ride, aimed at securing time so that reserves could get into the rear positions well before the start of the attack.

Plans of that sort regularly ran foul of Hitler's refusal. The same refusal was given to plans to bring back formations from the Kurland Front, to the Eastern Front in the *Generalgouvernement*. Also refused was the shifting of formations from the west to the Eastern Front, and refusal ended the discussions in the headquarters of *Heeresgruppe A*, in Krakow on 17 January. At that time, there could have been an opportunity to immediately transfer to the Eastern Front what was left of the formations after the end of the offensive in the west. The operations planned for 1 January 1945, i.e. *"Operation Nordwind"*, and *"Nord-Elsass"*, caused a delay. After that, there was still a chance to immediately send experienced formations to the Eastern Front. However, by Hitler's orders, they were sent to Hungary.

At the start of the New Year, *Heeresgruppe A* was defending 780 kilometres of front with 31 divisions at the front, and 5½ mobile divisions in reserve, giving an average sector of 25 kilometres for each division. On the *Heeresgruppe Mitte* front, the average divisional sector was only 16 kilometres, and for *Heeresgruppe Nord*, only 8.5 kilometres per division.

On 9 January, Guderian presented Hitler with yet another report on the situation of the Eastern Front, and pointed out the flagrant inferiority of the German forces. Nevertheless, Hitler turned down the shortening of the front by limited withdrawal. The reserves and mobile formations between Memel and the Carpathians remained limited to 12½ divisions, some of which were not fully prepared.

At the start of January 1945, *Heeresgruppe A* comprised four armies with a total of 1,816 artillery pieces, 18 *Panzer* that were ready for action, 616 combat-ready *Sturmgeschütze* and *Jagdpanzer*, and 793 anti-tank guns. In the *Schwerpunkt* of the 4th *Panzer-Armee* were 96 guns, and 474 *Panzer* and *Sturmgeschütze* for a front length of 187 kilometres. The 9th *Armee*, on the other hand, i.e. *Heeresgruppe Mitte*, with a front length of 222 kilometres, had 586 guns, and 323 *Panzer* and *Sturmgeschütze*.

In fact, the Soviet command planned its first advance from the Baranow bridgehead, with over 400,000 men, 8,700 guns and mortars, and 1,700 tanks and self-propelled guns on a 240 kilometre front. However, it had also prepared for an advance on Berlin from the Warka bridgehead, using a corresponding troop concentration. From the Baranow bridgehead, in the great bend of the Vistula, in co-operation with the neighbour to the north, the advance was to wipe out the German forces in the Kielce – Radom area and not, as the Germans thought, head towards Berlin. Instead, it was to advance initially towards Breslau. Half of the forces from the other bridgeheads were to advance to the northwest, to take the German forces near Warsaw in the flank and rear. The other half was to advance on Kutno and Posen. The Soviets planned to attack with 2 armies and 2 tank corps, from the Pulawy bridgehead on a 13 kilometre wide sector. They intended to advance generally west towards Litzmannstadt (Lodz). However, a part of the forces would be taking part in the envelopment of German forces near Kielce in co-operation with the north wing of the 1st Ukrainian Front.

The Soviets set the start of the attack for 20 January. They decided that by then they would be finished with the troop concentration, and in addition, expected favourable winter weather. On 9 January, the Western Allies requested that the start-date be moved up in consideration of the difficult situation in the Ardennes. Accordingly, the Soviet headquarters advanced the date of the attack, so that the 1st Ukrainian Front would attack on 12 January. Moving the starting date up caused no difficulties, as the preparations were well advanced. The troops were filled out with personnel and had a complete training programme behind them. The weather forecast appeared more favourable for the advanced starting date, than for the previous date in the second half of January.

The Start of the Attack

The General Staff of the army calculated the Soviet superiority at 11:1 for infantry, 27:1 for armour and 20:1 for artillery. The Soviet superiority in the air was great enough to control the airspace. With such force-ratio, from the very outset, even with the most extreme devotion of the troops and the best thought out and effective leadership, there was no chance of German success.

On 12 January, after 5 hours of artillery preparation, the Soviets initially broke out of the great Sandomierz bridgehead west of Baranow, in the front of the 4th *Panzer-Armee*. With great impact the Soviets overran not only the stationary divisions but also the relatively strong mobile reserves behind the front. Held there by Hitler's express orders, they were included in the Soviet preparatory fire and then drawn into the ensuing confusion so that there was no possibility of a planned commitment. The front of the 4th *Panzer-Armee* was broken through and torn apart. The Soviet advance was beyond containment, the more so as the Soviets immediately sent their operational armoured formations forward into the breach that they had smashed. Their main body advanced west to the Nida River, and their north wing turned in towards Kielce.

The next day the Soviets broke out of the Magnuszew and Pulawy bridgeheads against the south wing of the German 9th *Armee*. At the same time they committed weaker forces to a thrust north of Warsaw, preparing from the north to encircle the city, which had been declared a *Festung* or fortress. Despite a hard fought defence, the 9th *Armee* too, was unable to prevent the Soviets from breaking through to the west and turning their strong forces against the deep flank and rear of the 9th army's northern wing that remained at the Vistula.

On 15 January, Hitler ordered a two-division *Panzer-Korps, Panzer-Korps "Großdeutschland"*, to immediately be transported by rail from East Prussia to Litzmannstadt (Lodz). From there it had to advance to the south, and by attacking, close the gap caused by the penetration in *Heeresgruppe A*. Therefore a new front could be established. That corps was then lacking in East Prussia and spent precious days in transport on the railways. By the time it detrained Soviet troops had already reached the Litzmannstadt area. The divisions were caught up in the retreat. Soviet records of the available German troops proved seriously inaccurate, when compared with German records. They did not, however, make the same mistake that Hitler did of underestimating enemy forces. Instead, they more often overestimated them.

The Russians described the intended artillery preparation against *Heeresgruppe A* as 1½ days. After the start of the attack, however, the Soviets broke through the first position and part of the second position within a few hours, and advanced 6 to 8 kilometres. Thus, on the first day of the offensive, with the help of the 3rd Guards and 4th Tank Armies, which had, in the meantime, been committed, they advanced to a depth of 20 kilometres, tearing a 35 kilometre wide gap in the German front.

In the breakthrough sector of the Baranow bridgehead, they attained a concentration of 220 guns per kilometre by the 6th Artillery Division. The 1st White Russian Front achieved a density of at least 240 guns per kilometre of front, with 4 artillery divisions in its *Schwerpunkt* area. According to Russian statements, on the day of the attack, between 230 and 250 guns per kilometre were ready for action in the *Schwerpunkt* areas. There was a total of 32,143 guns and heavy mortars, 6,460 tanks and self-propelled guns, and 4,772 aircraft, with a total of 2.2 million men.

The massing of Soviet troops was so strong that the corps and army held back about one third of their forces as a second echelon. Assignment of independent tank and assault gun brigades or regiments, to the armies of the first echelon, was to enable the rifle divisions to break through the German tactical defence system. Tank and mechanical corps, or tank armies, were held ready for later commitment, to broaden the breakthrough in the depth of the area, and eliminate the German operational reserves. In that way, the plan was to avoid premature commitment of the operational armoured formations that would have to carry the force of the thrust of the attack into the depth of the German rear area. They would also prevent the manning of a rearward containment position by the Germans.

PART B

The Great Soviet Winter Offensive

VI

Prelude

The German View of the Situation

At the start of the year the overall situation of the German army was extraordinarily unfavourable. Instead of strengthening the Eastern Front against expected further Soviet attacks, Hitler obviously assumed that the Soviets would not attack during the cold winter months, in spite of the experience of previous years. Accordingly, he had ordered numerous battle-experienced formations to the west, for the Ardennes offensive. However, that did not succeed. American bombing, especially of the Rhine bridges, prevented the supply of fuel that was needed to keep the German armour in particular, continuing its advance. After initial success, the offensive ground to a halt. Instead of transferring the formations thus freed to the Eastern Front, which was *Generaloberst* Guderian's special concern, Hitler initially decided against withdrawing the formations. Perhaps he hoped that he could bluff the Americans by maintaining the numbers of troops in the west. It finally turned out that the southern portion of the Eastern Front in Hungary was closer to Hitler's heart than the Eastern Front in the *Generalgouvernement* in Poland. When the formations were finally released he did send them to the Eastern Front, but to Hungary, whereby they were lacking for *Heeresgruppe A.*

The *Heeresgruppe* faced the Soviet offensive with completely inadequate personnel and armament. In the meantime, reconnaissance had identified a major concentration of armour and artillery, but also in formations. The only remaining hope was for severe storms or some other such accident. Hitler expressed the opinion that the Soviet attack forces must have been crippled by previous offences, and ridiculed the portentous reconnaissance results as "the greatest bluff since the time of Genghis Khan."

The impending conflict was inevitable, the more so after diplomatic feelers from the Soviet Union in the spring of 1944 proved unsuccessful. Goebbels proved not unfavourable to such approaches, as he had recognised that the war could no longer be won. Hitler, however, expressed the opinion that a strong German position was the prerequisite to a compromise peace, and that, in turn, could only be attained through a successful military blow. All negotiations, then and later, ran up against the demand of the Western Powers for unconditional surrender.

Hitler projected a possible compromise peace on the basis of discord between the enemy powers. Hitler's plan for the Ardennes offensive may well have rested upon that basis. He convinced himself that a defeat of the Western Allies would deepen the differences between East and West, the more so if the relief offensive, demanded of the Red Army by the West, did not begin in timely fashion. For the Germans, after a success in the west, formations would at the very least be available to then be thrown into the Eastern Front.

German Concerns

With headquarters at Krakow *Heeresgruppe A*, under *Generaloberst* Harpe, anticipated with concern the impending Soviet offensive. Harpe had to acknowledge
there would be an attack in the great bend of the Vistula, between Warsaw and
Krakow. He also had to recognise the certainty of extremely thorough reconnaissance of the German situation, by the Red Army and by Russian and Polish agents
in particular, in the area behind the German line of defence. It had to be expected
that the Soviets had learned much, and had profited more, from their experiences
in earlier offensives. The German defence, too, had to profit from its most recent
experiences and discoveries in defence, against an attack using modern means of
combat. Accordingly, the tactical defence had the mission of smashing the attack,
to the greatest possible extent before it reached the main line of resistance. At the
very least, the German army had to contain the enemy's thrust into the depth of
their main defensive area. They had to weaken the Soviets. The operative reserves
would be echeloned in the rear of the combat area. They would then be able to decisively strike the enemy if they succeeded in breaking through the main defensive
area, but before they could break into the depth of the battlefield. Regardless of the
clearly extraordinary inequalities of forces, the *Heeresgruppe* still hoped that it
could succeed in carrying out the plan. However, hopes for that success fell flat
when the supreme commander, i.e. Hitler, withdrew several armoured divisions
and sent them west for the Ardennes offensive, whereby those units would no longer be readily available.

A senior German officer surveys a column of half-tracks

Chief of the General Staff Guderian was particularly concerned regarding the German troops. Therefore, as mentioned earlier, he arranged for the activation of 100 fortress battalions and 100 batteries that were, as a precautionary measure, to man the rear positions. However, by Hitler's orders, almost 80% of those battalions, 78 in fact, were sent to the west. At the same time, Guderian was concentrating on constructing systems for rear positions, with A–B–C–D positions all the way back to the border of the *Reich*, positions built, in part, by civilian labour. Those positions were supposed to provide backstops for the troops in the event of a retreat. Guderian wanted to equip those facilities with captured guns. But only 2,000 captured guns of small calibre, with limited supplies of ammunition, ended up in the positions behind the Eastern Front.

Guderian conceived the formation of a *Landsturm* or home guard, as a makeshift replacement for any withdrawal of the majority of his planned fortress troops. It was an idea that later bore fruit in Hitler's activation of the *Volkssturm*. A serious bottleneck developed, however, when it came to the weapons required for the *Volkssturm*. Complications also developed regarding the chain of command for the *Volkssturm*. Himmler managed to have the *Gauleiters* made responsible for the organisation, training, armament and equipping of the *Volkssturm*. In addition to the lack of arms and equipment, there was no possibility for realistic training by experienced officers and NCOs.

Guderian strove repeatedly for the withdrawal of the Kurland front, so that the formations there would be freed, and could be sent to the Eastern Front in the *Generalgouvernement*. Hitler did not allow Guderian's plans and concerns to have much influence on him. He merely ordered that 3 infantry divisions, 11th, 61st and 121st *Infanterie-Divisionen*, and 1 *Panzer-Division*, 4th *Panzer-Division*, be brought by sea to the *Reichs* territory. However, they did not go to *Heeresgruppe A* but to *Heeresgruppe Mitte*.

The troops themselves were engaged in the intensive construction of positions, with several lines behind one another, each having switch-positions and intermediate positions. Individual division sectors lacked the natural obstacles needed against enemy armour. There were no terrain elevations that would be useful for artillery observation. In addition, there was the problem of having an average of only 72 fighting men for a kilometre of front. That figure was for a depth, from the main line of resistance, all the way back to and including the regimental command post. During the weeks and months before the battle, the nights were filled with restless activity. In the entire depth of the division sector, men were preparing the terrain for defence. *Panzerjäger* i.e. anti-tank men, and pioneers who were not otherwise employed, reported for assault troop operations. They often brought in the prisoners so urgently needed to clarify the situation, with only minimal losses to themselves. Rear area services relieved the main line-of-resistance troops from building bunkers, so that the front-line troops could get a few days' rest at the soldiers' home in Radom.

Available German Forces

Formations at the front were not full of battle-experienced forces. The 344th *Infanterie-Division* in the 17th *Armee*, for example, was being refitted near the front. Then there was a *Sicherungs-Division,* i.e. security division, the 391st *Infanterie-Division*[1]. A *Sicherungs-Division* was a mobile *Landschützen* (home guard) division usually employed in rear-area duties such as object protection and area security. Seen in retrospect, the *Heeresgruppe* accomplished wonders with respect to training the troops, to the construction of positions, and to tactical operational planning. Being tied to the pre-existing shape of the front, virtually ruled out any flexible fighting retreat using the deeply echeloned system of positions.

The organisation of the system of positions in depth was supposed to provide the army with a certain backstop. However, that presumed an adequate strength of the security forces manning those positions which, for the most part, was lacking. On 1 January 1945, *Heeresgruppe A* had over 65 security battalions, 16 of which were its own battalions, in the command area of the *Generalgouvernement*. Only 8 battalions, however, were securing the A–1 line. All the other battalions were involved in other assignments behind the front, such as protecting stretches of railway, securing objectives, or combating partisans.

The troops waited nervously for the Soviet attack. They also felt, as did all front-line soldiers from time to time, that something bad was in the air. Indeed, they knew the German formations were hopelessly inferior to the Soviet forces facing them. *Generaloberst* Guderian was the one who said that, in the event of an attack against the German Eastern Front, in its present state of weakness, the front would collapse like a house of cards. Despite all that, the troops had faith in the tactical effectiveness of the *Großkampfzone.* They expected to take about 6 hours, during the night, to occupy the front zone before the start of the enemy offensive.[2]

However, as part of their comprehensive reconnaissance activity, including among other things the use of captured maps, the Soviets had gained a thorough picture of the layout of the German positions. They knew the tactical details, even the situation of the static divisions, right down to battalion level. The tactical arrangements of the *Großkampfzone* were thus well known to the Soviet command.

The troops eased their anxiety with the indefatigable construction of positions, aiming to do everything imaginable to increase the strength of the defences. Personnel had been replenished, replacements trained, equipment repaired, reserves of ammunition and fuel established. Regardless of the shortages, especially of fuel, the troops had certain 'black' stocks, i.e. the painfully accumulated, carefully hoarded, off-the-record reserves for emergencies. Those stocks enabled many actions that would otherwise have been impossible. Judging from previous experi-

---

1   Translator's note – A *Sicherungs-Division* was a mobile *Landschützen* (home guard) division usually employed in rear-area duties such as object protection and area security.

2   Translator's note – This requirement for 'advance notice' of enemy intentions was more realistic than it might sound. Past experience based on capture of prisoners for information purposes, defectors and indicators in the form of certain enemy activities suggested that the units right in the front line usually could expect about 24 hours advance awareness of an impending major attack. Even though it may not have been put to good use, in the event, the front-line units generally had that same awareness in the case of the impending great offensive.

German infantry carry ammunition supplies through a trench. Only extremely well constructed field fortifications could withstand the firepower that the Red Army could bring to bear by 1944-45

ence, such stocks gained significance. But static dumps of fuel and ammunition were mostly located at railway unloading points, and thereby exposed to enemy air attacks. Moreover, in a successful advance following main roads, the Soviets would come upon such points, making the dumps no longer available to the Germans when they were needed.

During the period of calm before the storm, the soldiers were greatly concerned about their situation. They worried about how the war could end without further outpouring of blood. Day after day, disturbing news arrived from their homeland, telling of destroyed houses and family members who had been killed. But there were also regular reports of carpet bombing on Berlin and other cities. Such reports gave rise to the realisation of the absolute air superiority of the Western Powers over the *Reichs* territory. That meant they could attack every transportation hub, every industrial plant, and could seriously impact on the production of logistical materials and their transport to the front. Such goods were urgently needed by the troops for continued fighting. Nevertheless, far to the east of the *Reichs* border, their duty clearly was to hold their positions in the event of an attack. They had to keep the Soviets away from the home territory. The behaviour of the Red Soldiers had become clear, with the recapture of the area of East Prussia that had fallen into enemy hands in the summer of 1944 at Nemmersdorf.[3] Citizens of other parts of the *Reich* could expect no better when the Soviets came.

The Soviet Concentration

The Soviet concentration of troops, in the individual sectors of the bridgeheads, had been identified with near certainty by German reconnaissance. That was on the basis of the usual unmistakable signs, such as registration of artillery fire, filling of the bridgehead billeting areas with new formations, and movement of armoured formations close to the front. German air reconnaissance was supplemented by monitoring the enemy's radio traffic, and the interrogation of prisoners. Those, however, did not give any clear insight into the timing of the Soviet plans. Judging by the experience of previous winters, constant cold would spur the Soviets to attack. The varying levels of fog would impact on the opportunities for using the Red Air Force.

At that point, the German command calculated Soviet superiority at 11:1 for infantry, 7:1 for armour, and 20:1 for artillery. The last was based entirely on the number of guns alone, not taking into account the vast amounts of ammunition available to the Soviets. The number of German divisions on the Vistula front was a delusion, when comparing formations committed. Hitler continually had new formations activated instead of replenishing existing ones. The infantry divisions then had only 6 battalions, and several of the newly activated *Volks-Grenadier-Divisionen* had only 2 regiments of 2 battalions each. That amounted to fewer than 6,000 men at full complement. At full strength, German companies had only 150 men, the Soviets on the other hand, as many as 600.

In addition, the Soviets had superiority in the air, enabling them to completely control the airspace. From the very outset, the given force ratio excluded the success that Harpe hoped for, even with the most extreme devotion of the troops, and the most well thought out and effective leadership. The troops and officers could only hope for unforeseen events.

Figures for strengths, released later, revealed that the Soviets had 15,100 tanks and self-propelled guns, and 15,815 military vehicles of all types. The German 4th *Panzer-Armee*, on the other hand, had 318 combat ready tanks and 616 combat ready *Sturmgeschütze* and *Jagdpanzer*, along with 793 anti-tank guns and 1,816 artillery pieces. On the German Eastern Front, the entire manpower complement was under 700,000, as against 6,298,000 Red Army soldiers.

---

3   Extensive and intensive familiarity with a vast array of personal narratives, documents and other material allows me to unequivocally endorse the unbelievably horrific accounts of vicious, brutal murder, pillage, destruction and rape perpetrated by vast numbers of mostly second-line and rear-area Soviet soldiers upon helpless civilians and injured or captured German soldiers as they moved into areas with German inhabitants. A widely known early example was that cited above, where German troops recaptured an area of East Prussia from the Soviets and discovered, to their horror, what had been done to the local inhabitants, mostly women, children and old men. Citizens of other parts of the *Reich* could expect no better when the Soviets came.

The greatest difficulty for the Germans was the inadequate supply of petrol, which seriously limited their mobility. As mentioned earlier, production of aviation petrol in the synthetic fuel plants had dropped from 180,000 tons in March 1944, to 5,300 tons in September 1944. Production of motor-vehicle petrol dropped in the same period from 184,000 tons to 40,000 tons. To put that in perspective it must be realised that, thanks to the tremendous deliveries of American trucks, without any shortage of fuel, the Soviets were blessed with far greater mobility than the German formations. Essentially, they moved on foot with horse drawn guns and vehicles.

German front line infantry divisions used every minute to dig trenches. Building a well thought out system of strong-points should have made it possible to continue to put up resistance, even after a successful enemy penetration. A rear position extended at a distance of 4.5 to 9 kilometres behind the main line of resistance, with several intermediate positions in the intervening space. The rear position offered the opportunity of using the advantage of the "main defensive area". The troops manning the foremost line could be pulled back to that position at the start of the Soviet artillery barrage.

In their preparations, regardless of extremely thorough reconnaissance, the Soviets overestimated the German forces, in contrast with Hitler's error of underestimating theirs. Upon that basis they prepared their attack.

Considerations regarding expected Soviet Tactics

All German considerations necessarily turned on what tactics the Soviets would use in their various attacks. Captured documents gave rise to reasonable expectations. The extent to which those instructions, which were based on previous experience, would be common to and used by all Soviet formations remained to be seen. Rules for action were developed on the basis of captured Soviet tactical plans being used to counter the current Soviet tactics.

At the start of the Soviet attack, the extent of Hitler's erroneous picture of the situation, and the effects of the resultant previous troop movements, was already clear. Events on the following day would only further substantiate that error in other sectors. In December 1944, *Heeresgruppe A* had been forced to give up 3 divisions to its southern neighbour i.e. 96th *Infanterie-Division*, 357th *Volks-Grenadier-Division* and 8th *Panzer-Division*, for which it received only the 320th *Volks-Grenadier-Division*. An additional infantry division i.e. the 344th *Infanterie-Division*, was *en route* from the Western Front. The attachment of the Hungarian 5th *Armee-Korps* and the German 17th *Armee-Korps* with two groups of divisions could not make up for the essential lengthening of the front in the Slovakian Erzgebirge. At the start of January, more formations were withdrawn from *Heeresgruppe A*.

At the start of 1944, by way of adequate armoured formations, *Heeresgruppe A* had available 2 *Panzer-Korps*, with 6 mobile divisions, i.e. 8th, 16th, 17th, 19th and 25th *Panzer-Divisionen* and the 20th *Panzer-Grenadier-Division*. In addition, the *Heeresgruppe* had available as a *Kampfgruppe*, the badly battered 10th *Panzer-Grenadier-Division*. The *Heeresgruppe* had to give up the 8th and 20th *Panzer-Divisionen*. In July 1944, *Heeresgruppe A* still had 200 fighting men per kilometre, with a front-length of 610 kilometres. In January 1945, it only had 133 fighting-men per kilometre, with a front-length of 700 kilometres. Military considerations had generally been pushed aside, thus weakening *Heeresgruppe A* and *Heeresgruppe Mitte* in favour of *Heeresgruppe Süd.* Hitler, it seemed, was more concerned about the advance of the Soviets in Hungary towards his own former Austrian homeland, than about the advance of the Soviets on the central front. Then the situation around Budapest developed, with the encirclement in the city of about 70,000 men of the Hungarian 1st *Armee-Korps* and 9th *SS-Gebirgs-Korps.*

Regardless of that situation, *Generaloberst* Harpe, Commander in Chief of *Heeresgruppe A*, anticipated with concern the Soviet offensive that would cer-tainly bring an attack at the great bend of the Vistula, between Warsaw and Krakow. He had established ground rules for the defence, in accord with recent experience and knowledge of modern means of combat. As noted earlier, the tac-tical defence had the mission of smashing the attack before it reached the main line of defence. If possible, that would at the very least, contain it in the depth of the main defensive area. If the Soviets thrust through the main defensive area, he hoped so to weaken them, that the reserves echeloned in the rear area, would be able to decisively smash the enemy in the depths of the battlefield. Despite the obvious inequality in the force-ratio, initially the *Heeresgruppe* believed it might possibly succeed in carrying out the plans. But Hitler, the supreme commander, withdrew more armour and *Panzer*-divisions to the west, for the Ardennes offen-sive. Those formations and units did not return in time to the Eastern Front, so that hope too, foundered.

Another plan was put out for discussion under the code-name *Schlittenfahrt*, i.e. Sleigh Ride. According to that plan, shortly before the start of the Soviet offen-sive, the front line was to be pulled back several tens of kilometres, thus rendering all of the Soviet preparations for the attack illusory. The commander of the 9th *Armee, General der Panzertruppe* von Lüttwitz, considered that a fall back of about 20 to 30 kilometres would suffice to negate the months of Soviet preparations for their attack. That, however, would involve the evacuation of Warsaw. A prerequi-site for carrying out that plan was the timely evacuation of equipment and supplies between the Baranow and Warka bridgeheads, i.e. Operation *'Entlausung'*, or de-lousing. With that evacuation, the 9th *Armee* and the 4th *Panzer-Armee* would be freed of all unnecessary equipment in their planned withdrawal. Hitler turned down the proposal for shortening the front by limited withdrawal. Despite Guderian's efforts, between Memel and the Carpathians, the reserves and mobile formations remained limited to 12.5 divisions, in part not fully prepared for battle. The *Heeresgruppe* therefore had to receive the offensive attack from its current positions.

As the most important mission, all that remained was to create a main de-fensive area. That had long been under discussion but, apparently, had made only slow progress through the levels of command. For example, the 6th *Volks-Grenadier-Division* should have pulled the troops back out of the foremost po-sition shortly before the start of the attack. The junior officers argued against that measure because of the good state of improvement of the positions. Appar-ently those levels of command had not yet experienced the effect, on unfortified trenches, of destructive fire that used all calibres. The troops had gained that

experience at a variety of locations on the Eastern Front. That must have become known, so that good improvement of positions may have encouraged a
certain feeling of security. However, that would not lead to the avoidance of
great losses. Experience had shown what would happen when such a barrage of
destructive fire, of all calibres, with profligate amounts of ammunition,
pounded their unfortified trenches. Those losses should have been avoided, by
pulling back the foremost line immediately before the start of the attack. In the
event, such firepower later led to losses of approximately ¼ of the troops in the
trenches.

VII

Start of the Soviet Offensive

Employment of Paratroops

A few days before the Soviet attack the alarm sounded in the quarters. Overnight, the Soviets had dropped paratroops in the area behind the German front. There was no question of them rolling up the front from the rear with so few individual soldiers, but rather of reconnoitring the terrain behind the front line, with its assembly areas and positions. The aim was to cause insecurity. Furthermore, the paratroops had to scout the usability of bridges and routes, in preparation for the Soviet advance, or even block them to prevent German troop movement at the start of their retreat. The *Wehrmacht* had used that same tactic during the advance in 1941. Among the paratroops dropped were some in German uniforms. They had the mission of causing confusion among the retreating German columns by issuing false orders sending them in wrong directions.

There was less concern about espionage by the Polish civilian population. The partisan movement in the *Generalgouvernement* proved less active than it had been earlier in White Russia. Furthermore, many Poles knew what they could probably expect if the area was conquered by the Red Army.

Soviet Attack Formations

1st White Russian Front, supported by the 16th Air Army

North of Warsaw:	47th Army
South of Warsaw:	1st Polish Army
Warka Bridgehead:	61st Army
	5th Shock Army
	3rd Shock Army (2nd Echelon)
	1st Guards Tank Army
	2nd Guards Tank Army
	2nd Guards Cavalry Corps
Pulawy Bridgehead:	69th Army
	33rd Army
	1st Tank Corps
	7th Guards Cavalry Corps (Reserve)
	9th Tank Corps

1st Ukrainian Front, supported by 2nd Air Army

North of Sandomierz:	6th Army
Baranow Bridgehead:	3rd Guards Army
	13th Army
	52nd Army
	5th Guards Army

	4th Tank Army
	3rd Guards Tank Army
	59th Army (2nd Echelon)
	21st Army (2nd Echelon)
	25th Tank Corps
In Support:	7th Guards Mechanised Corps (Reserve)
	4th Guards Tank Corps
	1st Guards Cavalry Corps (Reserve)
	31st Tank Corps

The Attack in Detail

Breaking Out Of the Baranow-Vistula Bridgehead

The bridgehead was bound on the north by the German 42nd *Armee Korps* i.e. 4 infantry divisions, one *Pionier-Brigade*, and on the west, by the 48th *Panzer-Korps* i.e. 3 infantry divisions. The 48th *Panzer-Korps* had to bear the burden of the defence along with the 304th, 68th and 168th *Infanterie-Divisionen*. The terrain of the attack had its boundary to the south on the Vistula, and in the north on the ridges of the Lysa Gora, which rose to a maximum of 600 metres.

The *Schwerpunkt* of the attack was identified as being directed against the 48th *Panzer-Korps*. Therefore, the 72nd *Infanterie-Division*, stationed southeast of Opatow, was to be withdrawn, and moved to the sector of the 48th *Panzer-Korps* by order of the commander of the 4th *Panzer-Armee*, *General der Panzertruppe* Gräser. However, the attack caught the 72nd by surprise, as it was on the move, so that it could not go into action with the 48th *Panzer-Korps*. One infantry regiment each, from the 359th *Infanterie-Division* of the 17th *Armee* and the 168th *Infanterie-Division*, was located on the right, i.e. the southern, and on the left, i.e. the northern corps boundaries.

On 11 January, at about 23.00 hours, the 4th *Infanterie-Division* brought in a prisoner who said that the attack was set for 12 January, at 03.00 hours. Thereupon the division artillery fired off 1/3 of its available ammunition, in concentrated artillery strikes, on infantry and artillery firing positions. Intercepted radio messages indicated that the firing had a significant effect. In the event, at 03.00 hours on 12 January, the Soviets delivered massed artillery fire on the main defensive area, alternated in hurricane like surges, from 08.10 hours to 10.30 hours. The Soviets had 267 guns per kilometre of front, with what appeared to be a completely inexhaustible supply of ammunition. The guns fired for all they were worth, at a rate of fire of only 4 rounds per tube per minute; for the medium calibres the rate of fire must have certainly been 6 to 8 rounds per minute. That would give a minimum of 70,000 rounds for the artillery preparation at the minimum rate of fire, in a single hour, and on a single kilometre of front. According to later Soviet statements, a total of 32,143 guns and heavy mortars were available for the Soviet offensive on the Eastern Front, along with 6,460 tanks and self-propelled guns and 4,772 aircraft. The entire strength of Soviet manpower, on the Baranow bridgehead front alone, amounted to 2 million men.

A German soldier awaits Soviet armour. He is equipped with a *Panzerschreck* (literally 'tank terror'). The official designation was *Raketenpanzerbüchse* 54, although many of the soldiers referred to it as *'Ofenrohr'* (stove pipe). This was a heavy weapon, served by two men, and could penetrate up to 9 inches of armour

The Soviets reduced the time allowed in their plans for the artillery preparation. Ahead of schedule, they committed their infantry forces against the foremost German positions. Then they moved against the German second position, and attacked with armoured support. The thrust took place with such great force, utilising the early morning fog and the planned gaps in the artillery preparation, that in short order, the attackers had thrust 6 to 8 kilometres through the German lines of defence.[1] Committed right behind the first waves of the attack, the armoured forces of the Soviet 3rd Guards and 4th Tank Armies thrust onward, to a depth of 20 kilometres. A 35 kilometre gap in the German front was torn wide open.

---

1   Translator's note – The Soviets developed and applied the practice of carefully leaving gaps in their massive artillery preparations through which infantry forces could advance while the barrage was in full force and the German defenders were taking cover. In the midst of the thunderous barrage of exploding shells the defenders would be unaware of those lanes in which shells did not explode. In some cases it has been reported that the lanes were at an oblique angle to the front, which would have made them even less likely to be noticed. Thus the advancing Soviet infantry would be in the German trenches before the defenders emerged from their bunkers at the termination of the barrage.

The massing of Soviet troops on the battlefield was so strong, that they initially had to hold back about 1/3 of their forces, as a second echelon, to then commit them as the next wave. They assigned independent tank, and assault gun brigades of regiments, to the armies of the first echelon. That assisted the rifle divisions to break through, with subsequent enlargement of the breakthrough in the depth of the area, and to eliminate the German operational reserves. They wanted to avoid premature commitment of their armoured formations, but at the same time, to carry the force of the attacking thrust into the depths of the German rear area. They had to thwart occupation of a rear containment position by the Germans.

During the Soviet artillery preparation, the German divisional artillery carried out their "rigid" plan of fire that had been decided on before the start of the attack. However, the German artillery found itself exposed to an increasing level of Soviet air attacks, and to the fire of heavy Soviet artillery. That led to the destruction of many guns, which weakened the artillery defence. Despite that, the Soviets too suffered not inconsiderable losses in the battle for the positions. Those losses went unmentioned in later Soviet literature. By Hitler's orders, the reserves had been brought up close behind the main line of resistance. They were then exposed to the second wave of the Soviet artillery preparation. As the higher command apparently did not have a clear picture of the situation on the first day, no concrete orders came for commitment of the reserves, or how they were to be used. Above all, the German command could not tell whether the Soviets intended, as Generaloberst Harpe believed, to cut off the German troops in a pocket, at the Vistula, or if they were aiming for the Upper Silesian industrial district. However, there were no available operational German reserves to plug the gaps. That allowed the main Soviet body to advance westwards to the Nida River. There they turned to the north on Kielce, to cut off the formations of the 48th *Panzer-Korps* that were still in the main line of resistance.

The next day, the Soviets continued their attack, moving out from the break-in area where they had made gains on the west front of the Baranow bridgehead. Using 4 armies, a tank army, and 2 to 3 independent tank corps, they significantly deepened their penetration. With that, the Soviet attack from the Sandomierz–Baranow bridgehead was a complete success. As a result of the difficulties in communications on that day, the highest levels of the German command had no clear idea as to the extent of the penetration.

Attack from the Warka Bridgehead

On 14 January, at 06.30 hours, the Soviets started their extended attack from the Warka bridgehead, using the 61st Army, 5th Shock Army and 8th Guards Army. The attack opened with an artillery preparation on the positions of the 8th *Armee-Korps*, especially against the front of the 6th *Volks-Grenadier-Division*. While the 30 minute fire preparation was in progress, Soviet advance battalions, were taking advantage of the thick ground fog. They broke into the forward German trench system with tanks and assault guns. In so doing, they used the tactic of utilising narrow gaps left by the artillery preparation. They attacked through the German main line of resistance and infiltrated between the strongpoints. Fog, at places lim-

A Soviet 122mm M1942 howitzer in action. This was the Red Army's standard divisional howitzer during the war.

iting visibility to barely 100 metres, aided the attackers in making the most of the moment of surprise.

After the first success of the advance battalions, the Soviet fire preparation extended to a depth of 6.5 kilometres, from 08.15 to 08.30 hours. The primary aim was to suppress the German artillery, while the main body of the Soviet armies entered the battle, under the protection of a double rolling barrage. The rear positions extended at a distance varying from 4.5 to 9 kilometres behind the main line of resistance.

Meanwhile, several switch and intermediate positions had been constructed in the intervening terrain. Indeed, because of the good construction of those positions, lower level officers expressed a desire not to evacuate the forward positions at the start of the attack. In anticipation of the disruption of communications that would result, during the enemy artillery preparation, the German artillery had worked out a "rigid plan of fire". With that help, depending on the evaluation of the enemy's primary direction of advance, rapid-fire concentrations could be developed. There too, the intention was to counteract the feared loss of observation as a result of enemy action, or bad weather conditions.

As a result of the fire-to-destruction, the 6th *Volks-Grenadier-Division* and the 251st *Infanterie-Division* suffered unusually heavy losses. The *Schwerkpunkt* was on the centre and also the left wing of the 6th *Volks-Grenadier-Division* i.e. *Infanterie-Regimenter* 18 and 37.

The superiority of the enemy force in that sector proved to be at least as great as in the breakthrough sector of the Baranow bridgehead. While the concentration of 8 artillery divisions there had consisted of 220 guns per kilometre, in the Warka bridgehead there was a concentration of 230 to 250 guns per kilometre. Concentrated in a 240 square kilometre area, were about 400,000 men, with a total of over 8,700 guns and mortars, and 1,700 tanks and self-propelled guns. The Soviets had to build a whole series of bridges and crossing sites over the Vistula. At the start of the attack the Front had more than 3 to 4 daily units of fire of ammunition.

By about 09.30 hours, on the first day of the attack,[2] the Soviet assault had already attained a deep penetration. By noon, it had reached the level of the regimental command posts. Employed on the right wing, *Infanterie-Regiment* 58 succeeded in a hasty counter-assault, in fighting free its staff. Thereupon, what remained of the regiment, forced a breakthrough to the south into the switch position that was about 9 kilometres south of the main line of resistance. The 6th *Volks-Grenadier-Division* suffered heavy losses, so its sector had to be counted as broken through, even though a few nests of resistance still carried on the battle at the level of the artillery protection positions.

In that situation, the 40th *Panzer-Korps* under *General der Panzertruppe* Henrici,[3] was supposed to launch a counter-attack. At 07.40 hours, it received orders from OKH to assemble southwest of the bridgehead, behind the sector of the 6th *Volks-Grenadier-Division*. Then came the *Armee* order, to take an assembly position for a counter-attack towards the north or northeast, depending on how the situation developed. At about 10.30 hours, the two *Panzer-divisions* i.e. 19th and 25th *Panzer-Divisionen*, reached the specified assembly position area. Even before the operation could begin, the 19th *Panzer-Division* was exposed to a heavy enemy attack east of the Warka–Radom railway line, during which it knocked out 51 enemy tanks. Along with the *Sturmgeschütz* brigade of the 6th *Volks-Grenadier-Division*, in a fighting retreat, they brought the Soviet armour to a halt by the evening of 14 January, causing heavy Soviet losses. However, the 25th *Panzer-Division* did not launch its counter-attack as it found itself under Soviet attack. Between the 2 *Panzer-divisions* was a gap that could not be closed. The effort had to be made to provide relief for the infantry forces who were fighting in the main defensive area.

On the evening of 14 January, the 40th *Panzer-Korps* and the remnants of the 6th *Volks-Grenadier-Division* held a continuous line east of the Jedlinsk–Bialoberzigi road. Meanwhile, the 251st *Infanterie-Division* of the 8th *Armee-Korps* still held a small bridgehead southeast of the Pilica River, in their struggle to defend the west bank of the river.

---

2   Translator's note – Remember, the attacks from the Warka (Magnuszew) and Pulawy bridgeheads started a day later than the attack from the Baranow bridgehead, so their first day is the second day of the earlier attack.

3   Translator's note – Do not confuse *General der Panzertruppe* Henrici, commander of the 40th *Panzer-Korps* with *Generaloberst* Heinrici, commanding *Heeresgruppe* A.

17 Situation of *Heeresgruppe A* on the evening of 17 January 1945

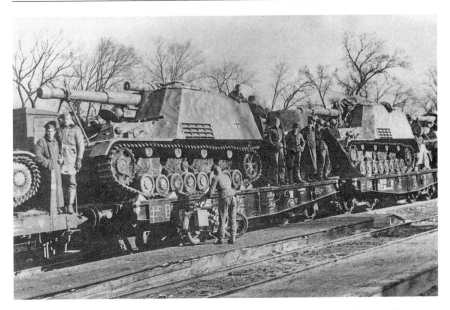

German *Hummel* self-propelled heavy howitzers loaded on board a train for transportation. This vehicle served principally with *Panzer* divisions.

Attacks from the Magnuszew-Pulawy Bridgehead

The Soviets broadened their attack from the Warka or Magnuszew bridgehead, with attacks from the nearby Pulawy bridgehead. The Soviet forces that had broken out of the Warka bridgehead advanced primarily to the west or northwest, towards Kutno–Posen as objectives. That was contrary to German expectations of a Soviet turn to the south to envelop the German forces on the Vistula. There was no immediate identification of such a direction of assault for the Soviet elements that had broken out of the neighbouring Pulawy bridgehead. With respect to that sector, the 17th *Infanterie-Division* was forced to attack with local reserves and a *Kampfgruppe* of the 10th *Panzer-Grenadier-Division*. No help could be expected there from the 19th or 25th *Panzer-Divisionen*, since those divisions each had only 1 *Panzer* and 1 *Sturmgeschütz-Abteilung* apiece, with about 50 tanks and a number of *Sturmgeschütze*.

On the morning of the first day of the attack, the Soviet 33rd Army achieved a deep penetration of the 214th *Infanterie-Division*. That led to the capture of Ciepielow, about 14 kilometres west of the main line of resistance. The division commander led an improvised counter-attack that proved to be fruitless. The introduction of a *Kampfgruppe* of the 10th *Panzer-Grenadier-Division* at 10.00 hours did, indeed, regain the commanding position near Ciepielow. However, it was soon forced into the defensive there and split into several groups. Finally, it had to fall back in a fighting retreat towards Radom. Reports told of about 100 enemy tanks knocked out in that fighting.

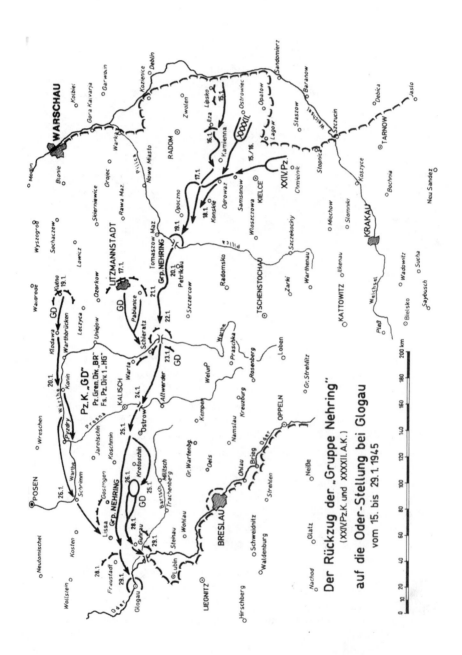

18 The withdrawal of "*Gruppe Nehring*" (24th *Panzerkorps* & 42nd *Armee-Korps*) to the
Oder positions at Glogau from 15 to 29 January 1945

At 13.00 hours, the Soviets had to commit another tank corps. It broke through the front at the boundary between the 17th and 214th *Infanterie-Divisionen* and captured the transportation hub at Zwolen. It thereby broke through the rear containment position in the sector of the 56th *Panzer-Korps*. As evening drew on, those spearheads approached the city of Radom, raising the possibility of encircling the elements of the 17th and 45th *Infanterie-Divisionen* that were still at the Vistula.

On the evening of 14 January, it could be said that the 9th *Armee*, with great pains and sacrifice, had prevented the Soviet breakthrough in the centre. However, the southern wing of the army i.e. 56th *Panzer-Korps*, had been broken through, and could no longer offer any resistance to the attacker. The main bodies of the 8th *Armee-Korps* and the 56th *Panzer-Korps* had either been wiped out or surrounded. Portions of the armoured reserves had suffered heavy losses. Isolated groups were working their way to the west among the Soviet spearheads.

On 15 January, the Soviets launched a new advance, committing the 2nd Guards Tank Army. They gained a 4 kilometre deep bridgehead over the Pilica River, east of Bialowrzegi. A German counter-attack there knocked out isolated enemy tanks but achieved no tactical success. By the evening of 15 January, the Soviets attained the line north of Mogielnica–Grojec, thereby threatening Warsaw from the south.

The 45th *Volks-Grenadier-Division* had been committed in that area, but could no longer establish contact with the 19th *Panzer-Division* by attacking. They were cut off, and all but a few fragments were wiped out. Remnants of the 56th *Panzer-Korps* attempted to build a line of defence at the east edge of Radom. However, the city then fell to the Soviet 49th Army and 11th Tank Corps. That meant the remnants of the 56th *Panzer-Corps* had to fall back to the Przysucha area, about 33 kilometres west of Radom. Similarly, the *Kampfgruppe* of the 10th *Panzer-Grenadier-Division* had to start a retreat, in the face of overwhelming enemy pressure. Finally, it could no longer maintain its coherence. Its commander was captured by the Soviets.

Extension of the Soviet Front of Attack

The Soviets on the northern front of the Baranow bridgehead contented themselves with knocking out the divisions of the 42nd *Armee-Korps* that were committed there. That meant the 291st *Infanterie-Division* was initially able to hold its position at the boundary next to the 48th *Panzer-Korps*, which had been broken through. Meanwhile, the Soviets broadened their attack front. On 15 January, the Soviet 38th Amy of the 4th Ukrainian Front attacked in the sector of the 17th *Armee*. Preparations for defence against the Soviet attack had foreseen, and thoroughly prepared for, a counter-attack by the 24th *Panzer-Korps*. Because the attack orders were issued too late it did not take place. The Soviets attained an 8 kilometre wide penetration of the 545th *Volks-Grenadier-Division* of the 11th *SS-Armee-Korps*. That was the moment when the 78th *Volks-Sturm-Division*, the 320th and 545th *Infanterie-Divisionen* and some temporarily attached troop elements from the Slovakian front, were moving into the adjoining left sector of the 59th *Armee-Korps*. At that point, on 16 January, the Soviets were able to force back the front of the 17th Armee about 30 kilometres to the west, behind the Dunajec River sector. The 68th *Infanterie-Division* lost its commander and two regimental commanders in crossing the Dunajec. The 359th *Infanterie-Division* had escaped in the fall back to the Dunajec. It was supposed to secure the open north flank, i.e. north of the Vistula, and receive the remnants of the 304th *Infanterie-Division* of the 48th *Panzer-Korps*. The hastily refitted 344th *Infanterie-Division* received orders to move towards Krakow. The marches took place in the fierce cold of –18° C (0° F), and amid heavy snowstorms over miserable roads and lanes. They were under constant threat of the envelopment of their flanks by overtaking Soviet armour.

The Soviets extended the front of their attack to the north, as far as the sector of the 73rd *Infanterie-Division*. It was stationed east of the Vistula, north of Warsaw. There, the Soviet 47th Army attacked, with the mission of capturing most of the area north of the Vistula that was still held by the Germans. That, in turn, exposed the Warsaw area to a double-sided envelopment.

Development of the Situation

On the morning of 15 January, *General* von Lüttwitz had already asked the commanding general of the *Heeresgruppe* for permission for the 46th *Panzer-Korps* to fall back to the west, towards the A–2 Position. The request included the evacuation of Warsaw. However, by evening of that day he had still not received the desired answer. The threat to Warsaw, from the north and south, made it apparent that the rapid evacuation of the "Fortress" was unavoidable. On the evening of 15 January, the 9th *Armee* ordered the 46th *Panzer-Korps* to fall back from the Vistula, while the "*Festungskommandant* Warschau" i.e. fortress commander continued to defend the city. Eventually, the commander of the 9th *Armee* received authorisation for the *Festungskommandant* to immediately evacuate Warsaw. The 46th *Panzer-Korps* would also break out towards Sochaczew, to retain contact with the southern wing of *Heeresgruppe Mitte*, near Hohenburg. In spite of Guderian's protests, Hitler suddenly ordered that the defence of the city continue, thus revoking all evacuation orders. As the evacuation was in full progress, the commander in chief of the army could not allow anything more to interfere. By noon of 17 January, the Soviets occupied the city of Warsaw with the 1st Polish Army. On 17 January, the elements that had garrisoned Warsaw linked up with the other elements of the 46th *Panzer-Korps*. At that time, it was falling back to the Bzura River Position south of Wyszogeva i.e. the A–2 Position.

However, the extension of the front that was under attack, was not limited to just the area from north of Warsaw to the Beskides. It also stretched, on the right, to the 17th *Armee*, adjoining *Armeegruppe* Heinrici to the south. On 11 and 12 January, the offensive had started there with a heavy artillery preparation that included the German front facing south in the area of the Hungarian–Slovakian border. The *Schwerpunkt* was directed at the 1st *Ski-Jäger-Division*. The division's personnel were completely burnt out. They were down to 10 to 15 men, who were equipped only with machine pistols. However, with battalions covering sectors 10 kilometres wide, there was no possibility of an effective defence of the line against massed enemy attacks. A counter-attack on 14 January gained a certain amount of ground against almost tenfold Soviet superiority in troops and materiel.

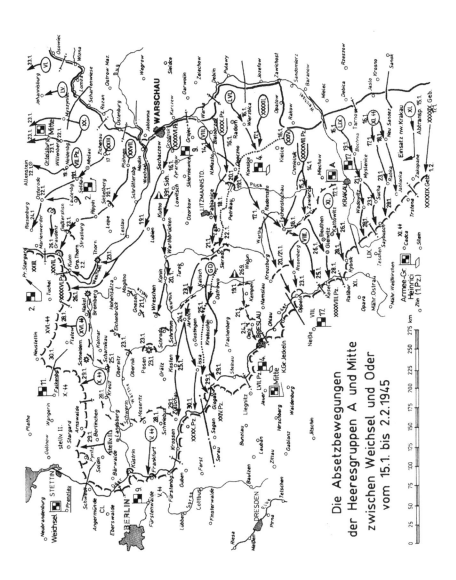

19 The movements of *Heeresgruppen A* and *Mitte* between the Vistula and Oder from
15 January to 2 February 1945

On 12 January, the situation also became critical for the adjoining 4th *Gebirgs-Division* southeast of Pelsöc, in the sector of the II./*Gebirgs-Jäger-Regiment* 9, when the Soviets launched an attack in doubled division strength. With great effort the *Gebirgsjäger* essentially were able to hold the hill position. But they were unable to prevent the enemy from bypassing to the right, in crossing the road at the level of Pelsöc and the Sajo River. Therefore the Soviets broke into the weak line of defence of *Gebirgs-Jäger-Regiment* 13. They took Pelsöc from the southeast, thereby surprising the elements of *Gebirgs-Jäger-Regiment* 91 that were still fighting to the east. In heavy fighting, the 4th *Gebirgs-Division* exacted heavy losses from the Soviets, reducing their companies from 100 men, to between 10 and 15 men. In 5 days of heavy attacks, the Soviets gained only 10 kilometres of terrain, without breaking through the German lines.

Because of the Soviet advance from the Baranow bridgehead towards Upper Silesia, Armeegruppe Heinrici was forced to evacuate its previous positions southwest of Kaschau, and between Kaschau and Jaslo In addition, the *Armeegruppe* had to give up formations to support the army groups retreating to the Upper Silesian industrial district. One troop element after another withdrew from the lines. They then made it to the Neumarkt-Makow area, south of Krakow, to the 11th SS-*Armee-Korps* on the right wing of the 17th Armee.

The 97th *Jäger-Division* also had to pull out of the Beskides front, and entrain for movement towards the Upper Silesian industrial district. Even earlier, the 75th *Infanterie-Division* was withdrawn from the 1st *Panzer-Armee* i.e. *Armeegruppe* Heinrici, to occupy the A–2 Position north of Krakow. There, however, it was bypassed by the Soviets. The 1st *Ski-Jäger-Division* also had to transfer to Silesia. The *Armeegruppe* received similar orders for the 100th *Jäger-Division* and the 208th *Infanterie-Division*. Transfer of additional formations, in the same combat sector, foundered on the fact that the 20th and 8th *Panzer-Divisionen* were still in action on the Hungarian front, and therefore were not so easily withdrawn.

First Provision of New Troops

In the meantime, Hitler may well have realised that his judgement of the Soviet strengths had not matched the facts. The Eastern Front had been broken through at various places by the Soviets, who then found the way to Berlin lying open for them. The only question was, from where could more formations come that could build a new line of defence?

Hitler had believed that the 9th Armee would be able to contain the thrust directed against it, at least to the Bzura River. He believed they could build a new front along the river. On 14 January, he ordered the immediate loading, and transport by rail, of 2 divisions under the command of *Panzer-Korps* "Großdeutschland". Their mission was to proceed to the Litzmannstadt (Lodz) area. They would immediately move south to close the penetration gap next to *Heeresgruppe A*, by attacking and building a new front. Although *Panzer-Korps* "Großdeutschland" was pulled out of East Prussia, its own organic *Panzer-Grenadier-Division* "Großdeutschland" was inextricably tied up in the heavy fighting near Praschnitz, in East Prussia. The corps command and some of the corps troops of *Panzer-Korps* "Großdeutschland" immediately entrained, along with the corps' own *Panzer-Grenadier-Division* "Brandenburg" and *Fallschirm-Panzer-Divison* 1 "Hermann Göring". The latter was taken from *Fallschirm-Panzer-Korps* "Hermann Göring". The corps en route was therefore missing at a critical moment in East Prussia, and then spent precious days on the railway. By the time it arrived, spearheads of the Soviet advance were already in the Kutno–Litzmannstadt–Petrikau area.

Instead of the planned, orderly detraining, concentration, and development of the corps as a coherent fighting unit, elements were caught up in the Russian advance. They were forced to detrain at stations scattered all the way from Kutno to Litzmannstadt and Petrikau, and were often drawn into battle in the immediate area. The intended thrust to restore the front was forgotten. *General der Panzer-Truppe* von Saucken himself arrived in Litzmannstadt on 18 January. It was clear to him that the original mission had been left behind by events. He decided that the best use of the fragmented *Panzer-Korps*, at least for the elements he could get his hands on, was to fight their way to the west. They would establish a firm German bridgehead at the Warthe River crossing at Sieradz. That would enable the wandering elements of Nehring's 24th *Panzer-Korps*, and the miscellany of other elements that had joined it, to make a safe crossing and passage of lines there.

As had happened so many times before, a change in personnel was supposed to make up for what was lacking in forces. In place of *Generaloberst* Harpe, whom Hitler blamed for the collapse of the Vistula front, *Generaloberst* Schörner arrived as commander in chief of *Heeresgruppe Mitte*. On 25 January, *Heeresgruppe A* was redesignated *Heeresgruppe Mitte*. Right then, Generaloberst Guderian's earlier prediction was happening, i.e. the collapse of the Eastern Front "like a house of cards". Where could the formations come from to build a rear defensive position? At that point, the supreme command was not even fully informed of the amount of territory that the spearheads of the Soviet attack had already won. They were still talking about a 6 to 12 kilometre depth.

Continued Soviet Advance

On 13 January, the Soviets had already crossed the upper Nida River in the Checiny area southwest of Kielce, despite the defence efforts of scattered hasty German counter-attacks. The Soviets made additional crossings near Wislica, Pinczow and Sobkod. Other forces simultaneously attacked the German bridgehead south of the Czarna-Nida River, against the 16th *Panzer-Division*. Moreover, the Soviets widened their attack sector. On 13 January, Soviet forces also enveloped the divisions of the 42nd *Armee-Korps* in the area south of Kielce, where the German divisions had hitherto maintained their positions. They still had the opportunity to advance against the east flank of the Soviet formations turning in towards Kielce.

While the Soviets bypassed those formations, and also those in action at the Czarna-Nida, they brought new forces into action, to feed the force of the attack from their depth. On that day they captured Jedrzejow, 15 kilometres west of the Nida. On 15 January, they took Kielce, thereby breaking the road and railway connection between Warsaw and Krakow, which happened on the third and fourth days of the attack.

The large number of Soviet penetrations and advances ruined any chances for the commitment of German forces against the Soviet offensive. The reinforced follow up attack of the Soviets, brought further deterioration of the German situation, especially as at that time, a planned reinforcement of the 4th *Panzer-Armee*, with elements of the 9th *Armee*, dropped out of the picture.

Locally, the 16th and 17th *Panzer-Divisionen* found themselves under attack from Soviet armour, without even having received commitment orders. It was only after darkness fell that, as they were standing by about 20 kilometres behind the main line of resistance, the two divisions received orders for a counter-attack. The delayed commitment proved outdated by events, as Soviet armoured formations had already broken through between the assembly positions of the two armoured divisions. That prevented them combining with the 24th *Panzer-Korps*. Elements of the 17th *Panzer-Division* fought their way west across the Nida River. Other elements of the division held a bridgehead, together with the 16th *Panzer-Division*, north of the Czarma-Nida near Morawica, with their front facing south. The 20th *Panzer-Grenadier-Division*, stationed further north, did not take part in that fighting and joined the retreat of the 42nd *Armee-Korps*.

A new counter-attack by the 24th *Panzer-Korps* remained illusory, as the Soviets brought up forces during the night and broadened their area of penetration. On the northern front of the bridgehead, the Soviets were content to pin down the divisions of the 42nd *Armee-Korps* that were committed there. The 291st *Infanterie-Division*, on the boundary with the 48th *Panzer-Korps*, was initially also able to hold its positions. The situation was similar to that of the 19th and 25th *Panzer-Divisionen*. The Soviets had separated the two, with newly committed advancing armoured forces.

Thus isolated, and no longer controlled by higher levels of command, the encircled German *Kampfgruppen* were forced to operate on their own. The difficulty for the division commanders was that they were unable to issue any sort of orders for retreat of the formations. Such orders had to be sent, ahead of time, to the OKH i.e. Hitler. They had to allow enough time so that counter-orders could reach the elements concerned. Hitler kept the enforcement of his directive under sharp scrutiny. For example, he had the *commandant* of Warsaw court-martialled because of his evacuation order.

The retreat of the 24th *Panzer-Korps* thus developed into a "wandering pocket". The formations of that army corps gathered up individual smaller marching elements of other divisions. Together, they had to aim for the crossing of the Oder near Glogau. Those were instructions that had been given from above. A new line of defence was to be erected there, and a new main line of defence formed.

That retreat of the wandering pocket followed no orderly plans. The Soviets ruthlessly thrust on to the west towards their intended objective, Berlin. They had no concern for flank security. Thereby the German formations, working their way west, often ran into Soviet tanks blocking the way. In that uncertain situation there was considerable confusion. In many cases the German batteries unlimbered and opened fire. However, the Soviets cared little about any elements of German formations staying in place, or moving. Their mission was to gain ground to the west.

Frequently, the Poles had turned local signs to point in wrong directions, sending individual elements and vehicles the wrong way so that they then fell into the hands of the Red Army. Not all the groups of moving vehicles had road maps. The logistical troops moving west suffered particular losses. They were unable to defend themselves and so were shot to pieces by the advancing Soviet forces. The Polish residents also pursued the more or less defenceless elements. Scarcely any soldiers of the overrun, or misdirected isolated vehicles, or smaller groups, ever returned from Soviet captivity. Evidence was given to inquiries that most of those who fell into the hands of Polish guerrillas were killed by them. It was so easy to prevail against isolated defenceless people.

The Advance Continues

Adding yet more to the confusion were the additional Soviet attacks. Branching off the advances from the Vistula bridgeheads the Soviets also attacked the south wing of the Heeresgruppe front i.e. *Armeegruppe* Heinrici. There they also achieved several local penetrations of 208th *Infanterie-Division*, *Kampfgruppe* 3rd *Gebirgs-Division*, 4th Gebirgs-Division, 24th Hungarian *Infanterie-Division*. They also broke through the 49th *Gebirgs-Division* on both sides of Moldau, with a penetration of the 2nd Hungarian *Ersatz-Division*. They broke through the 17th *Armee* northwest of Debica, the 59th *Armee-Korps*, and also the 4th *Panzer-Armee* and 48th *Panzer-Korps* between the centre of the 304th *Infanterie-Division* and the north wing of the 168th *Infanterie-Division*. That *Armeegruppe* was thus forced to fall back to the west. Later it had to give up more formations to the 4th *Panzer-Armee*.

As a frontal defence then seemed hopeless, the individual corps had then to concern themselves with gaining ground westward to the Oder. The Soviets paid little attention to those "wandering pockets". It appears that they had set their highest priority on the fastest possible advance to the west, committing their best formations at the spearheads of the assault formations. The less combat effective formations had to secure the rear areas.

The more or less disordered remnants of the 24th *Panzer-Korps* linked up with elements of the 42nd *Armee-Korps* in the Gowarczow area, north of Konskie, after the latter had evaded Soviet encirclement. The 42nd *Armee-Korps* began its withdrawal to the west on 15 January and, initially, maintained its integrity. Constant enemy attacks, and unequal rates of movement of the divisions, forced the *Armee-Korps* to dispense with co-ordinated command. The corps staff was captured. Elements of the attached formations were able to continue fighting for a short time. It was particularly bad for the infantry divisions because of their limited mobility. The 291st *Infanterie-Division* was smashed on 23 January, west of the Pilica River. However, surviving elements of the division were able to fight their way through to the Oder.

On the night of 20 January the elements received their first air-drop of petrol.

In the central sector, the Soviet advance continued unchallenged. The Soviets reached the lower course of the Pilica. They crossed the river near Maluszyn and captured Tschenstochau and Radomsko on 17 January. On 19 January, the first attack spearheads of the Soviet 3rd Guards Tank Army crossed the border of the German Reich. During the night of 21 January, the 6th Guards Mechanised Corps of the Soviet 4th Tank Army reached the Oder north of Steinau, Southeast of Glogau.

On 15 January, the Soviets achieved an 8 kilometre wide penetration of the 545th *Volks-Grenadier-Division* of the 11th *SS-Armee-Korps*. On 16 January, as a result of the unrelenting enemy pressure, and in light of the necessary withdrawal of an infantry division, the 17th *Armee* likewise pulled its lines about 30 kilometres back to the west, behind the Dunajec River sector. That freed the 359th Infanterie-Division to secure the open northern flank of the army, north of the Vistula, and to receive the remnants of the 304th Infanterie-Division of the 48th *Panzer-Korps*. The 344th *Infanterie-Division*, which was still in the process of refitting, moved towards Krakow. On 19 January, the Soviets captured Krakow. At that time, the battle began for the industrial district of Upper Silesia. On 22 January, elements of the 24th *Panzer-Korps* ran into rear guards of *Panzer-Korps* "Großdeutschland", *Panzer-Grenadier-Division* "Brandenburg", at the Wartha River, southeast of Sieradz.

As noted above, forces were transferred from the southern wing of the *Heeresgruppe* to the Upper Silesian industrial district. The 359th *Infanterie-Division* moved from the front of the 59th *Armee-Korps* to the area northeast of Krakow. The 344th *Infanterie-Division*, hastily refitted in the Tarnow area, went directly to the defence of Krakow, while *Panzer-Armeeoberkommando* 1 had to give up the 75th *Infanterie-Division* and 97th *Jäger-Division* to cover the Upper Silesian industrial district. Then came the transfer of the 100th *Jäger-Division* to the Heidebrek area in Silesia, while *Heeresgruppe* Süd had to set the 8th and 20th *Panzer-Divisionen* to march from Hungary to Silesia. Then, in addition, two divisions were relieved from the Western Front for transport to the Eastern Front, namely the 712th and 269th *Infanterie-Divisionen*. The other major formations freed by the ending of the Ardennes Offensive, were the 6th *SS-Panzer-Armee* I and II. However, over Guderian's strongest protests, *SS-Panzer-Korps* did not go to the central front, but to the Southeast Front, to *Heeresgruppe G* in Hungary. By the end of January, the 39th *Panzer-Korps*, with the 21st *Panzer-Division* and the 25th *Panzer-Grenadier-Division*, along with the *Führerbegleit-Brigade* and the *Führergrenadier-Brigade*, reached the Frankfurt-Oder–Cottbus area. In addition, 4 divisions were brought by sea from the Kurland bridgehead to the *Generalgouvernement* in Poland.

There was a great shortage of experienced front line troops to man the long front. By January, it was evident how difficult it was to fill the huge gap of practically 600 kilometres that existed there. Indeed, in the preceding year, the Eastern Front had frequently experienced similar situations as had just occurred on the central front. Building a defensive front at the Reichs border dropped out of the picture. By the end of January, Soviet spearheads were already over the Oder River near Küstrin and Frankfurt-Oder, thus advancing within 60 kilometres of Berlin. All that was left of *Heeresgruppe A*, capable of combat defence, was its southern wing, with the 17th *Armee* and the 1st *Panzer-Armee*. The latter, however, was trapped by the Soviet attacks in Slovakia and southern Poland.

VIII

Hasty Measures of Defence

On 14 January, at the request of the Chief of the General Staff of the Army, Guderian, the *Reichsführer SS*, Himmler, issued the "Call-up Order for the Entire *Volkssturm* in the East", initially for the first levée. Despite organisational and technical transport difficulties, by 20 January 32 *Volkssturmbataillone* had been activated from the Warthegau, with an average strength of 400–500 men, and sent to *Heeresgruppe A*. On 16 January, instructions went out to activate additional *Volkssturmbataillone z. b. V.* i.e. *zur besondere Verwendung*, meaning for special assignment. They were to be used outside the current borders of the Gau, the main territorial unit in the Nazi Third Reich. The rapidity of the Soviet advance did not allow those *Volkssturm* units to occupy the planned defensive positions in time.

The Kreis was an administrative district in Germany and Austria, roughly similar to a county. In Kreis Posen, 21 *Volkssturmbataillone* were available on 18 January. Most were to be used along the B–1 Line, west of Krakow, and east of Kalicz. As Soviet armoured spearheads had already rolled over the line in several places, and army formations were still en route from the West, the *Volkssturmbataillone* provided only very inadequate manning of the B–1 Line. Sometimes the sector widths were of 10 to 12 kilometres per battalion. The B–1 Line had been planned to accommodate 14 divisions. As then manned, the position did not constitute any significant hindrance for the Soviet formations, causing no more than brief local halts.

On 17 January, in the rear army area of *Heeresgruppe A*, there were 37 of the army's own security or *Volkssturm* battalions. Some were in the B–1 Line, some in the immediate rear area. Inadequately armed, and without combat experience, they were not employed within the framework of regular army divisions. They were left to stand on their own, so that, despite heavy losses in action, they had only limited combat effectiveness. Nevertheless, when they were later used in defence of encircled cities and fortresses, they achieved amazing successes in defence.

With the speed of the Soviet advance, the many planned transfers of German troops could no longer halt the retreat of *Heeresgruppe Mitte*. It was not until the beginning of February that most of the German reinforcements reached their intended areas. There they were immediately employed in building a new front. By 12 February, no fewer than 33 divisions had been assigned to the Eastern Front. In light of the hopeless situation, it is amazing what the replacement army achieved in assembling and forwarding new formations.

Guderian repeatedly pressed for the evacuation of the Kurland front, in which 22 divisions of *Kampfgruppen* and two *Panzer-Divisionen* were tied down. They could only be transferred to other front sectors by sea, a complicated and time-consuming process. Meanwhile, the Red Army could shift its units back and forth on land, at any time.

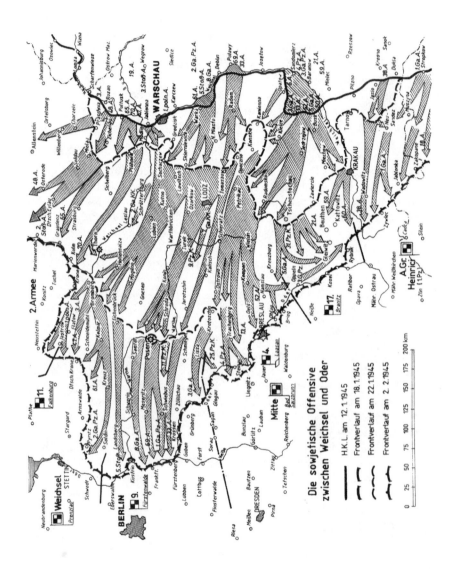

20 The Soviet offensive between the Vistula and the Oder

The redesignation of *Heeresgruppe A* to *Heeresgruppe Mitte*, on 25 January, could not increase the defensive power in the East. That depended far more on the provision of troops.

Building a Defence at the Oder

The remnants of units, particularly the "wandering pocket" of the 24th *Panzer-Korps* along with the remnants of the 42nd *Armee-Korps* that had been attached to it, moved westward by groups, large and small, towards the Oder line. The elements of *Panzer-Korps* "Großdeutschland" that had been brought from East Prussia and committed to the north, also had to move west. They took with them what was left of their fuel supplies, in order to restore their mobility. However, above all else, they had to wait for additional troop elements to be sent from the West, so that with their help, they could restore a continuous front.

It was essentially the formations en route from Slovakia, mostly by rail, that were needed to build up forces in Upper Silesia. *Sturmgeschütz-Brigade* 300, attached to the 48th *Panzer-Korps*, arrived on 16 January. Soviet armoured spearheads halted it, 30 kilometres from the border of Upper Silesia, in the Sosnowitz area. It was finally cut off. However, with the help of other troop-remnants picked up along the way, it marched to the west and southwest respectively, via Pinczow and Wulbrom. They formed a defensive barrier each day, breaking out at night to the west, from the pocket that had been formed in the meantime. Close to the eastern border of the Reich, at the B–1 Position near Ilkenau, it held off the Soviet spearheads for almost three days. That was achieved in part, through repeated successful counter-attacks with the help of the *Volkssturm*, who were poorly equipped with infantry weapons. The brigade then moved to the area 30 kilometres east of Beuthen.

At that time, the first transport trains carrying the combat elements of the 97th *Jäger-Division* arrived, and were unloaded near Kattowitz and Myslowitz. As with other formations, weapons received from the homeland did not arrive in time for battle preparation nor, in particular, for tuning of the radio equipment before going into action. The replacement troops were hurriedly thrown into infantry battalions, to reconstitute the formations returning to the Oder area with new personnel.

On 18 January, the Soviets captured Krakow, after the *Heeresgruppe* command post was transferred from Tschenstochau to Oppeln. At that point, Soviet armoured spearheads were already in Kreis Lublinitz, and finally in Kreisen Guttentag, Rosenberg and Kreuzburg. On 16 January, they turned up 25 kilometres from the Kreis capital, to the west. The troops of the Red Army had thus advanced to the Upper Silesian border, north of the industrial district, and had already driven wedges into the Silesian interior. Resistance came from alerted replacement troop elements, and remnant groups from dispersed army formations, along with hastily called up Volkssturm, and police units with makeshift equipment.

The commander of the 8th *Armee-Korps*, *General* Hartmann, was given the mission of building a new line of defence east of Oppeln. For that, he had to come up with forces, and then throw them into the Breitenmark area to join what was left of the 168th Infanterie-Division of the 48th *Armee-Korps*. Until then, it had not been

A column of German StuG IV assault guns. The vehicle at far right of photo is a
Panzerbeobachtungswagen IV, a special armoured observation vehicle,
and a variant of the Pz.Kpfw.IV.

known to be present. Elements of the army weapons school of the 4th *Panzer-Armee*
were already fighting in defence to the south. Near Rosenberg, there was a
Sturmgeschütz-Abteilung, with infantry protection from a screen of police, fresh from
walking their beats in Breslau. They may not have been able to halt the Soviet advance, but they could still delay it. Contact with the attacking Soviet formations,
over the course of several days, also provided a certain amount of intelligence information regarding the identities of the formations attacking on the Soviet side.

For the defence in the next days, until 20 January, there were remnant formations of the 68th and 304th *Infanterie-Divisionen* of the 48th *Panzer-Korps* along
with several remaining *Sturmgeschütze* of *Sturmgeschütz-Brigade* 300. There was
also the 75th *Infanterie-Division*, which made it by rail to Miechow, 60 kilometres
east of the Reichs border near Beuthen. There it held a sector northwest of Krakow
in the approaches to the industrial district. At that time, only the first half of the
combat elements of the 97th *Jäger-Division* had arrived on Upper Silesian ground.
The same was true for the 712th *Infanterie-Division* that was being brought from
the West, from the lower Maas River.

There were desperate hopes for the arrival of the 20th and 8th *Panzer-
Divisionen*. As to the Soviet wedge in the area, 12 kilometres north of Bleiwitz/
Hindenburg, their much needed presence appeared doubtful.[1] With that wedge

---

1   Translator's note – The Upper Silesian industrial district centered on the Beuthen–
    Hindenburg–Gleiwitz–Kattowitz cluster of industrial cities.

the Soviets initiated the envelopment of the industrial district, employing 33 rifle divisions, 5 tank corps, 1 cavalry corps and 1 tank brigade.

Combat Action Shifts from the *Generalgouvernement* to Silesia

The Soviet advance repeatedly ran into areas that were free of troops, in which their progress was simply a matter of using motor vehicles. In that way, the formations of the Red Army showed extreme superiority over the Germans. Due to a shortage of petrol the Germans relied for their movement, in part, on the railways. The infantry formations were on foot, with all their guns and heavy vehicles being horse drawn. Following the German example in various campaigns, such as in France, the Soviet armoured spearheads thrust westward to gain ground without concern for the exposed flanks. Locally, they expected to reach the Reichs border and the Oder ahead of the retreating, dispersed German formations. In those circumstances the Reichs border itself offered no basis for building a line of defence. That remained to be done at the Oder. Even that did not present an insurmountable obstacle for the Soviets. In some places they could use bridges that had not been destroyed. Elsewhere they built bridges. Earlier years of the war in the east had shown that the Soviets had considerable experience in overcoming rivers as obstacles.

It was then that the lack of adequate lines of defence came back with a vengeance. In years gone by, Hitler had wanted nothing to do with strong lines of defence. Based on his experience in the First World War, he was sure that in a dangerous battle situation, a soldier's thoughts would turn to the rear, and of his making it back to a rear defensive position. That would then give soldiers a short break to take a breather. But in 1944, that thought pattern had already proved calamitous for the 4th *Armee* and 9th *Panzerarmee* of *Heeresgruppe Mitte*. Having ad-

A column of Soviet IS-2 heavy tanks

equate reserves in readiness would have been a sufficient countermeasure, but that was exactly what was lacking. Recollections were of the number of formations that had been lost in earlier great battles as, for example, in the collapse of *Heeresgruppe Mitte*. It was lost, complete with equipment that could not in any way be replaced from the homeland. Such replacements as could be gathered up from the homeland, had mostly extremely brief infantry training. They had neither the experience in arms, nor the steadfastness that had marked the formations active at the start of the war.

Hitler ordered that any and every order for withdrawal or retreat had to be reported to the Führer headquarters. Sufficient time had to be allowed for possible counter-orders to reach the troops, before the original order could be executed. That completely tied the hands of the commanders at the front. The only remaining possibility was to utilise the principle of movement in the main defensive area. The foremost lines would be pulled back, before the start of the enemy artillery preparation, to spare those manning the trenches from that fire. Incomprehensibly, however, the formations made no use of that opportunity, apparently because the responsible officer may well not have experienced the advantages of such a tactic.

The rigid holding of the front thus excluded utilisation of the area for defensive purposes. At the same level, were Hitler's halt orders and, above all, the decrees regarding creation of so-called "*Feste Plätze*", i.e. strong places. Those were open towns or cities, particularly at critical transportation junctions, that were to be held and defended as if they were fortresses, in order to delay the Soviet advance. However, if such places were actually to be effective, in the sense intended by Hitler, they would have to be properly provided with troops, weapons and, above all, adequate supplies of rations and ammunition. Those too, were lacking.

The garrison of "*Fester Platz Thorn*" broke through to the west on 2 February 1945. The garrison of "*Fester Platz Graudenz*" came under heavy Russian attack on 2 February, and was completely cut off on 16 February. Finally, in desperately fierce house-to-house, indeed room-to-room fighting, they fought over every foot of ground, until the last fighting element was cornered in the last room of the old Courbière Fort. *Generalmajor* Fricke held rigidly to Hitler's orders to "fight to the last man". Festung Graudenz finally surrendered on 5 March 1945. "Fester Platz Posen", on the other hand, held out longer and proved notably significant, the defenders making good use of the old fortifications from an earlier day. "Fester Platz Posen" held out for a long time, thereby holding up the Soviet advance, and thus the preparations for crossing the Oder and the further advance on Berlin.

The inhabitants of the first stretch of land in central Silesia to be invaded by the Soviets, were faced with the decision of whether they should evacuate or remain in their homes.[2] There were those who believed that the German propaganda about the conduct of the Red Army must be exaggerated. Others thought that, as they were actually entering German territory, the Soviets would prove to be freed of

---

2   Translator's note – Treks were mass evacuation movements of the civilian population, whole villages taking to the road on foot and with whatever transportation they could utilize, ranging from baby-buggies to tractor or horse-drawn farm carts and wagons and trucks. Some were well planned ahead of time, many were last-minute flights.

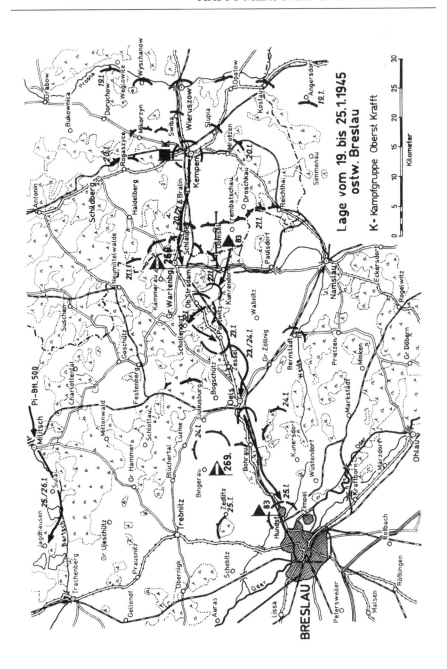

21 Situation 19–25 January 1945 east of Breslau

their frenzy to rob and destroy, and their sexual urge to rape. Everyone knew of Ehrenberg's exhortations that declared an "open season" for raping women. The first evacuees left their homes in bitter cold. Some of them were then caught in the destructive American and British air attacks on Dresden.

The most important mission for the German command was the formation of a line of defence. There was no mistake in the perception that Stalin set great store on capturing the Upper Silesian industrial district. That meant that the Soviets would either make a direct frontal attack on it, or would attempt to envelop it from the north. German formations brought from eastern Slovakia by rail could block the frontal attack. They could at least delay it, in co-operation with the first *Volkssturm* units to be committed. The Soviets were initially denied a breakthrough to the south, to the Moravian Gate. But they would eventually break through into central Silesia.[3]

Consideration of how to deal with the situation suffered from difficulties regarding jurisdiction. In the end, it was the *Gauleiter* of the Nazi Party, in their function as "*Reichsverteidigungskomissaren*" i.e. Reichs Defence Commissioners, who ended up with the highest power of command. That resulted in a shift of the entire responsibility from the *Wehrmacht* to the Party. In fact there were major problems of jurisdiction. At the end of 1944, Party officials had called up great numbers of Hitler Youth, for the construction of positions east of the Reichs border. Considering the way that construction of rear positions had been previously neglected, the work had to be achieved as quickly as possible. The positions would have fulfilled their intended functions if sufficient forces to man them had been there at the right time. However, that was not in the sphere of responsibility of the political leaders, but rather of the military commanders.

The people of Silesia had enjoyed a long quiet period before coming under air attack by the Western Powers. However, in 1944 it began. Every family had taken some share in the war commitment and had also suffered losses. Above all, the Silesian divisions had repeatedly been committed, and proved themselves at decisive moments in the entire war in the East. At home, schoolboys served as Flak helpers at the anti-aircraft guns, initially merely for daytime service, later for night defence too. Parallel to those duties for the boys, the girls cared for refugees and wounded in the hospitals.

Again and again, problems of jurisdiction came up when it came to evaluation of the situation and the commitment of available forces. It goes without saying that at various levels the *Wehrmacht* commanders had had different experiences in action from the *Gauleiter*, or other political functionaries. That difference came up regularly. There were difficulties, not only regarding the commitment of available formations, elements or individual weapons, but also regarding logistics. Repeatedly, the *Wehrmacht* commanders had first to prevail over Party functionaries. Hit-

---

3   Translator's note – The *Märische Pforte*, the "Moravian Gate", was the historical name for the age-old route of conquest that led through the fertile lowlands between the western Beskides and the mountains of Silesia into central Moravia and beyond. The major transportation links from the east ran through this depression to Preßburg (Bratislava), Vienna, Brünn (Brno) and Prague.

A crew prepares a Nebelwerfer rocket launcher for firing. These weapons could deliver a formidable amount of firepower.

ler placed more trust in his Party functionaries than in his Generals. He had been at odds with them for a long time and would have happily dispensed with them.

At an even earlier date, Hitler had already made clear his conviction that the will to resist was the decisive criterion for the steadfastness of a body of troops. But apparently he did not accept, even though it might be present, that it depended for its effective realisation upon specific prerequisites, namely, a sufficient body of troops, sufficient weapons and an adequate supply of ammunition. The Party leaders could not help with that. The *Volkssturm* men were called together, generally in civilian clothing that was not in any way adequate to meet the demands of the cold conditions. Weapons and appropriate ammunition were lacking. What use were Dutch carbines with Italian ammunition, or vice versa? Even worse, there was not even a carbine available for every *Volkssturm* man, nor an entrenching tool. The only time that the *Volkssturm* units could reckon on almost adequate equipment was when a *Wehrmacht* commander took them under his protection.

Soviet forces enter Silesia

German reconnaissance could certainly identify the formations and branches of the Soviet Army, even which troops were massed in individual concentration areas awaiting the great attack. But they could only presume what plans formed the basis of the attack, and thus, what were the objectives. One basic assumption was that Stalin wanted to possess the Upper Silesian industrial region, in an undamaged condition. Accordingly, a powerful advance could be expected from the Baranow

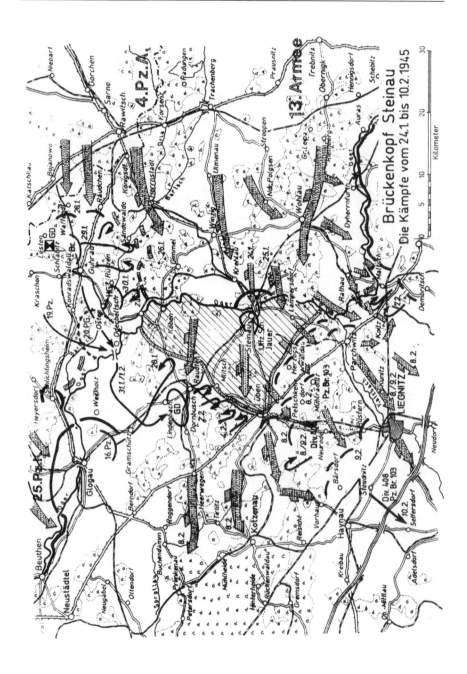

22 The Steinau Bridgehead, 24 January–10 February 1945

bridgehead, towards Krakow–Tschenstochau–Kattowitz, with possible additional relief attacks in Slovakia. Soon, however, it became apparent that the Soviet forces were essentially thrusting forward towards the northwest, with Berlin as their objective. At the same time, a branch movement developed from the main thrust, advancing towards the Oder and Silesia.

On 17 January, the Soviet forces of the 21st Army entered Silesian territory in Kreis Lublinitz of Upper Silesia. On 19 January, they crossed the Upper Silesian border formed by the Brosna River, also known as the Prosno or Prosna, between Kreuzberg and Rosenberg. Everywhere there was a lack of adequate defensive forces. There were German hopes for the return by rail of experienced battle formations from Slovakia. Additional hopes rested upon the prompt arrival of the 20th and 8th *Panzer-Divisionen* that were to be sent from *Heeresgruppe* Süd. In the meantime, defence of the Silesian borders depended on the *Volkssturm*, on elements of the replacement army, soldiers of the rear-area facilities of the field army, and on men fighting their way back from the Vistula. Thus the immediate defence depended on inadequately armed men who were lacking in combat experience. Therefore elements of the *Wehrmacht*, such as *Panzer-Jäger-Abteilung* 561, formed the backbone for the committed members of the Volkssturm men who had no experience, and were untrained for use as infantry.

Despite all that, they did manage to delay the advance of the Red Army for several days. However, on 20 January, Rosenberg and Pitschen had to be evacuated, and on the 21st, Kreuzberg. Such alarm signals required emergency units. The commanders of the replacement troop elements, and Party officers brought them in through the respective Gauleiter, throwing together men, who for the most part were without any infantry training. The result was a motley crowd of defence troops. The OKH assigned to *General der Artillerie* Hartmann the mission of commanding all forces to be activated in the Lublinitz–Wielun line. With them, he had to stop the enemy advance. He found elements of the army weapons school of the 4th *Panzer-Armee*, elements of the 168th *Infanterie-Division*, policemen straight from their beats in Breslau, detachments from the *Luftwaffe* and *Waffen-SS*, and army replacement units. Nevertheless, on 21 January, north of Oppeln, Soviet motorised infantry crossed the Oder which was frozen.

A *Kampfgruppe* of the 208th *Infanterie-Division*, under *Oberst* Krafft, arrived from Hungary. It was reinforced on 20 January by the 269th *Infanterie-Division*, arriving from the West. However, during the night of 21 January, the *Kampfgruppe* had to fall back on Oels. The 269th *Infanterie-Division* with all the attached elements, and the *Volkssturm*, fought until 28 January in the approaches to "*Festung* Breslau". They thereby helped the fortress commander to further organise the defence, until the Soviets east of Breslau suddenly broke off their assault. The Soviets bypassed the city on the north, and on 28 January, reached Steinau with their 4th Tank Army. Trebnitz, on the Oder, went up in flames. *Unteroffizierschule* (NCO) school Jauer had the mission of holding the Oder bridges at Steinau. The students had just occupied their positions east of the city when Soviet tanks rolled up. They were still able to blow up the railway bridge, but 4 Soviet tanks crossed the road bridge. After the Soviet tanks had been knocked out, it was possible to effectively destroy the bridge. It was impossible to block the Oder crossings, north and south of the city, so the Soviets reached the Oder between Kosel and Glogau. They crossed the river between Oppeln and Brieg, as well as on both sides of Steinau.

In other sectors too, remnants of German units that had found their way back to the Oder, crossed to the west bank. On 25 January, a reorganisation of the entire Eastern Front went into effect. *Heeresgruppe A* was designated *Heeresgruppe Mitte*, and *Heeresgruppe Mitte* became *Heeresgruppe Nord*. Formations between *Heeresgruppe Mitte*, in Silesia, and *Heeresgruppe Nord*, in East Prussia, were designated *Heeresgruppe Weichsel* i.e. Vistula. What had formerly been *Heeresgruppe Nord* in Kurland, became *Heeresgruppe Kurland*. Re-numbering of various field-post numbers ensued. The commander in chief of the 4th *Panzer-Armee* was *General der Panzertruppe* Gräser, whose command post was in Glogau. He immediately set about building a front along the Oder using the remnants of retreating divisions, soldiers who had lost contact with their units, and the *Volkssturm*. Contact was established with the south wing of the 9th *Armee* near Lissa, in the Warthegau. In the ensuing days, the 9th *Armee* then assumed command of the defence in the Oder sector, between Guben and Frankfurt.

Attempt to Defend at the Oder

A series of troop elements marching back from the *Generalgouvernement* crossed the Oder at Glogau. "Großdeutschland" reached the bridge on 22 January. The division staff of the 6th *Infanterie-Division* crossed the Oder in Glogau to take charge of the defence at the Oder on both sides of Glogau. At that point, there was little left of the 6th *Infanterie-Division* except for its division staff, and 2 of the 3 infantry regiments. The artillery, having been overrun, had dispersed. In large part they were destroyed or captured when the Soviets broke out of the Warka bridgehead. Glogau was an old bridgehead location. Its commander replenished the defences, had anti-tank obstacles constructed, and established weak advanced security forces 12 kilometres northeast of Glogau, in the Schlichtingsheim–Guhlau–Tschepplau line. Additional bridgeheads were built on the right or east bank of the Oder, particularly between Liegnitz and Sprottau. In part, they were made up of the remnants of the 6th *Infanterie-Division* that had returned, along with some *Volkssturm* units. They were collected under the designation "*Stab Panzertod*" i.e. "Tank-Killer Staff". Presumably, the name was given because a number of "*Tank-Destroyer Squads*", consisting of an officer and a handful of men armed with *Panzerfäuste*, and mounted on bicycles, were assigned to it. The *Panzerfaust* was a recoilless, disposable, lightweight, one-man anti-tank weapon, firing a large hollow charge grenade. Later models increased the range from 30 to 100 metres, the armour penetration from 140mm at 30° to 200mm at 30°. A portion of the gases, from the propellant charge in the disposable firing tube, vented to the rear to eliminate the recoil. There was not sufficient time to establish contact with all the *Volkssturm* elements. The greatest lack was in their means of communication. The formations generally depended for communications upon the available civilian postal and telephone networks.

A view of the dreaded German '88', a thorn in the side of Soviet armour until the end of the war

Oder Crossing near Steinau

Although the use of the *Volkssturm* east of the Oder was locally overtaken by events and happened by villages, it was without unified planning. The actual defence of the Oder then took a more planned form. In several sectors it developed mainly from the defence preparations near Steinau. Everywhere there were *Volkssturm* men, without weapons, distributed behind the levee on the west bank of the Oder. They were waiting for the impending point of the morning attack by the Red Army, at 07.30 hours. It was difficult, in frozen ground, to dig foxholes at suitable places that were deep enough to provide protection from infantry fire. A few "old hands" from the First World War had memories of extensive experience in that earlier trench war, and could provide good advice.

The Red soldiers approached the Oder from Ibsdorf, advancing in the short stages of a skirmish line through the terrain. The Germans defended themselves with their few available carbines, thereby thinning out the ranks of the attackers. Then their adversaries received support, initially from 6, later from 24 Soviet tanks and advanced further. The number of attackers simply increased. A German mortar fired between the attacking tanks, without causing them any noticeable discomfort. The tanks, using gunfire, set alight buildings that interfered with their field of vision and line of fire. The *Volkssturm* men lay in their foxholes with *Panzerfäusten*, and took aim at the first tanks that had opened fire to eliminate the observers they presumed to be in the towers of the bridge.

All of a sudden the ammunition exploded in a burning tank on the bridge. Two more tanks went up in flames after being hit by *Panzerfäuste*. In the meantime, Soviet infantry drew nearer and kept down the *Volkssturm* men with machine pistol fire. Then a tank that took advantage of shelter offered by buildings, climbed the bank of the Oder and crossed the Oder bridge at high speed. It was hit by a *Panzerfaust* and went up in the air. Additional enemy tanks followed at high speed on to the bridge. The *Volkssturm* men, unpractised and unaccustomed, fired on the tanks that followed. One *Panzerfaust* missed the second tank, another struck the rear of the third. The tank came to a halt and the crew bailed out. The crew then cut the connections to the detonators on the demolition charges attached to the bridge girders. A *Panzerfaust* aimed at the fourth tank fell short. The fifth tank finally crossed the bridge. It had been planned that the bridge would be blown after the fifth tank crossed over. That, however, did not happen.

The *Panzerfäuste* were expended. The *Volkssturm* men were forced to evacuate their positions and fall back with their wounded towards the railway bridge. 8 Soviet planes circled over the bridge during that fighting and fired on the *Volkssturm* men and their infantry weapons. In the event yet more tanks crossed the bridge on 24 January 1945. The defence thus achieved no lasting success. Individual Soviet tanks traversed the streets of the city and arrived at the city hall, which was full of refugees. There they directed their fire on the crowded civilians thronging out of the building, causing a gruesome bloodbath. As best they could, the maimed and wounded had to get away to the west. Some were dragged on sleds. They found no admittance at any hospital in Liegnitz or Goldberg. The first hospital to accept them was in Kauffau.

After Steinau, additional *Panzerfäuste* and Italian *Badoglio* weapons arrived for the defence, to equip additional elements of the *Volkssturm*. They were sent into action, in squads with *Panzerfäusten*, along roads leading westward from the Oder. The *Wehrmacht* reported for that day, "A Soviet *Kampfgruppe* committed across the Oder near Steinau with 30 tanks was repulsed after 24 tanks were knocked out." The *Volkssturm* men stayed in the various defensive positions without any supplies at all. The next day, they came under fire from Stalin Organs, also known as *Katyushas*. Stalin Organs were Russian multiple rocket launchers mounted on trucks.

Several elderly women persisted in believing in the combat effectiveness and striking power of the German *Wehrmacht* and, in their love of their homeland, stayed in their homes. The Red soldiers did not show any restraint in dealing with them. They suffered the same fate as all those who, after delayed evacuation orders, had tried to get away on evacuation trains or had stayed behind. The Soviets shot them down in rows, so that in many places a large part of the entire population lost their lives when the Red soldiers marched in. In general the Red soldiers, especially those of the second wave who were even worse than the first, were possessed with an unheard of destructive frenzy. In a few minutes they destroyed what had taken the inhabitants a lifetime to create. Furniture, dishes, linen or whatever was there was destroyed, or the house went up in flames. Much that was cherished in the way of valued furniture was thus destroyed. Some civilians had stayed put in hopes that it could not be that bad with the Russians, the more so as enemy radio broadcasts repeatedly urged the populace not to leave their homes and farms.

Nobody could imagine that Ehrenburg's calls for revenge would inspire Red soldiers to treat women in such a terrifying manner. The rapes started with 12 year old girls and extended to 80 year old women. The screams of those tormented people, who were often raped by a number of Red soldiers, rang through the villages. Where women had hidden, the Soviets set fire to the sheltering hay or straw stacks to get their hands on them. The hopes of the eternal optimists, that the destructive frenzy of the Red soldiers and their animal sexual lusts would abate upon reaching the territory of the Reich, proved to be wishful thinking.

The result of the defence of Steinau was that the Soviets crossed the Oder, on both sides of Steinau, and finally built a bridge of local materials near Lesewitz. There was fierce fighting around the cloister in which numerous refugees and wounded had taken shelter. The sugar factory in Kreischau changed hands several times. North of the city, too, the Soviets crossed the Oder. Other sectors of the bunker line held fast against them.

Additional Soviet Advances over the Oder

On the 7th or 8th of February, after crossing the Oder near Steinau with strong armoured formations, the Soviets thrust far to the west and southwest, passing south of Glogau. House-to-house fighting developed in Glogau, the garrison finally breaking out, but only a small number reached the German lines. On 9 February, strong Soviet forces with motorised infantry, advanced on Kotzenau and Primkenau. Lüben was already in enemy hands. However, on 12 February, the Soviets still had not made any preparations to cross the Bober River on both sides of Bunzlau. The Soviets then crossed the Bober near Kittlitztreben and pushed on to the west.

The remnants of the 6th *Volks-Grenadier-Division* had to attempt to establish contact, on the right and left, with the Latvian *SS-Division* and the *Bataillon* Erpenbach. It was made up of artillerymen who no longer had guns, nor communications personnel, and no *Volkssturm* companies. On the west bank of the Bober they found a homeland Flak regiment. They had an adequate supply of ammunition but lacked prime-movers for a proportion of their guns. *Bataillon* Erpenbach, along with "*Hetzer*", a fast-moving, new type of self-propelled gun, and SPWs of *Panzerjäger-Abteilung* Jänisch helped with the change of positions so that no guns were lost. Beginning in 1944, *Panzerjäger-Abteilungen* of infantry divisions were armed with the *Hetzer*. It was an effective tank-destroyer, armed with the 7.5 cm Pak 39 L/48 anti-tank gun, built on the chassis of the *Panzer* 38, the Skoda.

In bright moonlight, the Soviets thrust from the direction of Bunzlau, particularly from the north, into the movements of the 6th *Volks-Grenadier-Division*. In Birkenbrück they cut off *Bataillon* Erpenbach with its staff and 3rd *Kompanie*. *Hetzer-Kompanie* Dallmeyer assisted those elements in breaking out. German aircraft also joined in the fighting, engaging enemy armour with bombs and strafing. For the defence of the city, the city commander immediately committed a company that had been forced southward to Naumburg. Other elements had to break out west of the Queis River close to, and north of Sophienwald.

Provision of additional troops came, but only a few at a time. Between 13 and 16 February, a *Sturmbataillon* arrived for the relief of Naumburg, and the defence of the Queis sector between Naumburg and Siegersdorf. A replacement battalion came from Konstanz, and an infantry battalion with a battery of 6 light field howitzers arrived. Finally, the 17th *Panzer-Division* appeared under *Generalmajor* Kretschman, although with only a weak complement of armour. The Soviets forced the 17th *Panzer-Division* and 6th *Volks-Grenadier-Division* back to the Sophienwald–Altenhain railway line. The 17th *Panzer-Division*, however, moved back during the night of 17 February to Görlitz, leaving remaining formations to survive a hard fight with superior enemy armour. By then they were faced with 2 Soviet tank corps, which then turned south between the Queis and Neiße rivers.[4] Between Queis and Kießling the German remnant formations were finally faced with the main body of the Soviet 6th Tank Army of at least 3 tank corps. The attack in the Queis area moved south via Sächsisch-Haugsdorf, and from Güntersdorf to Hennersdorf, as well as from Oberbielau to Kießlingswalde. Apparently the Soviets had not recognised the difficulties of incorporating the arrival of infantry battalions, and in placing them for holding the line. That mistake was all to the good for the German formations.

On the morning of 20 February there was an armoured penetration near Hennersdorf, which repeatedly changed hands. There was no continuous line, so the Soviets had the opportunity, at any time, to advance westward between individually held localities. They gained ground to the south in Rachenau. A *Flak-Sturm-Regiment* under *Oberst* Lyncker arrived, and went into position to defend against armour adjoining the north edge of the city of Lauban. South of the elements of the Lauban *Kampfkommandant* there was fighting for the cemetery. Appointed to command a fortress or city, the *Kampfkommandant* was given special powers, including empowerment to attach to his command all troops and troop elements that came within his jurisdiction. The *Sturm-Bataillon* fell back across the Lauban–Görlitz highway to the hill south of Schützenau. A German armoured brigade was committed to the defence of Lauban.

---

4   Translator's note – There were two important rivers, each named the Neiße River, in Silesia, both of which are important in this history. The river mentioned here is the Lausitzer Neiße (also called Görlitzer Neiße) which finds its source in the Lausitzer Mountains southwest of Görlitz. It is completely different from the Glatzer Neiße that flows through the city of Neiße and joins the Oder between Brieg and Oppeln, south of Breslau.

PART C

The Advance into Silesia

IX

Advance into Lower Silesia

On reaching the Oder between Ratibor and Glogau, the Soviets had attained the objective of their attack in that sector. They had made it to the Oder on both sides of Küstrin, and then had to attempt to reach the Lausitzer Neiße River. The advance north of Breslau proved essentially stronger than the thrust south of Breslau. Because of the resulting opportunity to also turn north from Steinau towards Berlin, the German command assigned greater significance to that sector north of Breslau. However, it was difficult to get formations there that could build a German line of defence. A great number of exposed Oder sectors had to be brought into the considerations of the German command. All in all, however, the Germans had to build a defensive front on the Oder, regardless of the bridgeheads that the Soviets had already built.

Breslau Surrounded

The Soviets had already broadened and deepened their Steinau bridgehead, and concentrated their armoured formations there for continuing the advance to the west. The Soviet command had issued orders to press their advance north of the great forested area that stretched from Liegnitz–Lüben to Görlitz–Sagan via Primkenau, Sprottau, Sagan and Sohrau to the Lausitzer Neiße, to the Sommerfeld–Forst sector. Other formations were assigned to advance via Haynau, Bunzlau and Naumburg on the Queis to Görlitz, and provide further flank protection via Goldberg, Löwenberg to Lauban. The southern attacking wedge was to attack towards the southeast and link up with the Soviet army. Breaking out, and advancing from the bridgehead near Ohlau, they would thereby encircle *Festung* Breslau. The attack was strongly supported from the air.

The Soviets broke through the 4th *Panzer-Armee* defensive front by storm. Improvised formations, that were committed at the Queis by the commanders of the various sectors, could only briefly delay the Soviet advance. To the north, on the lower Queis, *Panzer-Grenadier-Division "Brandenburg"* and the 20th *Panzer-Grenadier-Division* delayed the Soviet advance, but could not stop it. The Soviets also crossed the Oder near Beuthen and Crossen. Liegnitz and Haynau were lost on 10 February, Jauer on 13 February. Sagan also fell. Thus, on 17 February, the front ran in the line Goldberg–Löwenberg, east of Lauban, Naumburg, along the Queis. On 18 February, the Soviet formations that had crossed the Oder near Crossen were 6 kilometres from Guben. On 19 February, those forces were pressing against Lauban, Naumburg and Sagan. That forced the commander in chief of the 4th *Panzer-Armee* to pull the front into the line west of Löwenberg, northwest of Lauban–Rothenburg to the Neiße west of Sorau, Sommerfeld and Guben, and then along the Lausitzer Neiße to its mouth in the Oder. That position was occupied on 21 February, and held until mid-April. With that, it was evident how far the Soviets had advanced south of Breslau, to the west and also the north of the

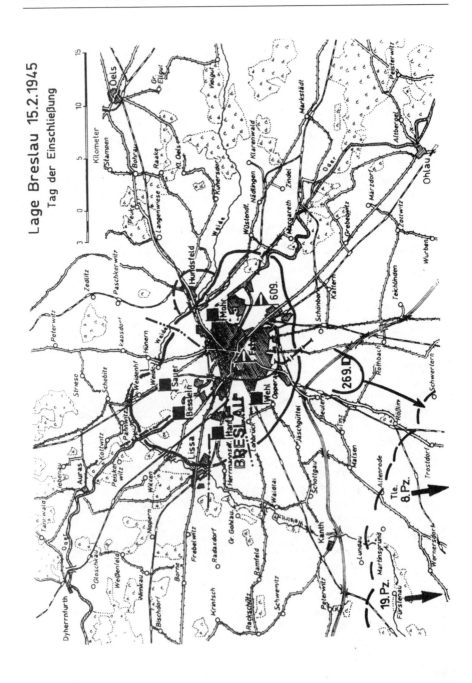

23 Breslau 15 February 1945 (day of encirclement)

city. In the meantime, the two arms of the advance linked up west of Breslau. Thereupon the *OKH* declared Breslau a *"Fester Platz"*, or *"Festung"*.

Battle for Breslau

The city that had been upgraded to a *"Festung"* had old infantry positions dating from 1914. By order of Napoleon, the city's other fortifications had been levelled in 1807. Most of the weapons that had been present in Breslau had been sent to the Atlantic Wall. It was only on 25 September 1944 that Breslau received a *Festungskommandant* i.e. fortress commander, *Generalmajor* Krause, but the only garrison was *Landesschützenbataillon* 599. In addition, came 6 fortress batteries, a fortress pioneer company, and a fortress communications company. There was an assortment of captured guns, from all nations, but for which there were no firing tables and aiming circles. In the course of time, all other logistical materials, such as petrol, heating fuel and clothing had to be provided for the city. Sufficient medical equipment and supplies were on hand, as was food. Later, the *"Festung"* received additional numbers of troops. They amounted to 5 divisions, 3 of which were positioned on the east and 2 on the west bank of the Oder.

The commander of the *"Festung"* had had the positions built, by the civilian population, in a 25 kilometre semicircle around the Oder bridges. There were not enough troops to adequately man the 120 kilometre length of the line of fortifications. Therefore, at the start of 1945, construction began on an inner ring around the pastureland. The *Festungskommandant* came up with ideas for additional defences, such as construction of concrete positions and trenches with obstacles, damming up the sewers, flooding the Ohle lowlands, and flooding the sewage farm north of the Oder. By the time it was encircled, the *Festung* contained approximately 50,000 men from the field and replacement armies, the *Luftwaffe, Waffen-SS* and police, as well as the *Volkssturm*. In addition, about 80,000 civilians remained, from the initially isolated inhabitants, who included refugees from the air war in the West. At one time, the total came to over a million people. There was practically no supply of ammunition because ammunition dumps, in contrast with ration dumps, were located at some distance from large cities. The railway was unable to exceed the demands already placed upon it.

The 609th *Infanterie- Division*, which had recently been activated in Breslau, was positioned southeast of the Oder as far as the line Hartlieb i.e. the built up area, Südpark, Gutenbergstraße, and Körnerstraße. In the western south sector was a *Luftwaffe* regiment with an *Abteilung* of heavy field howitzers. In the west was *Artilleriegruppe West*. On the east bank was a hastily formed alarm unit, supported by *Artilleriegruppe Nord*, with 5 light batteries and 1 heavy battery. Attached to those formations were several of the 26 combat battalions of the *Volkssturm*. Further individual troop remnants were also present, including a company of *Panzerjäger*. They were supported by *Volkssturm* construction battalions that had to build positions, dam up water and build an airfield. A technical battalion attended to electricity and water, and watched over the sewer network. The communications regiment maintained contact between the *Festung* and the outside. Two Hitler-Youth *Volkssturm* battalions were primarily concerned with counter-attacks, and, indeed had some success. In addition, *Fallschirm-Jäger* battalions of the

A fine close-up study of a crew preparing to fire a 7.5 cm Pak 40 anti-tank gun

I./*Fallschirm-Jäger-Regiment* 26 were flown in on 25 February, from formerly oc-cupying airfields, but without infantry training. On 6 March, there was flown in the II./*Fallschirm-Jäger-Regiment z. b. V.* i.e. *zur besondere Verwendung,* for special duties.

In the larger area around Breslau the Oder bridgeheads near Ohlau and Steinau held centre stage. The 269th *Infanterie-Division* was taken to Ohlau on city buses, but was unable to eliminate the bridgehead. The Soviet offensive broke out of the Steinau bridgehead on 8 February, and the Soviet 6th Army and 3rd Guards Tank Army, together with the 5th Guards Army, advanced from Ohlau to encircle Breslau. Therefore the German divisions that were south of the *Festung* were ordered to fall back to the south, but not all were able to do so. The elements that were unable to break out reinforced the *Festung* garrison. They included 6 *Sturmgeschütze* of *Sturmgeschütz-Brigade* 311, an *Abteilung* of heavy howitzers, and a battery with two 21cm heavy howitzers, with 50 rounds each. On 15 February the Soviets closed the ring of encirclement. The Soviet 6th Army, with three to four divisions, stood around the *Festung* in the south, southwest, west and north.

On 17 February the southern group began to attack between Klattendorf and Brockau. Southwest of the city the attackers penetrated the city, even crossing the great railway embankment in the southern part of the city. On 20 February *Hitler-Jugend-Sturmbataillon* 55 forced back the Soviets in Südpark. A Soviet launched on 14 February against the southwest and west fronts, with the Gandau airfield as its objective, failed. The defence achieved successes in the north. As February be-came March, the Soviets continued to attack in the south with undiminished vig-

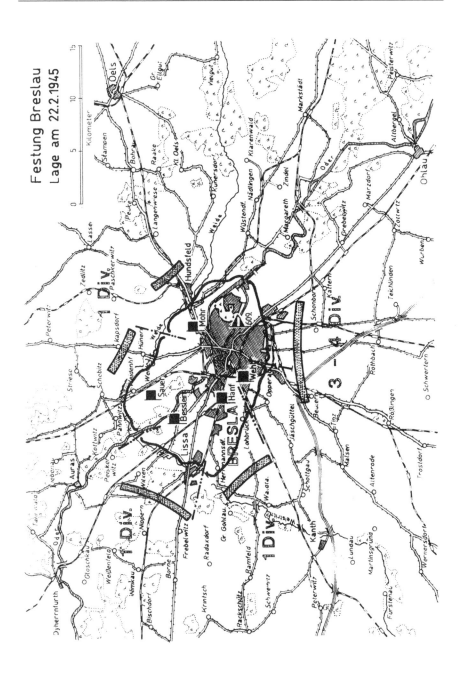

24 "*Festung* Breslau" 22 February 1945

our. *General der Infanterie* Niehoff, former commander of the 371st *Infanterie-Division* arrived as the new commander of Breslau. He strove for the relief of the *Festung*. The *Heeresgruppe* and 17th *Armee* had been forced to move the *Panzer* divisions to central Silesia. They had been intended for the relief, even though they were urgently needed elsewhere.

Fighting in the Area around Breslau

Elements of individual front formations arrived in nearby replacement garrisons. There they were filled out with personnel and refitted with new weapons. Thus *Panzer-Artillerie-Regiment* 19 received a series of new guns to attain full artillery combat effectiveness. The last attack against the Soviet bridgeheads near Koben and Steinau, with elements attacking the bridgehead near Ossig–Breslau, had failed, Afterwards, elements of the 19th *Panzer-Division* were set to march towards Breslau, guns and tracked vehicles by rail, wheeled vehicles by road. The Soviets had already crossed the *Autobahn* near Haynau, heading west. The train arriving at the railway station had to be unloaded in record time and the battery moved by road towards Woltersdorf. Action ensued near Saarau and Striegau. In the meantime the Soviets reinforced their bridgehead near Ohlau.

The elements of the 19th *Panzer-Division* that had entrained northwest of Breslau, and the vehicles that had proceeded via the *Reichsautobahn* Liegnitz–Kostenbluth–Kanth, arrived together near Wangern, southeast of Breslau. While advancing to the southeast the 19th *Panzer-Division* knocked out 18 T–34s. Supported by the I./*Panzer-Regiment* 10, elements of *Panzer-Artillerie-Regiment* 9, *Panzer-Jäger-Abteilung* 43 and *Heeres-Flak-Abteilung* 286, the division then broke through the Soviet ring of encirclement west of Breslau. They established contact

Two images of a Soviet gun line. The weapons are 122mm howitzers.

with the encircled formations near Tinz on 14 February. The penetration enabled a large number of civilians to flee the city towards Zobten. Several tens of thousand, indeed, probably several hundred thousands, joined the exodus, in bitter cold. There were old people and children without any supply of food. They reached the Lauban–Görlitz railway line and were transported out from there.

At that point the 19th *Panzer-Division* could have received orders to reinforce the *Festung* garrison. Instead of that, its orders were to continue to operate outside Breslau. The next day the ring around Breslau closed anew, despite the heavy losses that the three German *Panzer* divisions operating there had exacted from the Soviet armour. The 19th *Panzer-Division* was unable to conduct another assault to broaden the penetration in the ring around Breslau. Nevertheless, the 19th *Panzer-Division* made yet another attempt to break the encirclement. For that purpose it established a front facing northeast towards Breslau with observation posts on the peak of the Zobten. However, southwest of Breslau it could only establish visual contact with the defenders of "*Festung* Breslau".

The enemy attack, advancing south of Breslau, appeared less important to the German command than the northern arm of the envelopment. From the Köben and Steinau bridgeheads the Soviets thrust forward via Liegnitz. They used the ideally situated *Reichsautobahn* to move their strong armoured forces towards the southwest. Accordingly the 8th and 20th *Panzer-Divisionen*, along with the 19th *Panzer-Division*, were assigned as "corset stays" for the 17th *Armee*. It was an attempt to stop additional Soviet reinforcements for the ring around Breslau, that were moving in from the northwest. The change in direction, however, barred further possibilities for the relief of Breslau. Although it was possible to force the Soviets back from Kostenbluth, perhaps with the destruction of a number of enemy tanks, the Soviets still had several bridgeheads over the Oder through which they could send new troops.

X

Battle of the Upper Silesian Industrial District

During that time, an additional *Schwerpunkt* developed south of Breslau, around the Upper Silesian industrial and dwelling districts. Defence of the district essentially fell to the Commander in Chief of the 17th Armee, *General der Infanterie* Schulz. His army had been broken through, on 15 January, in the sector of the 545th *Volks-Grenadier* Division. Thereupon the 359th *Infanterie-Division* was withdrawn from the front to receive the 48th *Panzer-Korps* which was falling back. Two positions had been prepared for the defence of the Upper Silesian industrial district, the B–1 and B–2 positions. B–1 was approximately in the line Spytkowice–Olkusz–Zawiercie and the B–2 directly at the border of the region in the line Auschwitz–Chrzanow–Jaworzno–Zomblowic. Under the direction of the *Höheren Pionierkommandeurs* 11, General Dr. Beneke and the Organisation Todt, with the help of the Upper Silesian civilian populace, positions were constructed in strongpoint fashion. They consisted of concrete fighting positions, anti-tank ditches, barbed wire entanglements and the like, in the depth of the main combat area. The *Volkssturm* units that were called up to man the prepared positions were unable to reach some of them in time. The retreating troops only briefly occupied those positions and did not defend them. In some sectors, the *Volkssturm* battalions did not get to their positions in time, and were cut down in bloodbaths by advancing Soviet armoured spearheads. Construction of positions thus proved ineffectual in those sectors.

The 712th and 75th *Infanterie-Divisionen* arrived to aid the defence, which was nearly helpless against the opposing Soviet forces of the 60th and 59th Armies which had 16 rifle divisions.

The 59th *Armee-Korps* and 11th *SS-Armee-Korps* took over the lines of defence. They were in contact with the 1st *Panzer-Armee* that repeatedly sent individual battalions and batteries to support the 17th *Armee* front.

The northern front of the district followed the line Dombrowa – Beuthen – Gleiwitz, along the Adolf Hitler Canal to Cosel on the Oder. They also had contact with the remnants of the 48th *Panzer-Korps*, namely, the 304th and 68th *Infanterie-Divisionen*, as well as corps troops and other splinter-groups of the *Volkssturm* that made it back across the lines. The unit with most combat capability was *Sturmgeschütz-Brigade* 300. In addition, came the 67th *Jäger-Division* and, finally, the first elements of the 20th *Panzer-Division*, which came from Hungary. The Soviets did not wait for the arrival of additional forces. On 24 January, the corps faced the Soviet 4th Guards Tank Corps and the 31st Tank Corps. They immediately attempted to advance via Gleiwitz to Ratibor, to cut off the Upper Silesian industrial district to the north. Extraordinarily eventful fighting developed in the built-up areas of the individual housing developments, mine-shafts, factory buildings and the like. None of it materially affected the underground mining of coal. In those districts the Gau leadership had forbidden evacuation of the residents, in order to maintain production to the maximum degree possible. Thus the fighting took place in the midst of the population of Myslowitz, Sossnowitz, and Dombrowa, and also around Beuthen, Hindenburg, Gleiwitz, and at the canal.

Bringing up the combat elements of the 20th *Panzer-Division* gave rise to complications, in that, as the elements arrived, they were locally tied up in specific commitments. Thus they initially secured the area around Sossnowitz to the north, northeast, east and southeast and occupied positions near Zagorz. After assuming command of *Heeresgruppe Mitte*, *Generalfeldmarschall* Schörner immediately ordered a battery of *Panzer-Artillerie-Regiment* 92 of the 20th *Panzer-Division*, to Groß-Strelitz. Other elements were sent to Tuporowicze, in northeast Upper Silesia, to support the 168th *Infanterie-Division* that had neither motor vehicles, ammunition, nor rations. Remaining elements of the 20th *Panzer-Division* went into firing positions near Gorodok, as enemy forces attacked Tschenstochau over open fields. The attack continued to Krokenberg, 4 kilometres south of Tarnowitz, where *Panzer-Grenadier-Regiment* 112 of the 20th *Panzer-Division* had arrived in the meantime. The *Kampfkommandant* of the city had only 2 convalescent companies, 2 anti-tank guns, and several light machine-guns available. The civilian population had, for the most part, evacuated the city.

In order to avoid costly street fighting, batteries of *Panzer-Artillerie-Regiment* 92 went into position south of Krokenberg. From there they could engage the northern edge of the city, as well as raking the southern edge, and the southern exits, with direct fire. Thus they retained the possibility of falling back to the south towards Beuthen, in the event that Krokenberg could not be held.

A German StuG III Ausf G assault gun

Further Fighting Retreat

Panzer-Grenadier-Regiment 112 was surprised when it advanced to the edge of the woods to the north. There, Soviet troop elements that had infiltrated, and also elements of the Polish population, were ready to capture the city from the rear. Enemy forces emerged between the observation positions and the firing positions. They fired from cellars, houses and openings in the roofs. Finally there was nothing that could be done except to get out of a witch's cauldron through individual farmsteads and gardens, and then on byways. Racing along separate paths, the available combat vehicles reached the area of the new firing positions. A massive strike by the German batteries on the exit roads from Krokenberg, provided relief. East of the city of Krokenberg the other elements of *Panzer-Grenadier-Regiment* 112 fell back unscathed to Beuthen. The Soviets did not follow up the pursuit through Tarnowitz.

After detraining on 26 January, additional elements of the 20th *Panzer-Division*, particularly *Panzer-Regiment* 21, were involved in fighting in Kochlowitz–Sassnowitz, near Preiswitz. En route the tank crews had, in makeshift fashion, serviced their tanks and prepared them for action. After detraining they were able to immediately launch a strong counter-attack, thereby repulsing advancing Soviets, although in so doing, they were cut off. In the midst of that situation an order arrived from Hitler about holding a Ruda–Antonienhütte line. In a dramatic telephone conversation with *Generalfeldmarschall* Schörner, the division commander refused to carry out the order, saying, among other things, "I do not go along with this lunacy of holding hopeless positions. We are going to break out. As soon as this conversation is over, the commanders who are here with me will receive orders to fight their way through to Ratibor. When we are out of this danger you may, Herr Feldmarschall, have my head at your disposal." Without awaiting an answer, the division commander General von Oppeln-Bronikowski, put down the telephone handset.

The breakout from the pocket took dramatic form as the Soviet formations advanced between the grenadiers and the armoured group. Tanks no longer mobile, and already drained of fuel, were only there to cover the retreat as static fortresses. When tanks were needed, they were refuelled. Although less than fully combat capable, they could escort the infantry. The wheeled and tracked vehicles had to cross the tracks of the freight rail yard, harassed by Soviet armour. In so doing, a Stalin tank skidded on the railway embankment. Another turned over and exploded. Two other tanks were knocked out by gunfire. In a 25 kilometre night move, on foot through snow, the individual elements then made it through, to pass between the lines of waiting division elements. On the day they made it back, 28 January, they launched an immediate attack on Sohrau, about 30 kilometres from Kobier, and about 20 kilometres south of Kattowitz.

It showed how thinly spread the combat capable German elements were at that time. It could hardly be described as a Front. Everywhere the Soviets found opportunities to infiltrate and then cut off German units. It was not only true for the advance of the Soviets in Upper Silesia, but also for central and Lower Silesia.

Fighting in the Neiße Area

There was further fighting in the area south of Breslau around Bergkirch, Rudnik and Ratibor. The first elements of the 20th Panzer-Division also arrived in the Zobten area on 8 February, while a *Kampfgruppe* of the division took an assembly position east of Neiße. There they launched an attack early on 9 February, initially along the Neiße–Breslau road. The apparently unexpected appearance of German armoured combat vehicles created confusion among the Soviets. At about 12.00 hours the group took Groß-Briesen and Falkenau, about 18 kilometres north of Neiße. After hard fighting, the Germans threw the Red soldiers out of Schwarzengrund, a few kilometres distant.

Hitherto the direction of attack had read "north". But from then the German Kampfgruppen turned to the west towards Alt Grottkau, a few kilometres west of Schwarzengrund. The Soviets had studded the hill thickly with weapons, with their front facing west, so it appeared that the hill could only be taken from the rear. The Germans had about 30 tanks, SPWs and self-propelled guns, with anti-tank guns ready for action. The *Kampfgruppe* attempted to envelop its objective, moving through wet fields and meadows, making slow forward progress. The combat vehicles sank deep into the soft ground. Many stuck fast. The Soviets could observe the German movement from the hill, and thereupon turned round their west-facing *Pakfront*, an organised array of anti-tank guns under unified control. With its help they exacted serious losses. Finally the Soviets fired with tanks, anti-tank guns, artillery and Stalin Organs upon a nearly immobilised, and stuck in the mud *Kampfgruppe*. The German attack foundered on such ground conditions. Nevertheless, left to its own devices, a small group penetrated as far as Alt Grottkau.

Elements of the 20th *Panzer-Division* continued to fight the Soviets for another week in the Zobten–Jordansmühl area. Fighting developed around Heidersdorf, Strehlen and Rudersdorf, and later, in the Neiße area, north and south of the Glatzer Neiße, i.e. Kupferhammer, Groß Gießmannsdorf, Groß Karlshöhe, and Groß Grottkau. Near the last-named place an element of the division repulsed enemy forces advancing from Brieg, and then moved rapidly to the Zobten near Breslau, Ramkau, Rogeau-Rosenau, Steinfelde and the community of Zobten.[1] From that point on, the 20th Panzer-Division took part in breaking through the Soviet ring of encirclement to the city of Breslau.

Between 23 February and 14 March bitter defensive fighting developed, especially around the villages of Wolfskirch – Rogau – Rosenau. The Soviets committed a substantial amount of armour there, including T–34, KV–1, KV–2 and Stalin tanks. It turned out that after their tanks were knocked out, several enemy crews were unable to get out. Padlocks sealed the hatches. The Red air force also took part, destroying Ottmachau, which the Red soldiers had previously attacked

---

1   Translator's note – Regarding the Neiße area: The city of Neiße (pop. in 1939: 37,859) was the Kreis city of Kreis Neiße and was located on the Glatzer Neiße River. Regarding Zobten: The Zobten was a 718 metre hill and landmark, southwest of Breslau. The city of Zobten (pop. In 1939: 3,524) was located directly north of the Zobten hill.

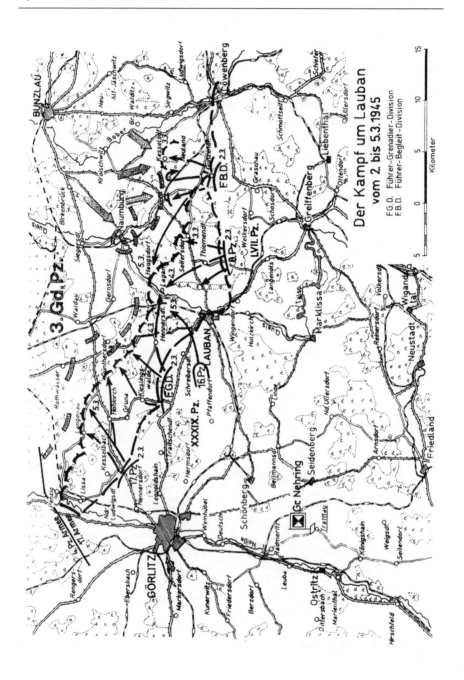

25 Battle for Lauban, 2–5 March 1945

without success. On 23 March, a German night attack on Heilersdorf came up against heavy infantry and artillery fire, as well as defending ground attack aircraft. The German troops finally evacuated the city of Neiße without a fight. The troops had the impression that the Soviet attacks let up. Apparently the Soviets withdrew forces and moved them towards Berlin.

All German actions suffered from logistical problems. Many actions had to be cancelled because of the shortage of fuel or ammunition. Supplies came forward to the troops, in part by rail, in part by motor vehicles fuelled by wood or gas converters, or alcohol. Among the ammunition arriving were shells with copper driving rings, from peacetime production, brought up in horse-drawn relay traffic from the supply dumps of the replacement troops. To conserve precious copper, wartime production shells had soft iron driving rings.

Conduct of the Troops

Regardless of the difficulties, the troops continued to hold their positions and fulfil their duties. Every single individual could clearly see for himself, as indeed could all men fit for duty, and even those with limited fitness, that the defence towards the east was the most important mission of the Wehrmacht at that stage of the war. They had to shield the German civilian population, to the greatest possible degree, from the orgies of the Red soldiers.

In those days there was great disillusionment regarding the Western Powers, as the British and American air forces attacked Dresden by day and night, a city that was filled with refugee vehicles and columns. The number of victims, in the tens of

A German 8.8cm Flak 41 deployed in the anti-tank role

thousands, cannot be determined. In order to prevent plague, the dead had to be piled in the market place and burned. Allied ground attack planes strafed the refugees that fled from the city to the meadows of the Elbe, creating yet another bloodbath there. There was no significant armament industry in Dresden, or other facilities significant to the war. In the opinion of the American commander in chief, it was merely a terror attack intended to cripple the powers of resistance of the German troops. However, the effect was the reverse.

The troops knew full well that the war was approaching its end, and indeed, with a forced surrender. However, nobody wanted to surrender to the East, after seeing what the Red Army had done to the German civilian population in all the places they had overcome, and how they treated prisoners of war. The willpower to resist to the east became stronger after that air attack on Dresden. Each one told himself that now, at that stage of the war, there were generally no longer any rules for the conduct of war. In any case, the rules of the Hague Convention on the Conduct of Land Warfare were no longer being observed by any of the enemy powers. Therefore, each must defend himself and the civilian population to the last.

Battle for Lauban

The railway line along the Riesengebirge via Lauban was vital to the Germans for troop movements and supplying the troops. Accordingly, the Red Army set Lauban as an attack objective. They captured the city, thereby blocking the railway line. In order to re-establish the link, the German command brought in formations from other sectors, including elements of *Panzer-Korps* "Großdeutschland" from the Stettin area.

Replacements also arrived to fill out the formations, including an infantry regiment newly activated in Saxony. An artillery *Abteilung* was activated from training personnel of the replacement army, in the course of the "Gneisenau" wave of activations. In addition, came remnants of the East Prussian 291st *Infanterie-Division*, the Elk-Division, which had been smashed on 12 January at the Baranow bridgehead, and small transports of replacements, including artillery replacements from Osnabrück.

Against strong motorised Soviet formations, equipped with armour, there had, indeed, in earlier fighting been isolated successes of a limited extent. But by then the German command intended to fight to free Lauban and the rail connection. At stake was the stretch of railway from Troppau via Lauban to Görlitz.

At first, entraining and detraining in the Lauban railway station was under well placed enemy artillery fire. Presumably the artillery observer was on the Silberberg, a commanding 281 metre high hill east of Logau. Therefore the 6th *Volks-Grenadier-Division* was ordered to capture that hill. It was called the "Nahkampfdiele", or " the close-combat floor". The 6th *Infanterie-Division* had changed its name repeatedly, from 6th Grenadier-Division, 6th *Volks-Grenadier-Division*, Division "*Panzertod*", and finally back to the 6th *Infanterie-Division*, and, indeed, with 20 to 22 infantry battalions. The 57th *Panzer-Korps* was in command of the impending battle, with the *Führer-Begleit-Division*, 16th *Panzer-Division* and two infantry divisions in the Lauban area, as well as the 39th *Panzer-Korps* with the *Führer-Grenadier-Division*, 17th *Panzer-Division* and 6th *Volks-Grenadier-Division*.

The attack of *Panzergruppe* Nehring on Lauban began on 3 March, at 19.00 hours. Initially, when darkness fell, and before the start of the German attack, the Soviets attempted to evacuate their frontal salient that reached to Lauban, in order to escape the impending envelopment. But it was too late. During the night the German attack began, and battered through to the Queis. Thus the German corps scuttled the Soviet intentions of breaking through to the south and southwest, via Lauban.

On 5 March, two *Panzer-divisions* worked together to capture the hills 7 kilometres north of Lauban. The 17th *Panzer-Division* was involved in particularly hard fighting. All the mobile formations in Silesia, especially Panzer divisions, had worked together in that attack at Lauban. The Soviets suffered heavy losses in armour so that they were not available for the following days. The Soviet command withdrew the remainder for refitting. 100 to 104 enemy tanks were confirmed as knocked out. There was substantial additional captured material, including 2 batteries of 12 cm guns, and 10 undamaged tanks. However, the formations that captured them had to turn over the captured tanks to the *Heeresgruppe*, for activation of an *Abteilung* consisting only of captured tanks.

The 208th *Infanterie-Division* arrived at Strigau which, after the usual pillaging, the Soviets had fortified. The division relieved *Polizei-Regiment* Schön of the 31st *SS-Freiwilligen-Infanterie-Division* "Böhmen und Mähren" and, on 9 March, attacked the city with *Infanterie-Regimenter* 337 and 309. The attack enabled the encircled city garrison to break out. During the fighting on 14 March, in snow squalls, Soviet ground attack aircraft strafed and bombed their own infantry.

There, as also in the villages around Lauban, the soldiers saw shocking pictures of Soviet licentiousness. The Soviets may well have viewed the populace as capitalists whom they had to destroy, along with all that had been built up in lifetimes of hard work. Dishes, furniture, even window panes were smashed, houses set afire, everything destroyed that man could destroy. Women were treated as fair game. Anyone who tried to shield them was shot. If the women and girls hid in attics and haystacks, the soldiers set the houses on fire to drive them out. Ranging from 12 year old girls to 80 year old women, they were serial raped by the drunken, howling Red soldiers. They indiscriminately shot inhabitants under the pretext that they were supposed to have been Nazis. The Soviets shot refugees left at the railway stations, after the departure of the last evacuation trains, as they did *Volkssturm* men and *Wehrmacht* members who fell into their hands. Many a civilian must have heard Goebbels' words about the "*Untermenschen*" or sub-humans, ringing in their ears. Everyone feared what would happen to the populace as a result of Ehrenburg's incitements. The fears evoked by German propaganda proved trivial, in comparison with the unbridled Red soldiers who then gained access to the populace.

Attack Operation across the Oder

East of the Oder, in Dyhernfurth, there was a chemical plant that had been evacuated at speed. A large amount of poison gas had been stored there. The evacuation order arrived too late, leaving not enough time for the poison gas to be rendered harmless and to be kept out of the hands of the Red Army. The risk of poison gas being used by the Soviets, caused the German command to call up an attack operation across the Oder. They had to reoccupy the plant, enabling the technical personnel who had worked there to destroy the poison gas stored in two subterranean vats. The plan was for the gas to be pumped through the factory pipe system, into the Oder. A number of formations became involved in the action. The plans included 1 company of *Fallschirmjäger* each, from *Heeresgruppe* Süd and *Heeresgruppe* Weichsel, 1 to 2 batteries of 8.8 cm Flak and *leichte* i.e. light *Pioneer-Sturmboot-Kompanie* 906, and 81 assault boats. A sudden concentration of artillery was to pound targets of identified heavy weapons, followed by a paratroop drop to occupy the factory site. Carrying out the intended task would require time. It was therefore vital not to alert the strong enemy armoured forces that were located 6 kilometres to the north, on the westward approach route. Reconnaissance showed that a railway bridge across the Oder had been blown up between two piers at the southern end. It would be necessary to cross the stretch of water to the undamaged portion of the bridge. The railway line passed 500 metres from a Soviet occupied farmstead, from which loud shouts of drunken Red soldiers could be heard. A railway siding branched off and would have to be the route to the factory during the night. Thus it was decided to dispense with the paratroopers. A parachute drop would have alerted armoured forces that were too strong to be held off, for the length of time required to dispose of the poison gas. A *Sturmboot* platoon with 25 boats would put a company of infantry across the Oder, further downstream, to feign a broad attack.

The operation went exactly as planned. The liquefied gases went into the Oder, thereby becoming harmless. In the plant nothing was left of the gas for the Soviets to analyse. At the end of work in the afternoon, 7 or 8 Soviet tanks appeared from the Dyhernfurth manor and advanced towards the railway embankment. An 8.8 cm Flak-battery had gone into position on the south bank with the barrels just above the level of the dike. It opened fire on the Soviet tanks. 6 tanks were instantly ablaze. An unhindered withdrawal route was cleared for the participants in that successful operation.

Further Fighting for the Upper Silesian Industrial District

It is important to understand that both the 11th *SS-Armee-Korps*, commanded by *SS-Obergruppenführer* Kleinheisterkamp, and the 11th *Armee-Korps*, commanded by *General der Infanterie* Bünau, were, for a time, involved in the fighting in that sector. According to the 11 January 1945 order-of-battle for *Heeresgruppe A*, later *Heeresgruppse Mitte*, given by von Ahlfen, *Der Kampf um Schleisen*, the 11th *Armee-Korps* with the 100th *Jäger-Division*, 253rd *Infanterie-Division* and 5th Hungarian Reserve Division was attached to *Armeegruppe* Heinrici. North of *Armeegruppe* Heinrici was the 17th *Armee* with the 11th *SS-Armee-Korps*, which included the 370th and 540th *Volks-Grenadier-Divisionen* and the 78th Volks- *Sturmdivision*, the 545th *Volks-Grenadier-Division* being en route, and also the 59th *Armee-Korps*.

On 29 January, the 11th *SS-Armee-Korps*, which had been broken through on 16 January near Jaslo, had to attach its two northern divisions, the 78th *Volks-Sturmdivision* and the 544th *Volks-Grenadier-Division* to the 59th *Armee-Korps*, as they had been cut off by the Soviet breakthrough from the corps headquarters. Accordingly, the 31 January order-of-battle showed *Armeegruppe-Heinrici* with, among others, the 11th *SS-Armee-Korps*, and 59th *Armee-Korps*, the latter including the 78th *Volks-Sturmdivision* and 540th *Volks-Grenadier-Divisionen* that had been turned over to it by the 11th *SS-Armee-Korps*. Adjoining *Armeegruppe* Heinrici to the north was the 17th *Armee* with the 11th *Armee-Korps*, which included the 75th, 371st *Infanterie-Divisionen*, 97th *Jäger-Division* and other formations.

On 6 February 1945, the sector of 1st *Panzer-Armee*, formerly *Armeegruppe* Heinrici, was extended further to the north. The 11th *Armee-Korps*, with the 75th and 68th *Infanterie-Divisionen*, the 1st *Ski-Jäger-Division* and the 97th *Jäger-Division*, which adjoined it to the north and which had been attached to the 17th *Armee*, was from then attached to the 1st *Panzer-Armee*. The 11th *SS-Armee-Korps* headquarters was then withdrawn and sent to another front, leaving the 11th *Armee-Korps* in command of divisions formerly attached to the 11th *SS-Armee-Korps*.

At the end of January and beginning of February, the Soviets tried in vain to break through the German positions in the Slovakian mountains. They even had support in the rear from the partisans of the forest areas of western Slovakia, who had resumed their activity. With the support of the civilian population, and under the direction of Soviet agents, the partisans fired from the rooftops of houses, on retreating German formations whose mission repeatedly consisted of eliminating mined partisan strongpoints.

The 1st *Panzer-Armee* was formerly called *Armeegruppe* Heinrici when the 1st Hungarian Army was tactically subordinated to it. On 29 January, it took over additional combat sectors to the north. Those included the command sector of the 11th *SS-Armee-Korps* in the area between the Slovak-Polish border and Saybusch, and the 59th *Armee-Korps* between Bielitz and Pleß. In the Saybusch area the Soviet attacks failed. However, the Soviets did win a crossing at the railway line from Auschwitz to Mährisch-Ostrau. It went over the valley of the river flowing from Bielitz to Pleß, and helped gain ground from Pleß to the west. In the course of 10 days, the Soviets gained 12 kilometres to the west, against the opposition of the 544th *Volks-Grenadier-Division* with attached elements of the *Volkssturm* included. The latter, however, were inadequately clothed and armed. They were then found to be of the greatest use in construction of positions to the rear.

In the Pleß area the Soviets realised the terrain was suitable for armour and therefore built a *Schwerpunkt* there. They concentrated several rifle divisions, reinforced them with armoured forces, and arranged support through the use of ground support aircraft. On 10 February, in an attack on the boundary between the 59th *Armee-Korps* and the 11th *Armee-Korps*, they broke through against the two German divisions fighting there, forcing them back to, and north of, the Schwarzwasser area, where they then came to a halt. Soviet attacks on both sides of Ratibor also failed to achieve a breakthrough. Counter-attacks near Schwarzwasser even led to a new line of defence. However, the centre division of the 59th *Armee-Korps*, the 78th *Volkssturm-Division*, which was committed south of the Vistula, was in danger of being cut off, and had to give up the high ground west of the Bielitz–Pleß line that had been so toughly defended.

The commander of the 1st Panzer-Armee again found the sector under his command was being extended to the northwest. The 1st *Panzer-Armee* took over the 11th *Armee-Korps* with the 75th and 68th *Infanterie-Divisionen* adjoining the north wing of the 11th *SS-Armee-Korps*, as well as the 1st *Ski-Jäger-Division* and 97th *Jäger-Division*, north of Ratibor. However, the formations involved, which had earlier fought in the Beskides, were no longer complete divisions, merely *Kampfgruppen*. In the sector north of the 59th *Armee-Korps*, in the Saybusch area, the headquarters of the 11th *SS-Armee-Korps* was then withdrawn and sent to a new front. That left the 11th *Armee-Korps* in command of divisions formerly attached to the 11th *SS-Armee-Korps*. The 49th *Gebirgs-Korps*, with the 545th and 320th *Volks-Grenadier-Divisionen*, 253rd *Infanterie-Division*, and 4th and 3rd *Gebirgs-Divisionen*, took over the entire mountain front, from Bielitz to south of Ruzomberok i.e. Rosenberg, in the Waag River valley, in Slovakia,

First near Rybnik, then north of Ratibor, and again in the Pleß area, the Soviets alternated their attacks, predominately with negative or limited success. However, the Soviets faced the 9 German infantry divisions of the 1st *Panzer-Armee* between Sohrau–Bielitz and Rosenberg, including 36 rifle divisions, and several armoured formations of approximately 160 tanks and 75 assault guns. The 4th *Gebirgs-Division* was engaged in hard fighting in its sector around Mount Skorusina, west of Zakopane, and the Magura, northwest of the Hohe Tatra. In the Waag valley the 3rd *Gebirgs-Division* fought in defence between 11 and 15 February. All Soviet efforts in that sector proved fruitless. The Czech brigades that the Soviets committed there suffered substantial losses.

From the selection of those sectors, it was apparent that the Soviets intended to gain the industrial district intact, by envelopment from the north and south. However, the German formations involved were extremely variable in combat effectiveness. Therefore the 3rd *Gebirgs-Division* had to give up elements to the north. The 253rd *Infanterie-Division*, which had been in the mountains south of Saybusch, exchanged positions with the 78th *Volkssturm-Division*, going into action near Schwarzwasser.

The weakness of individual formations, added to the Soviet change in *Schwerpunkt*, made it necessary to constantly move elements of troops. The 371st Infanterie-Division and 18th *SS-Freiwilligen-Panzer-Grenadier-Division* "Horst Wessel" went to the 11th *Armee-Korps*, which gave its right wing division, the 75th *Infanterie-Division*, to the 59th *Armee-Korps*. The Soviet attack by the 1st Ukrainian Front, from the bridgehead close to Leobschütz, gained ground near Groß Neukirch.

The Soviets achieved penetrations in a variety of places that were immediately contained by the Germans. However, on 21 February, the Soviets ceased their efforts. Between Saybusch and Sohrau the German formations had taken up new positions in the line of hills west of Saybusch–Skotschau, directly west of Schwarzwasser–Pawlowitz–Sohrau. There the two wings, in the mountains in the south and in the northwest, between Rybnik, Ratibor and Cosel, lost no ground. The Soviets failed to achieve their planned breakthrough into the Mährisch-Ostrau industrial district. In the 22 days of fighting after 30 January, they gained 20 kilometres, about 1/3 of the distance to Mährisch-Ostrau.

Red Army soldiers man a 45mm Model 1942 anti-tank gun. By this late stage in the war it was increasingly obsolescent. Note the horse-drawn limber in close attendance.

March Fighting

Repeatedly, troops had to be moved from one army to another, but because of petrol shortages most of the movements were by rail. It was amazing what was accomplished by the railways. It was no longer the "field-grey" or army-run railway, but the "blue" or civilian railway. Initially it had to transport tens of thousands of "Ostwall [East Wall] diggers" from Silesia to construct the "Ostwall". That required 100 trains every weekend, carrying 100,000 people, but without impacting on the commuter traffic. Over and above, came trains to evacuate first the Tarnowitz and Kreuzberg areas via Oppeln. In addition, there were shuttle trains from the northern industrial district to the nearby Neiße, Ziegenhals, Freiwaldau reception area. Until 20 January, to relieve overloading, there were also additional scheduled trains, running before and after the regular trains, returning to Breslau and Vienna. Approximately 1.7 million people came to the inner Reichs territory on the evacuation trains. And then there were the hospital trains.

Numerous troop movements each time required 65 trains for moving what was left of a single horse-drawn infantry division, and 40 trains for the *Kampfgruppe* of one *Panzer-division*. In addition, supplies had to be brought up. The Rybnik coal mines continued to produce coal until the end of March. The Mährisch-Ostrau coal district remained in production to the very end, the Waldenburg area until 8 May. Between February and the second half of April, the Karwien district east of Mährisch-Ostrau shipped 16,000 tons of coal and coke daily to the Reich, i.e. 12 railway trains of 60 wagons each. The railway had to convert one stretch from electric to steam power due to a shortage of electric locomotives. To secure the shipment of coal from the coal district, the *Oppeln Reichsbahn* directorate constructed a 1.5 kilometre detour curve, with a 10 metre bridge built of local materials. They added several culverts and signal facilities in the Jägerndorf sector, as the Ratibor railway station was under enemy artillery fire. The railway also repaired the Oderberg–Rybnik stretch after it had been blown up, putting it back in service within two to three weeks.

Ground Combat

The *Kampfgruppen* of the 19th *Panzer-Division*, the 10th *Panzer-Grenadier-Division*, and also the 20th *Panzer-Division* came from the Strehlen–Schweidnitz area to the north of Neiße. They had to halt the enemy armoured thrust, from Grottkau to the south. However, they themselves ended up on the defensive, and were unable to interfere with the Soviets' night crossing of the Neiße River near Rothaus, on 16 to 17 March. The attack of *Fallschirm-Panzer-Division* "Hermann Göring", south of Neiße towards the east, was not a success either. Individual elements of that formation did not come from earlier service in the Muskau bridgehead in time for the attack.[2] The battle for Neiße, 23 to 24 March, finally ended with the loss of "Festung" Neiße. However, south of Neiße, the front held that had been pulled back behind the river Biele sector, as did the front north of Neiße that faced east.

However, many soldiers lost their lives in the fighting around Neiße, and there were substantial losses in heavy weapons. Affected were the 344th *Infanterie-Division*, the 18th *SS-Freiwilligen-Panzer-Grenadier-Division* "Horst Wessel", also the 168th *Infanterie-Division* and the 20th *Waffen-Grenadier-Division der SS, estnische Nr. 1*. In addition, despite timely arrangements, evacuations of women, children and old people were caught up in the fighting.

---

2   Translator's note – Rothaus was located on the Glatzer Neiße about 10 kilometres northeast of the city of Neiße.

XI

New Battle for the Mährisch-Ostrau Industrial District, 8–21 March

At the beginning of March, developments had led the *Heeresgruppe* to give up, for the time being, their planned, additional, relief attack on the encirclement of Breslau. For that purpose, the troops of the 24th *Panzer-Korps*, with the 16th and 17th *Panzer-Divisionen*, along with the *Führer-Begleit-Division* that had been assembled there, had to move to the Leobschütz, Jägerndorf, Teschen area, as did the 254th *Infanterie-Division*. The 1st *Panzer-Armee* withdrew the 8th *Panzer-Division* from the front, and held it ready for commitment on the left wing of the 59th *Armee-Korps*. The 78th *Volkssturm-Division* also evacuated its positions south of Saybusch. Based on statements by prisoners, the new offensive of the Soviet 4th Ukrainian Front was expected on 10 March. Accordingly, on 9 March, the 59th *Armee-Korps* issued orders to occupy the *Großkampf* main line of resistance. The Soviet artillery preparation, and the use of ground-attack aircraft, pounded the evacuated German positions. The subsequent enemy infantry attack fell on empty positions. The later attack, against the *Großkampf* line of resistance, broke up into individual combat actions without concentrated systematic artillery fire. The Soviets did not commit the armour that they had assembled, giving the German formations a breather. Meanwhile the 16th *Panzer-Division* went into position via Freistadt, and the 8th *Panzer-Division* went into position east of Sohrau.

The Soviet plans were thwarted by the disruption of the Soviet attack preparations in the Cosel bridgehead, and the withdrawal to a *Großkampf* position. The Red Army had to start by reorganising its formations. The armour of the 4th Ukrainian Front remained inactive at first. In ensuing days, strong armoured formations again attacked north and south of Schwarzwasser. The 3rd *Gebirgs-Division*, which had repulsed the Soviets after falling back to the *Großkampf* main line of resistance, launched a counter-attack on 11 March, and recaptured its old positions. In so doing they captured an assault troop of the *NationalkomiteeFreies Deutschland"* in German uniforms[1]. It was only on the north wing of the 59th *Armee-Korps*, that the Soviets achieved a nearly 7 kilometre deep penetration towards Sohrau in the greatly weakened 75th *Infanterie-Division*. The 8th *Panzer-Division*, with *Gebirgs-Jäger-Regiment* 91, intercepted the penetration. A battalion of *Gebirgsjäger* counter-attacked, advancing 5 kilometres past the friendly lines.

On 15 March, a new battle broke out between Cosel and Grottkau. It hit the 11th *Armee-Korps* between Ratibor and Cosel on the north wing of the 1st *Panzer-Armee*. The corps was able to contain the Soviets on the first day. On the second

---

1 Translator's note – The *National Komitee für ein "Freies Deutschland"* was composed primarily of *emigré* Communists, but its subsidiary, the *Bund Deutscher Offiziere* was allegedly voluntary, non-Communist and exclusively devoted to overthrowing Hitler and restoring the traditional social order in Germany. (Ziemke, *Stalingrad to Berlin*, p. 149).

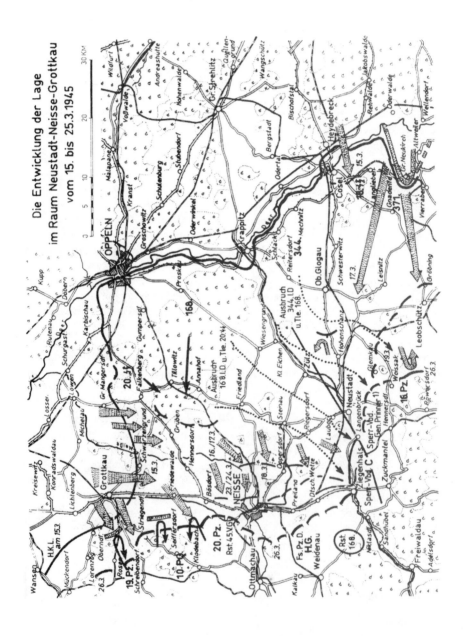

26 The development of the situation in the area Neustadt-Neisse-Grottkau,
15–25 March 1945

day of fighting, 16 March, the Soviets achieved deep penetrations towards Leobschütz. Immediately, the 254th *Infanterie-Division* had to be moved in from the central Silesian front of the 17th *Armee*, and the 1st *Panzer-Armee's* 16th *Panzer-Division* from the fighting front southwest of Schwarzwasser. Defence in that sector had special significance in preventing the Soviets from breaking through the Mährisch-Ostrau district. In addition, a breakthrough via Leobschütz to Jägerndorf would have assisted the south wing of the Soviet forces in the Cosel, Grottkau area.

On 16 and 17 March, the 4th Ukrainian Front concentrated all its forces again for a breakthrough. Southwest of Schwarzwasser, their efforts were repulsed in hard fighting by the joint efforts of the 544th *Infanterie-Division*, the 3rd and 4th *Gebirgs-Divisionen* and the 253rd *Infanterie-Division*. Also, northwest of Schwarzwasser, the weak 8th *Panzer-Division* together with the 75th, 68th *Infanterie-Divisionen* and elements of the 4th *Gebirgs-Division* prevented the enemy from making any progress. 65 Soviet tanks had been knocked out since the start of the fighting near Schwarzwasser. The 59th *Armee-Korps* held fast. The Soviets were able to continually throw new formations into the battle, thereby changing the force-ratio of the troops, on both sides, during the fighting. The greater mobility of the Soviets granted them a significant advantage.

Near Cosel there was the 344th *Infanterie-Division* with the *Kampfgruppe* of the 18th *SS-Freiwilligen-Panzer-Grenadier-Division "Horst Wessel"* that had come from Hungary. The Soviets pounded the German positions with extensive artillery fire, which helped them to finally break through to the west, south of Cosel. Various small communities achieved significance in the combat reports, namely Gnadenfeld, Schneidenburg, Schönhain, Drosselschlag and Matzkirch. On 17 March, the Soviets reached Borrowitz as the southernmost point, and achieved greater gains of terrain where *Reichsbahnstrasse* 145 swung in a bend near Gnadenfeld, between Leobschütz and Cosel. The events described above forced the 344th *Infanterie-Division*, with the *Kampfgruppe* of the 18th *SS-Freiwilligen-Panzer-Grenadier-Division "Horst Wessel"*, back to the northwest, to the Cosel–Krappitz area. Meanwhile, the 371st *Infanterie-Division* that was fighting south of the penetration, had to fall back to the southwest. The *Sturmgeschütze* of the 344th *Infanterie-Division* undertook individual attacks from Reinschdorf to Pirchwitz , south of Cosel. They secured Neumannshöh and fought near Kobelwitz, Juliusburg and Nesselwitz between Neumannshöh and Hartenau at *Reichstraße* 115, i.e. Cosel–Oberglogau, against the Soviet penetration. After the Soviets took Krappitz, contact was lost between the 344th *Infanterie-Division* and the 17th *Armee* and thereby, with *Kommando "Korpsgruppe Schlesien"*, 56th *Panzer-Korps*, with the 168th *Infanterie-Division* and the 20th *Waffen-Grenadier-Division der SS estnische Nr. 1*. To the south, contact was also lost with the divisions of the 11th *Armee-Korps* at the front.

At the same time, beginning on 15 March, the Soviets thrust south from Grottkau across the Glatzer Neißetowards Rothaus. On 17 March, the elements of *Fallschirm-Panzer-Division "Hermann Göring"*, that had in the meantime detrained, immediately launched a sharp attack against the western flank of the Soviet assault wedge that was advancing towards Steinau–Neustadt. However, after

Infantry assemble for a counter-attack in Silesia, 1945

initial success, the division had to go over to the defensive in the Kaundorf–Oppersdorf area, southeast of the Neiße.

In order to prevent a crossing of the next river, the Biele, the German command concentrated all available troop remnants to form a blocking formation. Essentially, it consisted of one fought out infantry battalion, and two construction battalions with a single heavy field howitzer. They were later reinforced with elements of *Fallschirm-Panzer-Division "Hermann Göring"*. The blocking formation, later reinforced with two *"Wespen"*, held a line from the city of Neiße to south of Ziegenhals. In the meantime, additional forces pushed on west from Krappitz. The Soviet formations that had broken in from Grottkau, advanced south towards Neustadt ,with the objective of linking up south of Deutsch-Rasselwitz with the forces that had broken in south of Cosel. The Soviets had thereby cut off several formations that had to attempt to free themselves.

The commander of the 344th *Infanterie-Division, Generalleutnant* Jollase, did not consider that he could break through to the *Korpsgruppe* of *General* Koch-Erpach of the 17th *Armee*. It was encircled to the north. In addition, on that day, 18 March, came the evacuation of Cosel, and the resulting confusion among the civilian population of Cosel and the immediate environs. All of that happened at night and in heavy rain. Only a few German formations were available for the defence, including several batteries of *Oberst* Kiewitt in the Nesselwitz area. They knocked out numerous enemy tanks and thereby delayed the Soviet advance. By 17 March, a total of 121 Soviet tanks had been knocked out on the entire offensive front.

The greatest misfortune was that of the civilians fleeing Cosel and its surroundings. When the Soviets could get their hands on them they unloaded their blind hatred on civilians. Tank tracks ground over the refugee wagons. Red soldiers unhitched the horses, rummaged through the contents of the wagons, and raped the women at every imaginable opportunity and place. They shot any who defended themselves, and the men who tried to protect them. Only a few managed to make their way through to the west. Such men as survived were later shipped off by rail to Siberia, from where only a few individuals returned. When a Soviet officer fell in combat in Plieschnitz, 20 men were seized and were immediately shot. The Soviets ransacked the houses, and shot civilians and wounded German prisoners of war. Only a few of the civilians returned to their villages at that time. Shocking reports came from several villages. The Red soldiers fired on all around them, regardless of whether they hit police officials, French prisoners of war, German prisoners, or wounded.

On the margins of the Soviet thrusts, the German formations that were not under direct attack held their positions, such as the 97th *Jäger-Division* and the 1st *Ski-Jäger-Division*. The 371st and 254th *Infanterie-Divisionen*, the 78th *Volkssturm-Division* and 344th *Infanterie-Division* had a difficult time. The latter, along with the 18th *SS-Freiwilligen-Panzer-Grenadier-Division "Horst Wessel"*, being forced back to the north.

New Soviet Advance

However, towards the south, the German command expected a further attack by the 1st Ukrainian Front and the 4th Ukrainian Front, from the Leobschütz area, in the direction of Troppau. They would try to get behind the German line of defence near Mährisch-Ostra.u. In addition, came the determination that the 2nd Ukrainian Front was advancing from Hungary, via Neutra to the northwest, towards the advance from Leobschütz near Troppau. From that came the conclusion that the Soviets had not yet given up their battle for the narrow space of Mährisch-Ostrau. Remarkably, the German combat success in that sector left them ready for action, with organisation and logistics, in spite of its shrunken division elements having limited mobility

However, there were only limited amounts of fuel that were often only brought up shortly before a movement was ordered. There was, generally, no shortage of diesel fuel. Thus, in order to remain mobile, the formations towed their petrol-driven combat vehicles behind their diesel vehicles from position to position. Thus came the unique picture of the field-kitchen truck towing an 8 ton prime mover, towing a heavy field howitzer behind it, to save fuel for the prime mover. The petrol driven combat vehicles, i.e. automobiles, trucks, prime movers, for the most part, had to make do with alcohol from former distilleries in the Polish *Generalgouvernement*, in the remnants of Silesia. No German soldier in uniform was permitted to go into Mährisch-Ostrau to avoid giving the Red air force any excuse to attack. In Mährisch-Ostrau not only was alcohol distilled for fuelling vehicles, ammunition was also made. When the railway was overloaded, supplies came to the troops by wood or gas driven vehicles. Transports arrived from replacement troop locations and training grounds, with peacetime manufactured ammunition, made with copper driving rings. Some even came from remote parts of the *Reich*. In any case, the troops on the Mährisch-Ostrau front got a short breather.

Encircled Elements Break Out

The formations cut off by the Soviet advance between 15 and 18 March, laboriously fought their way through, after the supreme command had refused to allow them to break out when the time was right. Thus, on 19 March, the 344th *Infanterie-Division* and the 18th *SS-Freiwilligen-Panzer-Grenadier-Division "Horst Wessel"* broke out across the Hotzenplotz River, on the initiative of the division commander of the 344th *Infanterie-Division*, Jollasse,.

Splintered elements of *"Korpsgruppe Schlesien"* had been cut off further north, and failed in their breakout to the west in the Neustadt area. They joined the columns of the 344th *Infanterie-Division* that was breaking out towards Deutsch-Rasselwitz. Deutsch-Rasselwitz was a little less than half way along the southern road from Oberglogau to Neustadt, and was defended by the constant fire of the Red Army. First, however, it was necessary to capture Deutsch-Rasselwitz, in order to break through the Soviet ring of encirclement there. Two kilometres southwest of Deutsch-Rasselwitz, the Hotzenplotz, its bridges blown, constituted a serious terrain problem. Through swampy ground the retreating infantry tried to find a suitable crossing point. There the 344th *Infanterie-Division* lost its heavy materiel, including all of the artillery, even the last *Sturmgeschütze* and some other vehicles. The leading elements of the formations reached friendly lines at the village of Hotzenplotz at about midnight.

Korpsgruppe "Schlesien", *General* Koch-Erpach, 56th *Panzer-Korps*, with *Kampfgruppen* 168th *Infanterie-Division* and 20th *Waffen-Grenadier-Division der SS estnische Nr.1,* had attempted to break out to the south at Neustadt, towards the Altvatergebirge. *Gruppe Wennsauer*, which had been encircled in Oppeln, joined it in breaking out, after Oppeln had been taken by the Soviets and set completely ablaze. The last position of the group was 12 kilometres southwest of Oppeln near Gumpertsdorf. It was attached to the command of *General* Schmidt-Hammer, commander of the 168th *Infanterie-Division*. *Gruppe Wennsauer* made it through the enemy lines during the night of 20 March near Altwalde, 15 kilometres northwest of Neustadt. The retreating group was then strengthened with about 3,400 men who later formed the blocking formation, the *Sperrverband*, of *Oberst* Capelle, and escaped from the pocket that encircled *Korpsgruppe Schlesien*.

Further to the south the Soviets also attacked. However, the formations there, the 97th *Jäger-Division*, 68th and 75th *Infanterie-Divisionen*, 8th *Panzer-Division*, 4th *Gebirgs-Division* and 253rd *Infanterie-Division* of the 59th *Armee-Korps* held fast against all attacks.

Further Fighting in the Leobschütz Area

"Gruppe von Einem", which was attached to the 8th *Panzer-Division*, was in the Katscher area and was assigned the mission of proceeding northward to support the 371st *Infanterie-Division*. However, during the attack it received orders to break off, in order to move further into the Leobschütz area. There, a large Soviet con-

German infantry and an assault gun move forward during a counter-attack

centration had been identified with the apparent intention of breaking through to the south, to Troppau. At 05.00 hours, the Soviet artillery began to pound the German positions in the Bladen – Neudorf area. The subsequent attack carried through to the plateau north of Bladen. It then rebounded from a hasty counter-attack by German armour, on a broad front, via Hennerwitz south of Bladen. With the hastily brought in 17th *Panzer-Division*, which knocked out 59 Soviet T–34s four kilometres south of Leobschütz, it smashed the Soviet attack. East of Leobschütz and on both sides of Hotzenplotz, the Soviets lost a total of 143 tanks. They did not let up on their attacks, so there was heavy fighting in ensuing days in the Leobschütz area. The German lines, however, held firm.

In a single day, 22 March, tanks of the 8th *Panzer-Division* and the *Führer-Begleit-Division* knocked out a total of 101 Soviet tanks in the Leobschütz area. On 23 March, the 715th *Infanterie-Division* under *General* von Rohr, which had been brought up from Italy, detrained. The division was inadequately armed and, above all, lacked any combat experience. The Soviets immediately broke through its line of defence, with the result that Hitler, incorrectly assessing the situation, decreed that members of the division had to set aside all awards and decorations. That day the Germans lost 1,200 men, many of them from the 715th *Infanterie-Division*. The following day the *Schwerpunkt* moved to Loslau, with artillery fire and attacks by ground attack aircraft. A counter-attack by the 8th *Panzer-Division* threw the Soviets back out of the city area away from the southwest edge of the city. After initial German tank losses *Panzers* launched a hasty counter-attack. The soldiers forced their way forward in hand-to-hand fighting. In the village of Kokoschütz, about 4 km west-north-west of Loslau, they forced the staff of a Soviet battalion to surrender, capturing a huge number of weapons, especially anti-tank rifles. In Krähenbusch, in *Kreis* Neustadt, which had fallen into Soviet hands, mass graves of 300 German soldiers of a *Pioneer* replacement battalion were found. A total of about six or seven hundred German soldiers were shot there.

The attacks in the sector of the 11th *Armee-Korps* and 59th *Armee-Korps*, particularly via Ratibor and Jägerndorf, were directed towards Troppau. There they also ran into elements of the 16th *Panzer-Division* which were supposed to be refitting with personnel replacements in the Troppau area. 42 burnt out Soviet tanks lay out in the fields. The 1st *Ski-Jäger-Division* put a company outfitted with captured T–34 tanks into action. At the same time, the 17th *Panzer-Division* arrived to support the defence in the Rogau area. The attack launched there met with initial success. But then they were bogged down near Feschdörfel, on the west bank of the Oder, in Soviet defensive fire.

After the unfortunate events involving the 715th *Infanterie-Division*, the 4th *Gebirgs-Division* had extended its frontal sector to the left. Despite that, it had to give up a battalion to the 68th *Infanterie-Division*. In a fighting retreat, the 8th *Panzer-Division* fell back to the Groß-Gorschütz area, 6 kilometres northwest of Oderberg. During the period from 10 March to 4 April, the Soviets lost 1,423 tanks and assault guns in the frontal sector, as well as 200 aircraft shot down.

At that time, however, the Soviet advance of the 2nd Ukrainian Front past Vienna towards Olmütz was already a threat. Therefore the 8th *Panzer-Division* was pulled out of the bridgehead and had to move to the Kremsier area, 83 kilometres south of Olmütz.

Fighting in the Oppa Sector

The fighting finally moved to the former Czech border bunker area in the Oppa River sector. A field training division, the 158th *Feldausbildungs-Division*, entered the fighting, but proved itself to be totally inexperienced in combat. Therefore, according to the results of reconnaissance, other formations again had to change their positions, including the 4th *Gebirgs-Division*, 97th *Jäger-Division*, 19th *Panzer-Division* and *Bewährungs-Bataillon* 500. The last of those was a probationary battalion, with minimal living standards. It was used for dangerous assignments to which officers and enlisted men were sent after committing military offences. *Panzer-Regiment* 27 of the 19th *Panzer-Division* knocked out 103 Soviet tanks and assault guns during the period of 15 March to 10 April, and destroyed or captured 104 guns. Nevertheless, the 19th *Panzer-Division* had to be withdrawn and moved to Brünn to lengthen the southern wing. The 17th *Panzer-Division* was also pulled out of its commitment sector and moved to Swoboda–Weißkirchen, as a reserve in readiness, after Czech partisans had interfered with the rear area services. The 344th *Infanterie-Division* entrained on 16 April in Ottmachau, to proceed to the 4th *Panzer-Armee* in the Spremberg area, south of Cottbus. The 20th *Panzer-Division* moved from the relatively quiet Neiße sector, to the Görlitz area.

In mid-April, the Soviets again started heavy attacks. 68 knocked out Soviet tanks remained east of Troppau. They had not achieved the breakthrough, but had forced the right wing of the German line back to Deutsch-Karwan on the Oppa River. Heavy fighting developed near Klein Hoschütz and Groß Hoschütz. The Soviets began with artillery, mortars and ground attack planes in the early morning, at 04.00 hours on 16 April. That same day, the Soviet attack on Berlin opened with 40,000 guns.

From 21 to 24 April, there was heavy fighting around Troppau. A massive Soviet assault temporarily smashed the continuity of the front on the right flank of the defence. The German formations, however, pulled themselves together again, on the other side of the Oppa River and prevented a deep Soviet penetration. On 22, 23 and 24 April, the bitter fighting continued to surge back and forth. After repeated attacks the Soviets forced their way into Troppau, on 25 April.

The divisions in the Mährisch-Ostrau sector had to repulse heavy Soviet attacks for several days. As a result of that attack the 16th *Panzer-Division* was again moved to the right wing, to Mährisch-Ostrau. The 371st *Infanterie-Division* evacuated the city on 1 May, after crossing the Oder. In the southern part of Troppau, the 16th *Panzer-Division* and *Führer-Begleit-Division*, along with the 1st *Ski-Jäger-Division* stood ready. The 17th *Panzer-Division* was at the northwest edge of Troppau, to prevent the breakthrough of the Soviets to Olmütz. With that, the battle for Upper Silesia ended, a few days before the capitulation of the *Wehrmacht.*

XII

Fighting on the Lausitzer-Neiße

In central Silesia the front on the Lausitzer Neiße had enjoyed a certain degree of quiet. Glogau had been essentially weakened as a fortress, and had quit the fighting at the end of March. It was less equipped for independent fighting than Breslau. The garrison broke out with great losses. On the other hand, in April it was possible to liberate Niesky, Weißenberg and Bautzen, thereby protecting Silesia's northern flank. On 16 April the Soviets began with two phases of bombardment and subsequent attack. They crossed the Neiße at two main places, on both sides of Rothenburg and south of Muskau as far as Forst. In both attack areas they broke through on 17 April. At the site of the northern breakthrough between Muskau and Forst, there was no more plugging the gap, so the Soviets had won free passage via Spremberg–Cottbus to advance against the south front of Berlin. The southern breakthrough wedge did not immediately penetrate the forces of the 20th *Panzer-Division* and *Fallschirm-Panzergrenadier-Division "Hermann Göring"* that it ran into. The *"Hermann Göring" Division* knocked out 65 tanks in a single day and went over to the defensive between Zodel, on the Neiße, and Ullersdorf, while the 20th *Panzer-Division* carried on with its counter-attack until 19 April.

On the southern flank of the gap, they had smashed and somewhat hindered the Soviets who continued their westward thrust, recapturing Niesky, Weißenberg and Bautzen. There the Soviets committed a larger armoured formation, the 1st

A column of German assault guns rolls towards the photographer

Polish Tank Corps, which had been activated by the Soviets. It developed as if on peacetime manoeuvres and rolled forward against Kodersdorf. When the first tanks were about 50 metres distant the German armour opened fire. In 20 minutes, 43 enemy tanks were knocked out. The rest showed white flags. 12 undamaged tanks fell into German hands, including three Stalin tanks. Within a few hours they were in service with German black cross markings on their sides.

On 20 April, in the area northwest of Görlitz, the reorganised elements of the 17th *Panzer-Division* arrived. They attacked to the northwest, to the right of the 20th *Panzer-Division*, with the 42nd *Infanterie-Division* as reserve. The assault liberated the formations and inhabitants who had been cut off in Niesky. Above all, the advance made it possible to regain full operational freedom in the Görlitz area, and free the Görlitz–Lauban railway from interruption. *Panzer-Grenadier-Division "Brandenburg"* received the mission of freeing Weißenberg, as soon as the division could be withdrawn and reassembled from the defence in the Rothenburg area. There, it been torn in two. On 21 and 22 April it attacked from north and south, freeing Weißenberg and destroying a Soviet division there. A large amount of booty was captured, about 200–300 trucks, knocked-out guns and a great many prisoners. The 20th *Panzer-Division* later managed to free the city of Bautzen, with the involvement of *Fallschirm-Panzer-Division "Hermann Göring"* attacking from the south. The overall battle exacted substantial losses from the Soviets, including the destruction of 355 enemy tanks, 322 guns of all sorts, destroyed or captured. About 7,000 dead were counted and 800 prisoners taken. Involved were the Soviet 94th Rifle Division, 7th Guards Mechanized Corps, 1st Polish Tank Corps, 16th Tank Brigade, 5th, 7th, and 8th Polish and 254th Soviet Rifle Divisions.

The attempt to interfere with the Soviet advance on Berlin from the south failed. The Soviets not only gained space for the advance on Berlin, but also to the west, towards Dresden. That fighting did, however, at least cause a delay that allowed more refugees to flee to the west.

XIII

Overview of the Situation

The hopeless situation of the *Heeresgruppe A* forces required consideration of whether such developments were really inescapable. The military professionals, particularly *Generaloberst* Guderian, had energetically warned against the repeated weakening of the Eastern Front. Hitler, however, had closed his mind against those warnings and stated that the Eastern Front would have to look after itself. He countered reports of the Soviet build-up and concentration with the remark that it was "the greatest bluff since the time of Genghis Khan". The force ratio was so unequal that, even by utilising special command skills, and new tactical techniques of commitment where possible, the German forces could not in any way hold fast. Guderian brought up the comparison with a house of cards, stating that, at the start of a Soviet attack, the Eastern Front would "collapse like a house of cards". And so it happened.

It would have been irresponsible for a military commander to place forces in such a hopeless situation of commitment, that could only bring about unheard of losses, without in any way justifying the loss of human lives. Hitler had earlier achieved great successes on the political level. But since the start of the war he had placed all his hopes on the military card that had failed in every respect. Hitler then rested all his hopes for a political change in the situation upon the success of the Ardennes Offensive. He thought it would make the Americans ready for negotiation, while at the same time ignoring the fact that the enemy powers on all sides had resolved to force Germany into unconditional surrender. It was exactly on those demands that all attempts to put out political feelers foundered, as did the resistance movement. The Western Powers had underlain the war with a missionary motivation to remove the National Socialist dictator. They ignored the fact that, in so doing, they went hand in hand with a far stricter and more ruthless dictator. Thus they thereby aided Stalin in his effort to extend Communism in Europe. Much too late, Churchill recognised that with his remark, "We butchered the wrong pig".

The military had propounded several plans to contrive a defence in the east. Essentially, those were connected with loss of ground, as with the *"Schlittenfahrt"* plan, and with the demand of the military commanders for greater freedom in their decisions for an elastic conduct of the war. Hitler persisted, however, in his orders that all ground must be held, and in the requirement for his permission, before any action order that could be linked with loss of ground.

Right up to the time when he was "put on the shelf", Guderian was unable to get through to Hitler with the serious warnings that he clearly presented. As for the advice of the general staff or of any commander in chief, it held little weight with Hitler. He had his own opinion regarding the military situation and gave that far greater significance than the opinions of experienced military leaders. It was upon that conviction that he based his militarily unjustifiable decree that the reserves would be held directly behind the front lines, and also the requirement that he himself must personally give permission for every withdrawal order. But he continued with his own orders to hold fast. There were, however, errors on various levels of the military command to the extent that the significance of the main defensive area was not recognised and the troops, such as the 6th *Volks-Grenadier-Division* and 45th *Volks-Grenadier-Division* were exposed to an extremely costly destructive fire. In fact, in that case, the division commanders had operational freedom that they had not made use of.

However the blame, for the costly development of the winter battle was not all due to Hitler's orders restricting the command possibilities for commanders at all levels. There was a shocking underestimation of the strengths of enemy forces as reported by reconnaissance. The commanders at various levels had to bear their own share of blame. As commander of a division, an army corps, or an army, every commander at those levels had to feel responsible for the commitment, and also for the preservation of their troop formations. Thus, they could not expose them to almost certain destruction, and the inescapable loss of terrain, along with the capture of large elements of formations. The commanders had opted for obedience to orders. In part, they may well have believed that, by carrying out an order, the responsibility was thereby moved on to the person who had issued the order. That, however, corresponds to a pattern of thought that one may ascribe to the very lowest levels of organisation of the troops, but not to commanders of larger military formations.

Generals observed the fate of many commanders who were involved in "resistance" to instructions, and saw what might, under some circumstances, happen to them if they failed to carry out an order. Sufficient awareness of responsibility and personal courage might have been expected of them, to come out in opposition to situations that they, as military professionals, judged to be a result of false evaluation. Their dilemma was particularly difficult when told to carry out orders that, based upon their military expertise, they judged objectively to be counterproductive, and uselessly endangered the troops. Even their oath of loyalty to Hitler could not relieve them of the responsibility implicit in their positions of command.

The troops continued to do their duty without limitation. It also appeared astounding that the logistical organisation still functioned at that time, in such minute detail, especially the railway traffic for movement of troops and their supplies. If there was a shortage of fuel, that was no fault of the logistic organisation. It was the result of air attacks on the synthetic petroleum plants, by which means the Western air forces seriously reduced fuel production.

After a great gap had been torn in the front in the East, moving new formations into position to build a new line of defence presented great difficulties. Entire armies of combat strength divisions had already been lost during the war, for the most part because of Hitler's stubborn attitude. That had happened at Stalingrad and in the collapse of *Heeresgruppe Mitte*, in Bessarabia, Budapest and in various other *"Feste Plätze"*. Hitler had promised a great resistive power from the declaration of numerous *"Feste Plätze"*. However, those places were open cities. They would then have had to be adequately supplied with personnel and weapons, and also with rations and ammunition.

The military replacement officers repeatedly gathered up men capable of military service, or those who appeared capable. But due to the shortage of time, they were given only extremely brief training, far less with infantry weapons than with *Panzerfäuste*. The replacements were assembled into infantry battalions, and sent towards the east to replenish formations that were coming to the Oder, or remained behind the Oder. In addition, the available troops themselves were searched through to find drivers, orderly room personnel, or others who were not unconditionally required for the unit's service in combat.

Among the replacement troops, companies were even formed of men with stomach problems or companies with hearing problems, who were, at least, supposed to take over static combat assignments. Despite the best intentions, in view of their brief and wholly inadequate training those "last levées", could provide no significant combat strength. In numerous places Hitler Youth had proved themselves efficient in the use of *Panzerfäuste*, particularly in Silesia. There they hid in gardens and under bushes, and engaged the approaching Soviet armour at short range. No one will ever be able to compile numbers to record the success of those efforts. The Red soldiers had extremely bad things to say about the Hitler Youth and, whenever they got hold of them, shot them out of hand.

Amazing, too, was the amount still being produced by industries in the way of weapons and other logistical goods and being provided to the troops at the front. The supply of rations to the troops, and also the civilian population, continued right up to the last day of the war, regardless of the constant daily and nightly air attacks. Troop movements did, indeed, suffer occasional delays as a result of bombing of the railway lines. But they did get through. So did a portion of the evacuation of East Prussia, at least to the extent that it could take place by sea.

However, in the context of the overall military situation, all the efforts of the homeland appeared inadequate in comparison with the massive superiority of the Western Powers and the Red Army, in personnel and materiel. Nevertheless, the will to defend remained constant to the end. Indeed, a large part of the reason was a result of the bombing attacks of the Western air forces upon open German cities, such as Dresden, with great numbers of casualties. The British bomber commander in chief, Harris, had promised that they would result in the demoralisation of the German troops, but it had the opposite effect, actually strengthening their cohesion and will to defend.

PART D

Final Battles

XIV

Fighting for the Moravian Gate

In the north, and in central Silesia, the Soviets set a priority on advancing to the west towards Dresden, and further on, turning towards Berlin. Meanwhile, in Upper Silesia the emphasis was on breaking through the Moravian Gate. An advance to that location was most important for better transportation, promising the Soviets a further advance into Bohemia. There they could take advantage of the rising unrest among the Czech population. In addition, the Soviet southern forces had entered the *Reichs* territory in the Ostmark, i.e. Austria. When successful, they could turn to the north and thereby advance to meet a German thrust coming through the Moravian Gate. Again, that offered an opportunity to cut off the German forces in Slovakia. Their westward retreat towards Bavaria would be blocked, as would their formations committed at the Moravian Gate.

In mid-March, the Soviets launched an offensive from Cosel towards Leobschütz, bringing them local successes. The German command hurled their decimated, but still mobile combat formations against each advance, in order to halt the Soviets. Despite hard fighting they were unable to break through at Oderberg and Troppau. Therefore the Soviets decided to bypass that blockage, by advancing from Leobschütz to Troppau. There, they struck the flank of the tough German defence around Oderberg that was provided by the 8th, 19th and 16th *Panzer-Divisionen* and 544th *Infanterie-Division*. With that, the defence of the Moravian Gate had again succeeded, despite continuing daily Soviet attacks with a smaller commitment of troops, in one or another sector of the front. They each began with an extravagant artillery preparation, according to Stalin's tactic.

However, the Soviet command planned well ahead. Their plans took shape after they captured Vienna on 14 April. The Soviet Army Group Plijew advanced north past Vienna, forming the 2nd Ukrainian Front. As quickly as possible, German formations had to be brought in from other sectors of the front. First came the *Panzer-Grenadier-Division "Brandenburg"* and *General* von Falkenstein's *Flieger-Division*, and then followed the 401st *Jäger-Division*, which received reinforcement from the 25th *Panzer-Division* by 10 April. The 16th *Panzer-Division* had also been transferred to the Brünn area, but in light of a new Soviet attack on the Moravian Gate, again had to return to their former commitment area.

On 11 April, to provide unified command in the southern sector, the *OKW* placed the northernmost *Armeegruppe* of *Heeresgruppe Süd* the 29th *Armee-Korps,* under the command of *Heeresgruppe Mitte*, of the 1st *Panzer-Armee*. On the 15 April, the same change of command sectors followed for the 57th *Armee-Korps.* In the meantime, during May the Soviets repeatedly attacked the German lines in the Mährisch-Ostrau area. Among other places, there were attacks in the area northeast of Troppau, where the German formations finally had to fall back to the lines of the former Czech fortifications. That line of fortifications had been disarmed in 1938/39, so the Soviets were able to take it by 22 April, and thereby, Troppau. After a fruitless counter-attack in the burning city of Troppau, the 17th *Panzer-Division* prevented a sideways envelopment of the burning city and, in particular, between Troppau and Jägerndorf. On 23 April, the 16th *Panzer-Division* in the meantime, had arrived in that sector and helped with tough resistance in the Tropppau–Wigstadtl area. They were in loose contact with the 1st *Ski-Jäger-Division*, the 4th *Gebirgs-Division* and the *Führerbegleit-Division*.

In the fighting from mid-April, with heavy use of artillery and armour, the Soviets had succeeded in gaining ground against the slowly disintegrating German formations. Until the end of April they were still denied a breakthrough to the Moravian Gate. Finally the Soviets attempted, on a large scale, to achieve it by drawing a ring around the defending German formations. There was no other way that the Soviet's intense thrust, from Jägerndorf to Troppau, and finally towards Hultschin could be explained. It was done in connection with the advance of Soviet forces from Hungary moving north, past Vienna on the east, towards Olmütz and Brünn. Those last movements in particular forced the German command to withdraw formations from the Mährisch-Ostrau sector, otherwise the Soviets would easily have been able to interfere with the supplies going to the fighting formations. At stake was more than just these supplies. There was also the need to hold open the escape route for refugees, travelling either on foot or by rail from Silesia, and also from north and east Moravia.

Indeed there was talk of unrest in the Czech hinterland. There had been isolated instances of partisans firing on German soldiers, as well as on vehicles and locomotives in the Mährisch-Weißkirchen area. But there was no interruption to the flow of supplies. Rail traffic from the Mährisch-Ostrau area, through Bohemia to the *Reich*, flowed satisfactorily, thanks to the strict organisation of the *Reichsbahn*. Refugee trains repeatedly ran from the Troppau, Freiheitsau, and Hultschin area into Saxony. It was the more remarkable since the American advance had not yet stopped the movement of refugees. Hospital trains and refugee trains also ran through Prague to Bavaria.

Extension of the Front to the South

The command was once again faced with the difficult task of extending the German front line to the south. The 49th *Armee-Korps* in western Slovakia had already given up many formations, sending them by rail to Upper Silesia. It had to quickly gain ground to the west, to prevent being cut off by the Soviet forces advancing from the south. The movements of that corps suffered increasingly from emerging partisan activity. Under Soviet command, the partisans carried out bridge demolitions, road blocks, and infantry fire on individual vehicles. Accordingly, all precautions had to be maintained during the movements of the troops in retreat. The German formations that moved from the 24th *Panzer-Korps* to the Olmütz area, were assigned the mission of holding Olmütz open for the passage of formations of the 49th *Armee-Korps*.

Opportunities for the command to call on formations in the Mährisch-Ostrau area steadily worsened. On 16 April, the 371st *Infanterie-Division* was to entrain in Ottmachau to go to the 4th *Panzer-Armee* in the Spremberg area, south of Cottbus. The 20th *Panzer-Division* entrained between 15 and 17 April in the Görlitz area. There was another command change. *General der Infanterie* Hasse replaced *General* Schulz.

New Soviet Breakthrough Attempt

The Soviets mustered a series of divisions to attempt a new breakthrough in the Troppau area, and achieved some success against the hard-fighting 1st *Ski-Jäger-Division*. Therefore the *Kampfgruppe* of the 17th *Panzer-Division*, that was standing in an intercepting position near Klebsch, had to rejoin the fighting. Knocking out 68 Soviet tanks northeast of Troppau, the German formations again repulsed the breakthrough attempt. The Soviets merely gained a foothold in Deutsch-Krawarn. The 16th *Panzer-Division* also fought a hard defence in the area south of Rogau. Groß Gorschütz fell into enemy hands. Southwest of Groß Gorschütz, and at the city exit from Uhilsko, the 16th *Panzer-Division* had a bitter fight against the Soviets that penetrated its positions. South of Rogau it was possible to contain the Soviet penetration in makeshift fashion. For the time being, Rogau itself remained in German hands. Despite the badly battered condition of their personnel, the German formations launched counter-attacks, as in the Klein Gorschütz area. In an extremely difficult combat situation, the 16th *Panzer-Division* pulled out of the combat sector for entrainment to Brünn. The 371st *Infanterie-Division* lost ground south of Behrdorf on 17and 18 April. A place named Haatsch changed hands repeatedly during the night of 20 April. It was known that the Soviets suffered substantial personnel losses in that fighting. In the following days, the battle continued against the remaining German formations, particularly against the determined fighting of the 1st *Ski-Jäger-Division*.

On 25 April, the attack also hit the positions of the 4th *Gebirgs-Division*, starting with a concentrated, sudden barrage that would be hard to surpass. Then followed fire from artillery, heavy infantry weapons, tanks and ground attack aircraft. The artillery regiment with its mountain guns, knocked out 8 T34s on the right wing. The Soviets engaged the 78th *Volkssturm-Division*, and broke through on the right to Mährisch-Ostrau. In fact, they opened a gap in the front that could not be closed, even on the following day.

Retreat of the 49th *Armee-Korps*

After the Soviets penetrated the *Generalgouvernement*, the corps situated on the right wing of *Heeresgruppe Mitte* had to repeatedly give up formations to the left wing, and also extend other sectors to the left. However, some formations of the corps were in circumstances that differed essentially from the formations in action to its left. The terrain was entirely different. Under Russian leadership, it offered many opportunities for partisan groups to attack, to disrupt rear area logistic services, and to ambush field-kitchens *en route* to feed the troops. Slovak locals led the groups through hidden woodland paths, ravines, caves and the like into the hinterland. The Polish resistance did not prove to be hostile to the Germans. They only spoke ill of the Czechs, possibly because of the disagreements about the Teschener Ländchen that bordered eastern Upper Silesia.

The 3rd *Gebirgs-Division* received supplies of weapons, and most importantly personnel, in the context of the *"Gneisenau"* programme. It reached a notable strength of 16,000 men. With the help of *Volkssturm* men, the division built positions with their *Schwerpunkt* near Skotschau, and at the Vistula bridges on the Bielitz–Teschen road, a fortified strongpoint.

The Soviets used assault detachments, in German uniforms of the *"Nationalkomittee Freies Deutschland"*, that made themselves unpleasantly conspicuous. Some of them were even captured. Their activity consisted of ambushing isolated combat outposts. The division commander concerned himself with the factory workers, so that coal production, and synthetic fuel production from coal and iron products, could continue. In April, the width of the front of the 3rd *Gebirgs-Division* was about 50 kilometres. The right wing was at the crest of the Beskides, with defensive flanks in the Jablonka area, near Freistadt. Czech Communists led the Soviets through the subterranean tunnels of the mineshafts, taking them behind the lines of the strongpoints of the division, near Korwin and Mährisch-Ostrau.

However, the German troops had been required to give up vehicles, so that later they lacked the transport to remove substantial dumps of *Teller* mines and artillery ammunition that were in the woods. Therefore on 4 April they had to blow up the dumps.

On 9 April, the Soviet advance from the south towards Brünn, forced the 3rd *Gebirgs-Division* to pull back its positions east of the Vistula. The combat situation of the 97th *Jäger-Division* and the 4th *Gebirgs-Division* made an extension of the width of the battalion sectors unavoidable. On 1 May, came the retreat to the Olsa River. The 3rd *Gebirgs-Division* had to fight its way quickly to the rear, after the Soviets had captured Freideck on 3 May. The Soviet attack came up against a strong *Pak* and defensive blocking position, facing *Gebirgs-Jäger-Regiment* 138, with their artillery mainly directed towards the west. In Freideck, the enemy blocking position meant that the railway tracks were blocked with steaming locomotives, trains filled with refugee columns, and troops wanting to push towards the west. All were waiting on the success of the attack.

At last, the opportunity presented itself for the division to detour south of Freideck along the slopes of the mountains. Accordingly, from 4 to 5 May, the division moved through the Kühlandchen, the source region of the Oder, via Misteck, Freiberg, Neu-Titschein, and later towards Mährisch-Weißkirchen and Olmütz. The Soviets pressed hard in pursuit from the east, forcing *Gebirgs-Jäger-Regimenter* 144 and 138 into heavy defensive fighting, the artillery often firing at will. *Panzerjäger, Sturmgeschütze* and *Pioniere* bore the brunt of the rear-guard fighting. On 5 May, the Soviets launched armoured attacks against Alt-Titschein. After those attacks foundered, they moved their *Schwerpunkt* to the west, to bypass the division.

On 6 May most of Neu-Titschein was lost. In order to gain a lead towards the west, the troops then had to cross the March River, with vehicles overloaded with women and children of the fleeing populace. On 7 May the Soviets were already near Olmütz. Elements of the division were placed under the command of the *Festungskommandant* to carry out a successful attack at the southern edge of the city. Thus the 4th *Gebirgs-Division* was able to pass through Olmütz. At about 01.00 hours the pioneers blew up the bridge. On 8 May the Soviets were back in Olmütz, and were again thrown out by the 10th *Infanterie-Division*. Armoured fighting raged back and forth around Olmütz. At that time the German formations even enjoyed fighter plane protection by Messerschmitts.

On the afternoon of the day of the surrender, the division staff was south of Olmütz at a crossing of large, fully packed railway yards near Brodek, on the east bank of the March. The *Pak* and *Sturmgeschütze* fired through the gaps between the wagons and still knocked out many Soviet tanks. The Soviets attempted, as in many other places, to force their way from the south into the marching column. After destroying combat materiel, in accordance with instructions on the occasion of a capitulation, the formations were made mobile. They were loaded on trucks, horse-drawn vehicles, or on horseback and bicycles, and continued west towards Deutsch-Brodt and Iglau.

After the surrender, Soviet ground-attack planes bombed the columns that they found, mostly stuck in traffic jams. Due to fuel shortages the vehicles finally stopped, so the only remaining movement could be by horse or on foot. Many managed to avoid capture, but the majority did not.

Fighting in the Mährisch-Ostrau–Brünn Salient

During that time the 8th *Panzer-Division*, together with the 16th *Panzer-Division* of the 24th *Panzer-Korps*, was engaged in several days of armoured combat south of Olmütz, and in the area south of Brünn. The 1st *Panzer-Armee* fought the last armoured battle of World War II at the historic site of Austerlitz. (On 2 December 1805, Napoleon I had won the Battle of Austerlitz, conquering the allied Austrian and Russian armies). Then the Soviets pushed on to the west. Therefore the main body of the 8th *Panzer-Division* had to fall back to the area west of Brünn. The 24th *Panzer-Korps* joined with *Panzer-Grenadier-Division "Feldherrnhalle"* and the 8th *Jäger-Division*. Due to the situation in the Mährisch-Ostrau area, the 16th *Panzer-Division* had to move back again to the Troppau sector. The 24th *Panzer-Korps* thus considered that it was no longer in a position to hold the Brünn area, and evacuated the city.

Nor was there any way in which the German troops in the Mährisch-Ostrau area could withstand the Soviet attack for any length of time. The remaining *Kampfgruppen* of the 371st *Infanterie-Division* was forced back to the southeast, via Hultschin to Wrablowetz, 6 kilometres from Mährisch-Ostrau. On 28 April, in the extreme southern angle of *Kreis* Ratibor, Bobrownik was lost. The miners in that area still worked shifts until 14.00 hours, as did their comrades in the Karwin district, east of Mährisch-Ostrau. Until well into April, the Karwin district had continued to mine, and have ready for shipment, about 16,000 tons a day of coal and coke.

In the sector of the *Kampfgruppe* of the 371st *Infanterie-Division*, the Soviets advanced 5 kilometres past the Upper Silesian provincial border. In its retreat from the Oppa River sector, the 4th *Gebirgs-Division* held another improvised position facing Wagstadt, making contact with both neighbours. On 1 May, the *Kampfgruppe* of the 371st *Infanterie Division* fell back across the Oder to Mährisch-Ostrau, and evacuated the city. As usual, its artillery covered the retreat. The last guns of the 371st *Infanterie-Division* pulled out under cover of darkness.

That same day, the 1st *Ski-Jäger-Division*, together with the 16th *Panzer-Division* and the *Führer-Begleit-Division* launched a hasty counter-attack to the north, in the area west of Mährisch-Ostrau. On the following day too, the 1st *Ski-Jäger-*

Division and the 16th *Panzer-Division* launched a joint attack near Brisau, 15 kilometres south of Troppau, the 16th *Panzer-Division* committing its last 6 tanks. The *Kampfgruppe* of the 17th *Panzer-Division* was in action in the Troppau area. On 5 May, they attempted to prevent the Soviet breakthrough to the south, to Olmütz. The *Kampfkommandant* of Olmütz, *General* Hax was given the mission of holding Olmütz until the elements of the 49th *Gebirgs-Korps* of *General* le Suire, which were then in retreat and still far to the east, reached Olmütz. There were, however, not many formations near Olmütz. *Panzer-Grenadier-Division "Brandenburg"* was brought in from Dresden, as was *General* von Falkenstein's *Flieger-Division* that had been intended for infantry service.

The Prague Uprising

After the Prague uprising on 6 May, the supply of troops, looking ahead, no longer seemed secure. The troops received orders from *Großadmiral* Dönitz to rapidly fall back, as far as possible, towards the west, saving the largest possible number of German soldiers. The intention was to spare them from capture by the Soviets. After that, the right wing front of the 17th *Armee* in western Upper Silesia began the move, starting with the evacuation of villages in the Neiße–Ziegenhals area. The 1st *Ski-Jäger-Division* fell back to Freiwaldau. The 40th *Panzer-Korps* received orders, during the night of 7 May, to continue its movement to the Landskron area.

Surrender

At midnight on 9 May, the cease-fire was to take effect. The *Wehrmacht* report for 8 May still reported, "Heavy defensive fighting southeast of Brünn and in the greater Olmütz area. *Generalmajor* Hax had carried out his mission of holding Olmütz until 12.00 hours on 8 May, although all the formations of the 49th *Gebirgs-Korps* had not reached the area by that time.[1]

The Soviets took immediate advantage of the situation to press onward in the Mährisch-Ostrau area, advancing via Sternberg. However, there the 10th *Panzer-Grenadier-Division* put a brake on the Soviet advance. At the same time, the Soviets also advanced from the south towards Iglau. The formations committed around Olmütz received orders from *Generalfeldmarschall* Schörner to abandon all heavy weapons and equipment, and seek safety for themselves with their manpower, to the west bank of the Moldau in the Budweis area. Difficult terrain, and scattered fire from infantry weapons of Czech civilians, complicated the night march. As the formations reached Iglau, early on 9 May, they ran into armoured spearheads of

---

1   Translator's note – *General* Nehring, who had succeeded Heinrici in command of the 1st *Panzer-Armee* , had ordered *Generalmajor* Hax to hold Olmütz until the last elements of *General* le Suire's 49th *Gebirgs-Korps* had passed through. *Generalfeldmarschall* Schörner underlined the importance of his mission with a teletype to Hax reading, "You will answer with your head that Olmütz will be held until 1200 hours on 8 May." *General* Hax fulfilled that requirement when he and his *Ordonnanzoffizier* left the burning city of Olmütz, which was under heavy artillery fire, on a sidecar-motorcycle on 8 May.

the Soviet enveloping force. They were advancing from the south, to intercept the westward marching German formations retreating towards Bavaria.

On 8 May, the 97th *Jäger-Division*, which was still near Prossnitz, southwest of Olmütz, set itself to march to the Deutschbrod–Iglau area, but did not get far. The Soviets intercepted it. The 3rd and 4th *Gebirgs-Divisionen* crossed the March River on 6 May. In echelons ahead to the east, elements of the 49th *Gebirgs-Korps* still fought on. Above all else, they hoped to hold open the route for the retreat of the 3rd and 4th *Gebirgs-Divisionen* to Olmütz. On 7 May, there was only a narrow gap still open. Yet again the 4th *Gebirgs-Division* had to make a front in the Olmütz protective position. The Soviets could not resist the opportunity to thrust into the marching German column.[2]

The 17th *Panzer-Division* fired off the remainder of its artillery ammunition from *Artillerie-Regiment* 40, and that of the heavy infantry weapons, and then blew up carriages and guns. The 1st *Ski-Jäger-Division* reached Landskron on 8 May. There they received orders by radio from the 40th *Panzer-Korps*, to set up a blocking position in the area south of Landskron. The division, however, then issued the order, "Concentrate in Wildenschwert". From there, they had to carry on the march to the west, 45 kilometres east of the line Königgrätz–Pardubitz. There, however, all roads were jammed so it seemed impossible to continue. In addition, the Soviets blocked the westward leading roads.

Even those formations that managed to reach the American area of occupation, such as the 17th *Panzer-Division* and the 4th *Gebirgs-Division,* did not remain in western custody, but were delivered up to the Red Army. They therefore followed the same sorrowful path to the "Gulag", as had the other divisions. Immediately following the capitulation, divisions in part disbanded, in part remained as coherent formations, but all had fallen into the hands of the Red Army.

The Last Great Offensive

On 30 April, the Soviets launched their last offensive to win the Moravian Gate, and also to capture the last part of the Mährisch-Ostrau industrial district. That was after three months of hard fighting for Silesian ground.

For the German command, the next priority was to hold open the route of retreat for the troops, and also for the refugees from that area. They also had to do the same for the supply route for the 17th *Armee* which was still echeloned far to the east in Silesia. Then there was the additional mission, of maintaining the supply route and route of retreat, for the German *Gebirgs-Korps* that was still in the

---

2   Generalleutnant Julius Braun, in his book *Enzian und Edelweiß, Die 4. Gebirgs-Division 1940–45* describes this incident: "The Russian motorized troops could not resist the opportunity this situation offered to thrust into the German column of march. Thus a 7.6 cm gun suddenly appeared over the road embankment. It came to a duel between a German mountain-infantry gun and the Russian. The mountain-infantry gun surprised the Russian gun with the first hit as it was still unlimbering. The Russian gun crew had hardly taken cover when an assault troop of the 3rd [sic.] *Gebirgs-Division* pounced on the gun and put a premature end to the attempt to, yet again, be dangerous. *Gebirgsjäger* on the day of capitulation!"

Beskides. In any case, cutting off the 17th *Armee* and the refugee columns walking with it out of central Silesia, could ensue in combination with the Soviet forces advancing in the Neiße area. By diverting the advance through the Moravian Gate to the north, the German 49th *Gebirgs-Korps* in Slovakia feared an advance through the Moravian Gate to the south. The 17th *Armee* prevented the possible Soviet advance, by pulling its right wing back to Kleinmurau into the prepared combat position of the Altvater-Gebirge. They thereby spared the 1st *Ski-Jäger-Division*, which made it to Mährisch Höhenberg, to prevent the Soviets from breaking into the Glatz basin.

In the meantime, the danger, to the south and from the south, mounted substantially after the Soviets captured Brünn. There were no German formations at all west of Brünn, leaving a yawning gap through which the Soviets could advance to Saxony. The 1st *Panzer-Armee* therefore rapidly moved the 19th *Panzer-Division* by rail to Olmütz and then, by road, onward to the area north of Brünn. Under constant strafing by circling Soviet aircraft, the elements of the 19th *Panzer-Division* entrained in a suburb of Mährisch-Ostrau, loading into the side of the wagons at a hitherto unheard of speed.

Nevertheless, the German line of defence from Mährisch-Ostrau to Brünn was full of gaps. At that point, the remainder of Silesia was still in the hands of German troops. That included portions of *Kreis* Leobschütz and the Hultschine Ländchen, along with parts of the Freudenthal, Jägerndorf and Freiwaldau vicinities. In Lower Silesia it included the *Grafschaft* i.e. county of Glatz, and the mountain foothills, with Reichenbach, Schweidnitz, Hirschberg and Laugan. In the Görlitz area was the part of Silesia lying west of the Lausitzer Neiße.

The fighting cost the Soviets heavy losses, mostly in manpower. Indeed, their losses in both men and armour were many times those of the losses that, sadly, the Germans too, had to mourn. The 1st *Panzer-Armee*, alone, reported knocking out over 1,000 tanks. The greatest losses, however, were among the civilian population. The evacuation orders either arrived too late or failed to arrive at all. So people had to walk on their own, but in any case, were poorly organised. They repeatedly suffered from problems with the terrain, the weather, and always were affected by combat operations. Refugees' vehicles lay on the roads, crushed under the tracks of tanks. Frozen children, women and old people were strewn in the roadside ditches. Civilians were shot in the villages.

XV

Last Days of "Fortress Breslau"

Between the Upper Silesian and Lower Silesian combat sectors *"Festung* Breslau*"* still held out. For the Germans, it was an off-the-cuff creation with respect to troops, weapons and ammunition. The major portion of the troops consisted of elements of the 269th and 70th *Infanterie-Divisionen* and their heavy weapons that had been forced aside into Breslau. In addition there were:

> *Unteroffizier-Schule*[1] Striegau
> *Fahnenjunker-Bataillon*[2] of the Gnesen war school
> *Aufklärungs Ersatz und Ausbildungsabteilung* 8 from Oels
> Six 7.5cm *Sturmgeschütze* of *Sturmgeschütz Brigade* 311
> One *Abteilung* (three batteries) of heavy field howitzers (15cm)
> One battery (two guns) 21cm heavy howitzers with about 50 rounds of ammunition
> Elements of *Pionier Bataillon* 269
> Elements of *Nachrichtenabteilung* 17
> Numerous horse-drawn vehicles of the 17th *Infanterie-Division*

On 12 and 13 February, the elements of the 269th *Infanterie-Division* that had been forced aside into the fortress, still tried to hold up the Soviet forces advancing from the Brieg and Steinau bridgeheads, and prevent them from linking up in the area south of Breslau. The attempt remained just that. South of the *Kampfgruppe*, the Soviets had already closed the ring around Breslau and the formations were cut off from their trains. The breakthrough planned for the night of 13 February failed. It was then a matter of organising the formations for effective defence, in all directions, and of working out an equitable distribution of the available weapons and ammunition. When the depots and railway freight yards were searched, 100 *"Ofenrohre"* with 6,000 rounds of ammunition were found.[3] In the Famo factory, *Panzers* were found that were being upgraded there.

---

1 Non-commissioned officer school.
2 Officer candidate battalion.
3 Translator's note – The term *"Ofenrohr"* usually referred to a German version of the American "Bazooka", but firing a heavier and more effective 88mm projectile weighing 3.25 kg and capable of penetrating 160mm of armor at 60°. However, von Ahlfen and Niehoff, in *So Kämpfte Breslau* (p. 35) refer to those as "100 *Ofenrohre"* (a tube on a carriage for close-quarters anti-tank combat)" and, in the lengthy section on Breslau in Becker, *Niederschlesien 1945,* (p. 125), it is stated that "The *Panzerjägerabteilung Breslau ... second and third companies were equipped with* *"Ofenrohr"*, the close-quarters anti-tank weapon on carriages ...".The reference is, apparently, not to the usual *Ofenrohr* but to the 8.8 cm *Raketenwerfer* 43/8.8cm, usually nicknamed *Püppchen*. Mounted on a simple, two-wheeled single-trail carriage with a protective shield and a simple breech-block with striking mechanism, the weapon had no traversing or elevating wheels on the carriage. The gun had to be held at the required elevation by the spade hand-grip and manually

Initially, the organisational measures, occasioned by the encirclement, appeared to promise a period of only three weeks in which the fortress could hold out. However, the inner city itself gave no impression of a main line of resistance. Even the trolley-buses were still running in the streets. Although there was no shortage of clothing and rations, weapons and ammunition were in short supply. Emergency weapons and ammunition had to be prepared from half-completed articles found in the factories.

Breslau had a large diameter sewage system. Accordingly, it was necessary to prevent the Soviets from using the sewers to make their way into the centre of the city. In addition, the sewage farm north of the Oder was flooded, to be able to reduce the forces on the northern front. The Ohle, which joined the Oder just above the Breslau city limit, had to be damned up by the technical company. That was on Breslau's southeast flank. The Soviets repeatedly attacked from the south, working their way from house to house, finally capturing entire blocks, so that the inhabitants of the city had to fall back to the centre of Breslau.

Given the weakness of the fortress's garrison, all conceivable opportunities for defence had to be utilised. Demolition of flyovers and erection of roadblocks prevented an immediate pursuit by enemy armour. The Soviet forces pressed forward, one house at a time, with massive expenditure of artillery ammunition, and strafing by the Red Air Force. Above all, the numerous rear area *Wehrmacht* members and old *Volkssturm* men, as well as the Hitler Youth, had to be instructed in handling weapons and infantry combat. Ammunition had to be flown in. At first it caused difficulties as the Soviets knew the radio beacon system of the German planes, so that first a counter-apparatus had to be provided. Landings ensued at the Gandau airfield, which were a thorn in the side for the Soviets, and against which they repeatedly advanced. Using mortar fire, the Soviets were also able to repeatedly interfere with landings, making it necessary for *Volkssturm* members to perform pioneer duties in clearing the airfield of wreckage, and levelling shell craters.

Gun barrels were flown in for wrecked tanks found in the workshops. In addition, many of the captured guns lacked sights and firing tables. Those too, eventually came in by air. In the Famo works an armoured railway train was constructed. It was used to go rapidly forward with guns, engage in the fighting, and then vanish just as quickly. Among others, its armament included fixed 8.8 cm *Flak*.

After the enemy captured the Gandau airfield, a landing place had to be made in the inner city. *General* von Ahlfen wanted to build it on the Fritzenwiese and at the stadium east of Scheitniger Park. In addition a 1,300 metre runway was to be built on the Kaiserstraße. It ran from southwest to northeast, requiring the removal

---

traversed on the traversing slide. The projectile was an 8.8 cm hollow-charge rocket that weighed 2.66 kg, similar to that used in the usual *Ofenrohr* but with the addition of a rimmed base fitting over the stabilizing fins. The rimmed base, which served to seal the breach upon firing, resembled a short cartridge case with a percussion firing pin that reached through to strike the percussion cap on the base of the rocket projectile in the centre, thus igniting the rocket motor. The sealed breach confined the rocket gasses in the tube, increasing the range to over 700 metres and eliminating objectionable back-blast. (See Ian Hogg, *The Encyclopedia of Infantry Weapons of World War II* and P. Chamberlain, H. Doyle and T. Gander, *Deutsche Panzerabwehr, 1916-1918 & 1930-1945*.).

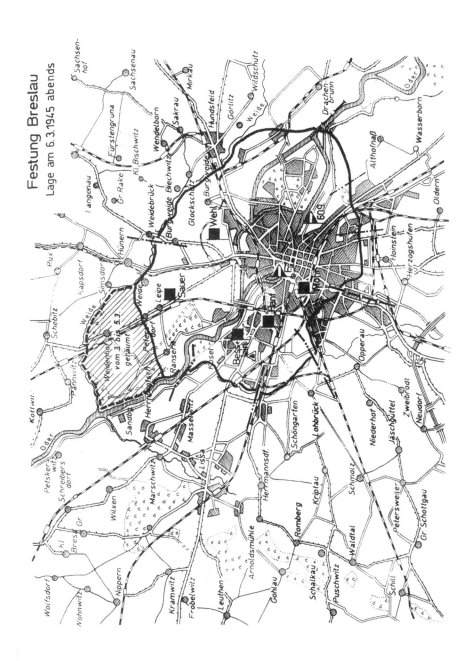

27 "*Festung* Breslau": situation on the evening of 6 March 1945

of pylons, streetlights and trolley-wires. Trees had to be removed from the central promenade, and a large number of houses on both sides had to be levelled.

Living conditions in the fortress steadily deteriorated. The flooding of the Ohle lowlands and the sewage farms, along with blocking the sewage system, provided increased security. A technical company repaired many interruptions of electric and water services that were particularly vital for the hospitals. Pioneers constructed a new "Inner Ring", building specific massive constructions for the battle.

On 5 March, *General* Niehoff flew in to replace *General* von Ahlfen as fortress commander. Construction of new positions also made it necessary to clear German dwellings and use them for other purposes. In the month of February, the forces in Breslau were not involved in a war of movement. The armoured companies of the *Panzerjäger-Abteilung* repeatedly engaged in street-fighting. The *Sturmgeschütze* had to deal with many Russian anti-tank guns. They remained constantly ready for action, day and night, and fired along the streets. However, during that time the most important mission was to build up the available combat forces, and take advantage of the resourcefulness of the troops, particularly in improving positions. Communications trenches were dug through the cellar walls of houses reaching to the foremost positions.

Technicians of all specialisms showed great ingenuity in strengthening the defence, particularly in manufacturing ammunition. About 100,000 empty, light field howitzer shells were found in a warehouse. Fuses for them had to be flown in. The detonating charges came from the numerous Soviet duds. For that, however, it was necessary to figure out how to transfer the charge from those shells to the light field howitzer shells, which required that the material be heated. The explosive charges had to be melted and poured into the empty shells. Several Goliath *Panzers* were found. The Goliath was a small, remote-controlled, tracked vehicle carrying an explosive charge. The few *Sturmgeschütze*, however, achieved the greatest successes in defence against armour.

On 1 April, the Soviets began to soften up the fortress with renewed massive fire. In the course of the next few days' fighting they finally managed to capture the airfield. That dealt a heavy blow to the defence, since that was how ammunition came in, and above all, how wounded were flown out. The living space of the remaining population and the fortress garrison continually shrank. The technicians, however, were able to maintain water and electric services, and even the telephone network within the city. Communications with the outside continued via decimetre wavelengths that the Soviets could not listen to. Inch by inch the Soviets pressed onward, first over the southern railway embankment, then over the embankment of the Posen railway bridge near the Nikolaitor railway station. The steady reduction in forces, and the shortage of ammunition, raised further difficulties in holding the fortress, which when requested received frequent support from German aircraft. As soon as they appeared, the Soviet planes vanished.

On occasion the Soviets used loud speakers. Over the available transmitter, they once sent a message to the civilian population calling upon them to prepare to move, at a specified time, in order to carry out an evacuation to the south from the fortress-ring That broadcast was made as if it originated from an official German source. Fortunately, in good time, people were told of the deception. At the time

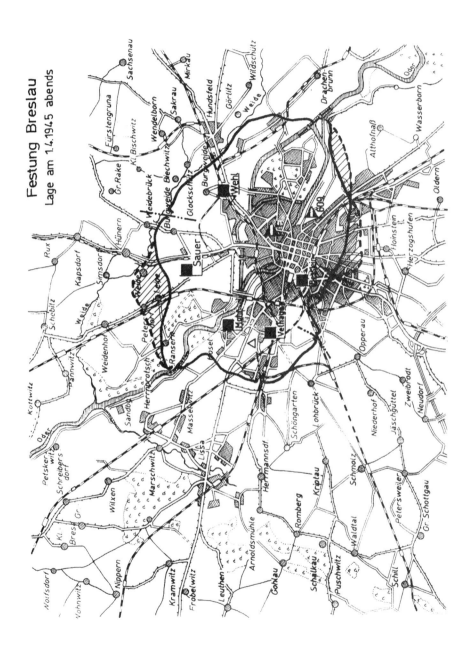

28 "*Festung* Breslau": situation on the evening of 1 April 1945

specified in the Soviet propaganda broadcast, the main street was subjected to a sudden, heavy concentration of artillery

After the April offensive had led to the loss of the Gandau airfield, the shortage of ammunition became more critical for the defenders. In addition, the Soviets initiated repeated loud-speaker propaganda with extravagant promises. However, earlier in the Russian campaign the men had learned that such promises were never fulfilled. In spite of all the difficulties, the lines of the fortress defence continued to hold into the last fortnight of April. The Soviets were unable to split the German forces, or break into the heart of the city. However, the German command had to expect that, with the fall of Berlin, Soviet forces would be withdrawn from there and sent to Breslau. Yet again that increased the inequality in the balance of forces. There could be no more thought of breaking out of the fortress. With their massive superiority in weapons and ammunition the Soviets could wipe out any such attempt in a wave of killing. After thorough consideration of the situation, *General* Niehoff reached the decision to surrender.

On 5 May, *General* Niehoff called the commanders of the individual formations to him and informed them of his decision. The last teletype from *Armeeoberkommando* 17 read: "Germany's banners are dipped in proud but sorrowful respect to the steadfastness of the garrison and the sacrificial courage of the population of Breslau." *General* Niehoff then negotiated with the commander in chief of the Soviet 6th Army of the 1st Ukrainian Front, General Glusdowski. The conditions agreed upon called for the surrender of the manpower, weapons, all combat materiel, transport and technical materiel. All officers and soldiers, who stopped resisting, were guaranteed life, nourishment and the possession of their personal effects. At the end of the war they were to return to their homeland. Officers were permitted to retain their swords or daggers. All wounded and ill were to receive immediate medical treatment from the Red Army. The entire civilian population was guaranteed safety and normal living conditions.

With that, the brave soldiers and long suffering civilian population started the same route of hopelessness as in other sectors of the Eastern Front. Some of the prisoners only returned to their homeland after ten or more years, if they survived that time in the Gulag. Some of the walking wounded survived the Gulags. The other wounded suffered the same fate as in other Silesian cities – they were promptly killed by the soldiers of the Red Army. The last commander of *"Festung* Breslau*"*, *General* Niehoff, remained a prisoner of war for ten and a half years. It is not possible to determine the number of prisoners of war who were killed in captivity.

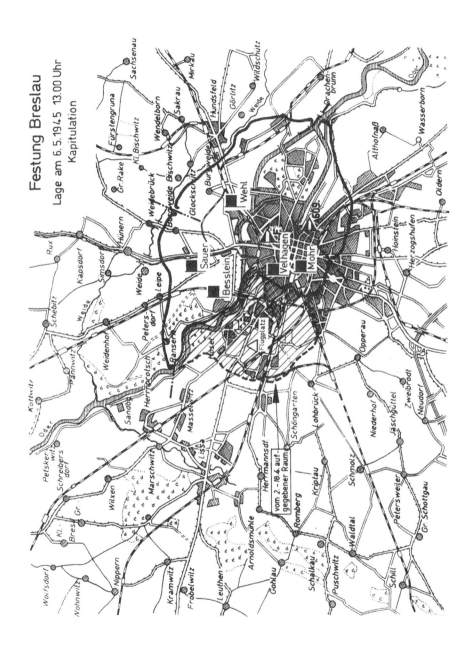

29 "*Festung* Breslau": situation on 6 May 1945, 13.00 hrs (surrender)

XVI

The End in Silesia

A Pause for Breath

A large part of the German forces that were retreating from the Vistula front, through the *Generalgouvernement*, arrived in Glogau on the Oder and there crossed the river. Also among them were elements of *Panzer-Korps "Großdeutschland"* that came from East Prussia and had detrained in the Posen area. They could not carry out their intended mission and were caught up in the retreat. In occasionally daring actions, they marched right across the Soviet routes of advance to make their way to Silesia.

On 22 January, as one of the first divisions to arrive in the Glogau area, the 6th *Volks-Grenadier-Division* as its first assignment, had to attend to security at the Oder and on both sides of Glogau.[1] The *Kampfkommandant* of Glogau initially held the old bridgehead on the north bank of the Oder, directly north of the road bridge, and improved the anti-tank obstacles erected there. Weak advanced security forces were located 12 kilometres northeast of Glogau, on the line Schlichtingsheim–Guhlau–Tschepplau. With the help of the *Feld-Ersatz-Bataillon,* the field replacement battalion of the 6th *Volks-Grenadier-Division,* the broadened bridgehead was built east of the Oder with the objective of securing the Oder crossing for the retreating elements of the 4th *Panzer-Armee.*

In Glogau itself, the division arranged for the reception of remnants of troops, their supply, and the further movement of the wounded. The division additionally reinforced the security and occupation of the Oder sector, between Glogau and Neusalz, and then the bridge positions at Beuthen and Neusalz, on the east bank of the Oder. Attempts to occupy old combat positions at the Oder, that had been fortified and improved during peacetime, ran into difficulties. The necessary organisation in the area was lacking to direct troops to those positions. The 6th *Volks-Grenadier-Division* assembled retreating individual soldiers into combat battalions, and assigned them to coherent formations that were marching through. As ordered, the division additionally concerned itself with organising a defence as rapidly as possible, in the sector assigned to it between Liegnitz and Sprottau. The time remaining, however, scarcely sufficed to establish contact with the approach-

---

1   Translator's note – The reader will remember that two of the three infantry battalions and a large part of the division's artillery had been wiped out in the initial Soviet breakout from the Warka bridgehead. As Großmann describes it, in his *Geschichte der rehinische-westfälischen 6. Infanterie-Division,* p. 258, what is referred to here as the 6th *Volks-Grenadier-Division* consisted of the division staff, a few hundred infantry, 320 artillerymen without guns, a nearly complete communications *Abteilung* without wire or equipment, and the remnants of the other division elements.

ing formations, especially as means of communications were lacking, and the division was almost entirely dependant on the available postal telephone system. Everywhere, the division had anti-tank obstacles erected at the entrances to and within the towns and villages, at locations apparently favoured by the terrain. The lack of friendly forces made it impossible to provide infantry security.

Remnants of divisions moving back from the east, and several other divisions, were initially committed to the defence of the Oder on its east bank. Commitment of others on the west bank, however, did not ensue. The counter-attack did not take place, as later planned, against the Soviet western bridgehead as far as Steinau. Before there could be serious commitment, the formations first had to be appropriately organised. The order in which their vehicles arrived, and thus the branches of the service, proved inadequate with respect to readiness for action. Elements of the formations that crossed the Oder at Glogau were used to hinder the encirclement of Breslau or, as the case might be, for its temporary relief. Other formations were assigned to delay the Soviet advance from Glogau to the west. Up to that point, the Soviets had placed their priority on encirclement of Breslau and also on Berlin, rather than advancing into Saxony. That meant that the weak and still partially disorganised German formations could at least delay the Soviet advance. -

Some of the formations that made the return, ran into replacement troops of other formations from which they were refitted with vehicles and personnel, to restore combat readiness. In any case, despite the loss of several localities, they delayed the Soviet advance to the west. That gave the German splinter groups a chance for organisation, and the reconstitution and arming of the formations.

Soviet Advance into Lower Silesia

On 5 February, the 6th *Volks-Grenadier-Division* received from the *Armee* the mission of intercepting a possible breakthrough of Soviet armoured forces. Across the Oder, in the depths of the army territory, they would act as a command staff in the rear army area, together with the *Volkssturm* formations that had been activated there. Those formations had been sent to face the anti-tank obstacles that had been built everywhere. Along with elements of the division that had arrived in the meantime, it established a line of defence at the Bober River, between Bunzlau and Kittlitzterben. They joined the artillery, without guns, that had been committed as a blocking battalion. It is unclear how this *Kampfgruppe* received the resounding designation of '*Stab Panzertod*'(literally, 'Staff Tank-Death'). In any case, the division concerned itself with organising a suitable defence, as rapidly as possible, in the assigned sector between Liegnitz and Sprottau. However, the remaining time barely sufficed for establishing contact with the *Volkssturm* formations.

After the Soviet crossing over the Oder near Steinau, and the failure of the German counter-attacks, the Soviets pressed on to the west and southwest with strong armoured formations. They bypassed Glogau, cutting off the defenders in the city, who later broke out with heavy losses. Lüben, Kotzenau and Primkenau fell into enemy hands, as the Soviets continued to advance to the south and southwest. The division received two newly formed *Panzerjagdverbände*. They lacked infantry training, but were well equipped with *Panzerfäuste*, submachine-guns and assault rifles, but had no *Jagdpanzer*. Anti-tank weapons, other than the

Panzerfäuste, were not available. Nevertheless, a series of Soviet tanks were knocked out. However, without long range anti-tank weapons and artillery a lasting line of defence could not be formed.

With the help of *Luftwaffe* ground personnel who lacked prior infantry training, and additional arriving *Volkssturm* squads it was, time and again, a matter of preparing new obstacles. A great ammunition dump was blown up near Linden. The Soviets halted briefly at the forest exits on both sides of Lichtenwaldau. That gave several defence groups a chance to establish more favourable positions south of the Kleine-Bober River. They were on the hills directly west of Thomaswaldau and just south of Ober- and Nieder-Schönfeld. Above all, it allowed an opportunity for the population of Bunzlau to evacuate. There was a Latvian *SS-Division* at the Neuhammer troop-training ground that served to reinforce the Bober line of defence.

Building a Defence

The division received welcome reinforcement with the arrival of *Jagdpanzer-Abteilung* 1183. It had been brought into action on a training ground in Bohemia, along with one *Jagdpanzer-"Hetzer"* company and several *Schützenpanzerwagen,* or *SPW,* that detrained in Bunzlau. There was also a battalion of the division that had earlier been detached, but was then re-attached.

The division learned only later of the presence between Bunzlau and Groß Kauschen of a battery of light field howitzers. It had been formed from an artillery replacement *Abteilung,* after the battery had already pulled out again and vanished. Unfortunately, the battery had neglected to inform the division of its existence. Thus the battery was not present to support the night attack of *Bataillon Erpenbach* on Thomaswaldau. Naturally, the division immediately endeavoured to locate the battery and secure it and its guns for the division. That took over three days. As noted below, those guns for the third time then formed the basis for the reconstitution of the division's artillery.

The night attack apparently took the Soviets by surprise in Thomaswaldau, which was on fire. They suffered substantial losses, including 6 tanks and several trucks. An additional *Jagdpanzer-Abteilung,* with the notable number of 22 *"Hetzer"* detrained in Bunzlau. In the attack they were another asset for the 6th *Volks-Grenadier-Division.* However, within a few hours that *Abteilung* was re-called, and sent elsewhere with rush orders. That forced the division to order its elements standing behind the Kleiner Bober River, to fall back to the city limits, and consolidate the positions there that had been planned for them. However, the police battalion that had been defending the northern edge of the city had vanished. That left the northern edge of the city with extremely inadequate defenders. Possibly, the assumption was that they too were included in the orders withdrawing the *Jagdpanzer-Abteilung.* In turn, that caused the 6th *Volks-Grenadier-Division* to pull its front line back from Bunzlau, after the last evacuation train for the population pulled out at 05.00 hours that morning. The division then fell back across the Bober, and blew up the Bober bridges.

The command relationships proved extraordinarily involved and disorganised, particularly between the army and *Luftwaffe.* Unexpectedly, the division suddenly came upon an entire homeland *Flak* regiment, outfitted with adequate ammunition and guns, but lacking sufficient prime movers for all the guns. It was a regiment that had not, until that point, been incorporated in the defensive fighting. It proved extremely difficult for the division to keep together the troop elements that, as they came across them, they had organised from dispersed troops. Other levels of command repeatedly interfered. The lack of means of communication perhaps prevented the division from learning that, during the fighting, some elements had been forced aside to adjoining formations. Under those circumstances it was not possible for the division to hold the Bober River sector. Indeed, it finally had to fall back to the Queis River line, near and north of Sophienwald, as well as Siegersdorf. There, too, however, enemy forces immediately attacked and forced them back to Altenhain.

In the ensuing days, heavy eventful fighting developed in the Naumburg–Siegersdorf–Sophienwalde area. In an effort to support the inadequate forces in that sparsely occupied sector, the division repeatedly released flood-surges from the reservoir near Marklissa, hoping to raise the low water level of the Queis River. Unfortunately, each time it was effective for only a few hours. Finally, a *Sturm-Bataillon* that had been activated by the *Armee* arrived on both sides of Naumburg. In the same courageous manner, *Bataillon Erpenbach* of the 6th *Volks-Grenadier-Division* was able to repulse repeated advance elements of the Soviet spearheads in Siegersdorf.

Fourteen-year-old Hitler Youth from Siegersdorf, Paritz and Thommendorf reported with the request for action. Clad in makeshift fashion in field-grey, they were sent with the patrols where their exact knowledge of the terrain proved advantageous. The youngsters knocked out several Stalin and T–34 tanks with *Panzerfäuste*. However, the division then sent those young men back to their camp of origin in the rear.

From 13 to 16 February, the division received additional reinforcements that were sent from the 4th *Panzer-Armee*. In addition to the *Sturm-Bataillon* that was committed in Naumburg, and for defence of the Queis River sector between Naumburg and Siegersdorf, a replacement battalion from Konstanz arrive. After a few initial setbacks, the battalion proved so effective that it was taken on as a regular part of the division and employed as *Füsilier-Bataillon* in the division formation. When it finally located the battery, the division received important weapons reinforcement with 6 light field howitzers. As mentioned above, the battery had vanished before the attack on Thomaswaldau. That battery's guns allowed the reconstitution of the division's artillery, the guns being manned by the division's own artillerymen who had been fighting as infantry. The situation then changed with the arrival of the 17th *Panzer-Division*, although it only had a weak complement of armour and relied on trucks that lacked off-road capability to move its guns.

The Queis Line

On 17 February, the 6th *Volks-Grenadier-Division* launched a joint attack with three battalions of infantry, a *"Hetzer"* company and the *Sturmbataillon*, along with the 17th *Panzer-Division*. The attack forced the Soviets out of Siegersdorf, despite the strong support that the enemy had from armour and Stalin Organs. The attack succeeded in forcing the Soviets back to the south edge of Sophienwalde. Unfortunately, it was not possible to evict the Soviets from the factory area north of Sophienwalde. The Soviets also lost heavily, in both men and materiel, in the advance of the 17th *Panzer-Division* to the Sophienwalde–Altenhain railway line. A single battalion knocked out 7 enemy tanks.

In the ensuing fighting, the 6th *Volks-Grenadier-Division* had to limit itself to taking advantage of every opportunity for an attack or counter-attack, immediately thrusting into any opening left by the enemy. The German forces were favoured in that situation by the methodical and slow conduct of the enemy command and troops. Thus the fighting around Lauban continued for the next 14 days. On occasion Russian voices cut into the telephone network, as there was no way of shielding it. Particularly vital was the extraordinarily alert German reconnaissance and their speedy reaction, which enabled them to instantly prepare appropriate defences against identified Soviet *Schwerpunkte*. As reinforcements at that time, the division received one battalion made up entirely of men with stomach problems, and another of men with ear problems. There was eventful fighting around Hennersdorf, and also around other villages. The Soviets broke through the 4th *Kompanie* of *Flak-Sturm-Regiment* 1. The enemy armour vanished to the north. Then, however, the armoured unit ran into another *Panzer-Division* with 6 *Tigers* and 10 *Panzer* IV. In the meantime, on 2 March, the 39th *Panzer-Korps* drew up close, to take assembly positions for a top-secret counter-attack on the enemy salient towards Lauban. Simultaneously, other German *Panzer*-divisions of the 57th *Panzer-Korps* were to attack that salient from the east.

Battle for Lauban

The *Heeresgruppe* enjoyed a major advantage in having the availability of a high capacity stretch of railway along the *Riesengebirge*. With that help, all formations could be supplied, and troop movements carried out through Lower Silesia and the Lausitz. The railway ran north of the mountain mass, and south of the fighting-front from Mährisch-Ostrau, via Neiße, Kamenz, Glatz, Hirschberg and Lauban, to Görlitz. In addition, another line ran from Kamenz via Königszelt to Waldenburg–Dittersbach.

In mid-February, when the Soviets captured Lauban, they cut the vital supply link between Görlitz and Greiffenberg. All that remained for supply purposes were the lower capacity lines of the Bohemian railway network. Therefore it was vital for the German command to recapture Lauban and restore the rail connection as rapidly as possible. An advance on Lauban would also prevent or delay Soviet plans for a further advance on the Neiße front, and thus their pursuit of their further main objectives, Görlitz and Dresden.

In 14 days of heavy, eventful fighting, up to 3 March, the 6th *Volks-Grenadier-Division* had conducted a fighting retreat to Lauban. It was achieved by means of flexible withdrawals, approximately on the line of the Queis River east of Lauban, the north part of Lauban, Schreibersdorf-East, and the southern west edge of Hennersdorf. All that happened under pressure of an attack by 3 Soviet tank corps. As a rule, the Soviets opened their attacks with 15–20 tanks, moving out on to the battlefield in a series of successively echeloned groups. That separation offered the opportunity of regrouping an otherwise inadequate anti-tank defence, in time for each of the expected armoured attacks. In the course of the last fighting in the area, between Hennersdor, Wünschendorf and Schreibersdort, over 100 Soviet tanks were knocked out.

On the night of 1 March, the German command launched a counter stroke that had not, apparently, been recognised ahead of time by the Soviet command. East of Lauban was the 57th *Panzer-Korps* with the *Führerbegleit-Division*, and the 8th *Panzer-Division* and the 16th *Panzer-Division*. They had come direct from re-fitting, but had not yet worked together to enable their elements to be synchronised. In addition, there were two infantry divisions. The left attack group, under command of the 39th *Panzer-Korps* and *General* Decker, consisted of the *Führer-Grenadier-Division*, 17th *Panzer-Division*, 6th *Volks-Grenadier-Division* and an additional infantry division.

The surprise attack initially gained ground in both directions of attack. Then, the eastern attack group of 57th *Panzer-Korps* ran into superior enemy forces that launched an unsuccessful attack, in front of and on the right flank of the *Führerbegleit-Division*. On the afternoon of 2 March, the left attack group of 39th *Panzer-Korps* took Ober-Bielau and the northeast and northern edges of the woods, albeit against strengthening enemy resistance. They then had the enemy forces in a "sack", in the so-called "delivery room". However, there was a danger that those forces would escape to the north, if time was lost in an attempt to achieve a "classical envelopment" with forces that were 8 kilometres from the route of retreat. Accordingly, the 39th *Panzer-Korps* immediately turned north in a new direction, towards Logau. On 4 March, the *Führer-Grenadier-Division* attacked eastward over the Queis. There they linked up with the 8th *Panzer-Division* on the Lindenberg hill. With that, a smaller pocket was closed. The *Führer-Grenadier-Division*, however, was tied up in heavy, eventful fighting in the Neuland–Kesseldorf–Gießmannsdorf area against superior enemy forces. They were thus unable to reach their attack objective of Naumburg. The battle for Lauban ended with the capture of the Silberberg hill, southeast of Sächsisch Haugsdorf, against a strong Soviet defence. With that, the rail connection was restored, and the damage caused by the fighting repaired on 9 March. The Soviets lost heavily in vehicles, particularly in armour. On the first day of the attack, the 17th *Panzer-Division* alone knocked out 80 T–34s. The 8th *Panzer-Division* tallied over 150 enemy tanks knocked out. The Soviet 99th Mechanized Corps lost 48 undamaged guns. After the battle, *Infanterie-Regiment* 58 of the 6th *Volks-Grenadier-Division* activated a *Pak* company from the booty consisting of 16 7.65mm guns. The artillery regiment activated 2 batteries of 12cm heavy field howitzers.

The fighting around Striegau was handled by the 208th *Infanterie-Division* alone. It ended with the capture of the city, which the Soviets had turned into a fortress, and the commanding hills to the northwest. In heavy, eventful fighting that lasted until 15 March, it was finally possible to hold the positions, smash the various breakout attempts of the Soviet garrison of Striegau, and to actually liberate Striegau. There were again fearsome sights of the treatment of civilians by the Red soldiers. On 22 March, in the Opperndorf area southeast of the city of Neiße, *Fallschirm-Panzer-Division "Hermann Göring"* received the same insight into the workings of the Red soldiers.

Fighting in the Neiße Area

On 18 March, elements of the 20th *Panzer-Division* were in the Neiße area, where the Soviets had advanced to Groß Giesmannsdorf, 5 kilometres west of the city of Neiße. There, elements of the 20th *Panzer-Division* held on for 3 days, launching hasty counter-attacks that finally forced back the Soviets. The 20th thus gained a defensive front in the line Nowag–Stephansdorf–Bielau.

Three companies of the *Panzer* regiment of the 20th *Panzer-Division*, with 10 armoured vehicles, took up a reverse-slope position, with their front facing the nearby pioneer training area. Most of the vehicles were *Jagdpanzer*. They were front heavy, due to heavy frontal armour, and became bogged down in the soft ground. An attack was launched at 03.00 hours in the early morning of 23 March against Heidersdorf, northwest of Neiße. It ran into a Soviet night attack that had just begun, and did not get through.

In the city of Neiße were *Volkssturm*, several alarm units, the city police and remnants of the 20th *Waffen-Grenadier-Division der SS (estnische Nr. 1)*, from the pocket east of Neiße. Early on 24 March, Soviet troops entered Neiße, whereupon the civilian population was exposed to the orgies of rape. The Red soldiers set fire to the city, destroying about 80% of all its structures.

The 19th *Panzer-Division* had to launch an immediate counter-attack to re-capture Neiße. Not all elements of the division made it back in time from other fighting. The attack failed. The division then launched an attack with *Panzer-Regiment* 27, along with the *SPW* battalion, forcing the Soviets to fall back. Between 22 and 24 March, the success of 6 to 7 kilometres in depth changed the situation near Neiße, at least south of the city. Large numbers of Soviet soldiers fled the city, offering only weak resistance. The German formations immediately pulled out of the front line again, to shift to Ziegenhals as reserves. The 19th *Panzer-Division* then engaged in an intermediate action in the area north of Jägerndorf, and then again at Oderberg.

Pilgersdorf, at the foot of the Sudeten, changed hands several times, finally ending up in Soviet hands. Suddenly, Soviet Il–2 ground attack planes attacked the town that was held by their own troops. Regardless of the ground troops' demands to stop, one plane after another continued the attack.

At that point, at the end of March, the Soviets had less interest in the advance north of the Riesengebirge. Perhaps that was because the German divisions there had behind them the terrain obstacles of the Sudeten, such as Waldenburg in Silesia, Hirschberg in Silesia, and Lauban. The Soviets finally pursued other objectives, using the formations advancing north of Breslau to the west. At the end of March, their actions were restrained in several sectors, probably to redirect troop formations to commitment against Berlin. The capture of Berlin seemed more significant to the Soviets than the westward advance.

Although the fate of Berlin was already looming, in mid-April the Soviets also pushed on over the Lausitzer Neiße and on towards Dresden. That advance, related to the advance from Mährisch-Ostrau in the "Moravian basin", and on towards Moravia, brought risks with it. The danger was that the 17th *Armee*, in its positions at the margin of the Riesengebirge, would be cut off if the Soviets advanced via Mährisch-Schönberg to the Glatz basin. Above all else, that would block the escape route for the retreats from central Silesia. The 17th *Armee,* therefore, pulled its right wing back to Mohrau, and shifted the main line of resistance into the prepared combat position of the Altvatergebirge. The 1st *Ski-Jäger-Division* was thereby released as a reserve. They were given the mission of shifting to Mährisch-Schönberg, to prevent penetration into the Glatz basin. The enemy spearheads advancing in that area were repulsed. More intensely than at the southern edge of the Altvatergebirge, the Soviets pushed onward in an east-west direction, their north wing against Sternberg. The commitment of troops, in the Olmütz area, was thus directly related to the Soviet effort to advance, south of the Riesengebirge, to the west. Thereby, they would simultaneously cut off the formations at the northern edge of the Riesengebirge.

The great frontal salient of the Altvatergebirge, reaching to Olmütz, could be held almost to the day of capitulation. However, with the loss of locally independent formations of the 49th *Gebirgs-Korps* being so great, they could not join the breakthrough to Olmütz. Nor could they get further to the west in time.

Defence at the Neiße

The line of defence at the Lausitzer Neiße held for a long time, approximately from 20 February until the new Soviet advance on 16 April. That offensive led in several parallel lines towards Cottbus, Spremberg, Senfenberg and Kamenz. It went past the existing German line of defence north of Bautzen, towards Riesa on the Elbe, and Torgau. The 20th *Panzer-Division* received no missions as a result of long-term planning in that region. Each time, its commitment was unexpectedly ordered, which placed substantial demands on improvisational ability. In any case, it was no longer able to carry out planned and prepared operations. There was no adequate supply of fuel and ammunition. Nor was there the prospect of any significant amount of renewed logistical support. The elements of the 20th *Panzer-Division* that were tied up in isolated actions, often had to dispense with the possibility of planned co-operation of their different groups. Repeatedly, they tried to delay the spearheads of the Soviet attacks. In the face of the immense Soviet superiority in personnel and materiel, they could attain no lasting success. Individual companies, indeed individual grenadiers, also the members of other specialist units, including pioneers and *Panzer* soldiers used as infantry, organised their positions for defence, and held fast. Again and again their self-reliance must, nevertheless, seem astounding.

XVII

Final Battles in Saxony

Offensive on 16 April

On 16 April the Soviets started their offensive. After preparing for three defensive missions, from 15 to 17 April, the 20th *Panzer-Division* found itself on the move again, but by night. During the day the vehicles had to be camouflaged against enemy observation planes. On 18 and 19 April, elements of the division fought Soviet forces surging into the Odernitz–Niesky–Wilhelminental–Kodersdorf area. Before the start of the German attack on 19 April, shells from a Soviet tank struck amidst a discussion group, instantly killing two of the participating pioneers and wounding several others.

The next day, on the occasion of Hitler's birthday, came orders to mark the main line of resistance with swastika flags. The troops got around that order by indeed, hanging out flags, but making sure that they could not be seen by any Red soldier from his position, let alone by any of their planes.

Soviet Advance on Cottbus

On 21 April the Soviets launched new attacks in the Muskau area. They broke through the German blocking positions and advanced on Spremberg and Cottbus. Warned during the night, elements of the 20th *Panzer-Division* moved out towards Görlitz. Due to the lack of fuel, the elements of the division brought most of their vehicles in tow, especially petrol driven vehicles. On 22 April they arrived at Landskrone, south of Görlitz. At that time the Soviets were on a broad front, stretching via Königshain, Niesky and Altmannsdorf to Bautzen. Görlitz itself proved to be free of the enemy. The artillery fired sudden concentrations on the location of the penetration point north of Görlitz. For that purpose, 10 stationary *Flak* batteries with abundant ammunition were attached to *Panzer-Artillerie-Regiment* 92. They provided the grenadiers with good breathing space. The German counter-attack gained ground and closed off the Soviets at the point of the penetration. However, the civilian population suffered heavy losses as they had not evacuated houses directly in the combat zone, and thus were drawn into the fighting. As soon as they left the cellars of their houses, to flee to the west, both friendly and hostile fire fell on them.

Further north, there were still German defensive forces such as the 24th and 40th *Panzer-Korps*. They crossed the Neiße to the west and south of Guben, and initially covered the area as far as the Spree River, staying until about 22 April. However, the 4th *Panzer-Armee* was responsible for the larger sector between Cottbus and Bautzen. It seemed out of the question to build a line of defence there as forces were lacking. Soviet forces, largely Polish, pushed forward to the west, thanks to good motor vehicles. They were supported by armoured formations. The

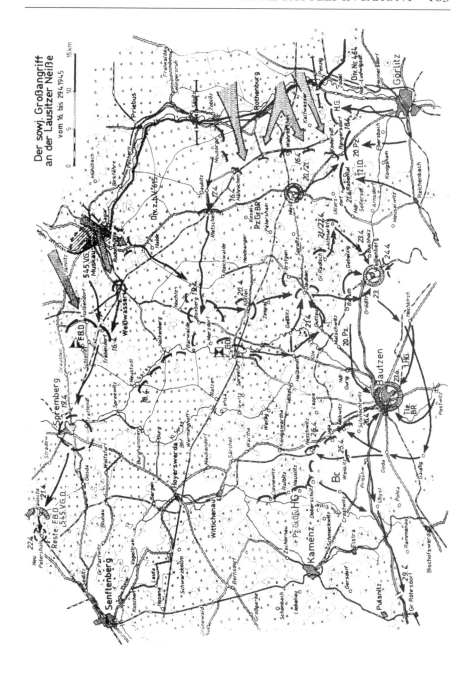

30 Great Soviet attack on the Lausitzer Neiße, 16–29 April 1945

artillery of the 20th *Panzer-Division*, in the Altmannsdorf area, had to fire to the west, while the *Flak* continued to engage the site of the penetration north of Görlitz. The *Panzer-Aufklärungs-Abteilung* of the 20th *Panzer-Division* cleared Königshain and Niesky of enemy forces. They were then bogged down facing the next village. Its occupation required a difficult night march through shattered villages and woods and past the north side of Löbau. The Soviets attacked Altmannsdorf from the north and west. Friendly artillery fire worked over the margins of the woods so that the Soviets fell back. That also limited their Stalin Organ fire to the built up area and the firing positions, until Soviet ground-attack planes joined in at daybreak. The *Panzer-Aufklärungs-Abteilung* of the 20th *Panzer-Division* attacked westward with 25 *Panthers* and broke through, followed by the artillery. The guns aimed direct fire into the enemy marching columns. Apparently that was a new experience for the Poles. They surrendered in droves. The Soviet 5th Tank Army encircled Bautzen, while the *Panzer-Aufklärungs-Abteilung* of the 20th *Panzer-Division* held on east of Bautzen, and the garrison of the city held fast.

Battle for Bautzen

While advancing on the Löbauer Straße, the *Panzer-Brigade* knocked out over 20 T–34s that were approaching from the right at extremely short range. Troops occupying the city had made themselves at home in the empty houses. It was not only the Red Army soldiers. The Poles, too, had raged fearsomely among the populace. Almost all the houses around the Bautzen fortress were ablaze. The place had to be liberated in hand-to-hand combat with drunken Poles. The Poles drove German women in front of them as living shields against bullets.

The German relief force first fought their way to the fortress, whose German garrison still held on. At that point the north part of Bautzen was still in enemy hands. The attack on the fortress was to start at 09.00 hours on 24 April. However, the assembly position was hit by a strong air attack, putting their attack on hold. A Soviet bombing attack followed. At 14.00 hours the motorcycle troops of the 20th *Panzer-Division*, attacking from the north, reached the fortress and established contact with its defenders, liberating over 10,000 soldiers and civilians.

Another *Schwerpunkt* of the battle developed northeast of Hochkirch, southeast of Bautzen. There an entire series of T–34s, in serviceable condition, fell into German hands, along with numerous trucks. An entire *Panzer* company could thus be activated, but there was not enough fuel to take everything with them. For the same reason, the command stopped the progress of a successful attack and pursuit of the beaten Soviets east of Elstra, between Bautzen and Kamenz. There was no fuel. Indeed, the question was where the fuel had come from for the movements of the motorised forces up to that point. Search detachments had been formed, to pump what was left from the tanks of destroyed filling stations.

Action at Dresden

The 20th *Panzer-Division* then received orders to proceed towards Dresden. Berlin had to be considered almost encircled, unable to be relieved from that side. Nevertheless, it seemed possible that the 20th *Panzer-Division* might yet be ordered to relieve Berlin from the south. All sorts of supplies were found in Bautzen, rations and fuel, so the formations could move out towards Dresden.

East of Dresden the columns turned off and went into action south of Großenhain. Adjoining on the left was the 10th *SS-Panzer-Division "Frundsberg"* with the Dresden–Berlin *Autobahn* as its boundary. *Panzer-Grenadier-Regiment* 112 was to occupy a position in the line Königsbrück, Ottendorf, Okrilla and Pulsnitz. The position was in open fields, with no significant roads, among small villages and rolling hills. Then, on 26 April, the report came that the Soviets and Americans had linked up in Torgau on the Elbe. In its own sector, the division expected a Soviet artillery division to arrive from the north, at the positions of the 20th *Panzer-Division.*

Therefore *Panzer-Grenadier-Regiment* 112 dispatched patrols, principally to capture the bunkers in front of the position on the Königsbrück troop training ground. It was presumed to be already in the hands of a Soviet advanced detachment. For that purpose pioneers set up several so-called *"Stukas zu Fuß"* i.e. rockets in wooden launching frames.

The troops learned little regarding the situation. Word had gone round that Berlin was in a hopeless situation. In the meantime, the Soviets attacked on both sides of the Berlin–Dresden *Autobahn*. According to statements by prisoners, those were forces that had already been withdrawn from Berlin. The fact that the 20th *Panzer-Division* held its positions did little good. In light of the scarcity of German defensive forces, the Soviet forces advanced in areas that were nearly free of German troops, so they could avoid attacking the positions of the 20th *Panzer-Division.* In the areas between the defences they found no significant opposition. Nevertheless, on 29 April they strengthened their attacks, in particular using artillery fire on the positions of the 20th *Panzer-Division.* Apparently they used the expected Soviet artillery division's guns of all calibres, from 7.5 cm cannon to heavy 22.9 cm howitzers. They fired with massive expenditure of ammunition and, indeed, in accord with the former German artillery manuals that they had taken over.

Preparation for the End of the Fighting

After Hitler's death *Generalfeldmarschall* Schörner issued new instructions. The Americans should only be opposed where there would be difficulties with the withdrawal movements of the troops towards the south and west. It would be critical to maintain resistance to the east, to the extent that the infantry divisions and refugees could be brought back via Dresden.

In the first days of May, the *Panzers* drove from Ottendorf–Okrilla, 20 kilometres northwest of Dresden, into the area of the 4th *Panzer-Armee* towards the Dresden–Lübben *Autobahn*. They went into action driving northwest near Groß-Dittmannsdorf, Würschnitz and Klein-Naundorf. On 3 May, other elements of the division moved on into Dresden, via the *"Weißer Hirsch"* i.e. White Stag, after they had brought all but one vehicle out of the previous positions.

This close-up view of a German 8.8 cm Flak gun shows a typical late war colour scheme supplemented by branches and twigs being used to break up the gun's silhouette on the skyline.

Fighting in Dresden

The sight of the destruction of Dresden gave rise to the conviction that there could be no hope of pardon with surrender. It became a matter of getting the columns of refugees into the mountains, in the hope that Schörner would keep his promise to make sure that nobody fell into Soviet hands. In the meantime the Soviets stood by, ready to attack with their armour. Swarms of Soviet bombers flew over Dresden towards Czechoslovakia, demonstrating their crushing superiority.

On the *Reichsstraße* to Dippoldiswalde, lines of refugees moved towards Bohemia between elements of a *Waffen-SS* division. As a precaution the batteries prepared new firing positions. The situation did not look good. One artillery *Abteilung* ended up in an enemy held village during its change of position, and remained missing ever after. The new position was near Frauenstein because the city itself was already in Soviet hands.

At that point the Americans were already in Karlsbad. Formations scouted minor roads to Brüx in the Sudetenland, in order to get all the men, vehicles and equipment that could be spared, over the mountains to Brüx and further on towards Karlsbad. The elements on trains were ordered to proceed there. The combat echelons merely formed the essential rearguard.

In the afternoon the Soviets attacked from Frauenstein, but 7 May too, passed with no order to retreat. The division intended to avoid being cut off. The Americans were to the west. The Soviets were coming from the north and east, so the only chance to escape seemed to be to reach the Sudetenland.

Elements of *Panzer-Regiment* 21 were ordered to block the Soviet advance near Neiße in Upper Silesia, and prevent them from crossing the Elbe towards Bohemia and Moravia. It was a mission that it could no longer accomplish. The Soviets proved to be faster. They had fuel, marched on whatever roads they chose, and brutally crushed the refugees fleeing on the roads. The German troops, on the other hand, had practically no fuel, and therefore had to drive in long strings of towed vehicles, and suffered other logistical difficulties. *Waffen-SS* formations and *Fallschirm-Panzer-Division "Hermann Göring"* also moved on the 20th *Panzer-Division's* route of retreat, along with many refugees. The roads finally proved to be hopelessly jammed and blocked.

Part of the armour still made it, via Dippoldiswalde–Bärenburg to Altenberg. Other elements, particularly the trains, went via Heidenau, Pirna and Bad Schandau to Tetschen–Bodenbach, in order to cross the Elbe there. The railway elements entrained on 6 May to travel to Teplitz–Schönau, as well as Luhdorf. There they came under enemy artillery fire.

Dux–Brüx were already in Soviet hands. Trains assembled in a village south of Berlin, and off-loaded superfluous equipment and ammunition. It was planned to move out at 19.00 hours and drive as a unit into American captivity. During a last preliminary discussion, Soviet tanks suddenly appeared, standing in a semicircle on a hill facing the village. The last vehicles could still turn and leave from the other end of the village. Most, however, were unable to get away again. They were immediately captured by the Soviets.

Swinging in a wide arc, the vehicles that had escaped drove towards Saaz, past the airfield and the blazing German aircraft, on towards Karlsbad, which they reached on 9 May. There they ran into long German columns from Bohemia that had the same objective of escaping capture by the Soviets. Bumper to bumper, the vehicles were locked in a stationary traffic jam when suddenly, tanks opened fire on them from a hill to the left. However, it was not Soviet, but American tanks that had received orders to open fire to provide exciting scenes for the American weekly newsreels. Columns followed with American military police who escorted the German vehicles to prisoner assembly points near Falkenau. The next morning they were moved on to the Eger airfield, where about 9,000 soldiers arrived with many vehicles. The first releases began after 10 days. However, the Americans turned over the entire Marienbad and Pilsen camps to the Soviets.

By order of the division commander, the *Panzer-Aufklärungs-Abteilung* of the 20th *Panzer-Division* moved out towards Prague. The German radio station, working around the clock in Prague, then transmitted that it was under siege and appealed for help. The *Panzer-Aufklärungs-Abteilung* did not reach its objective. Early on 8 May, other elements of the division including *Panzer-Artillerie-Regiment* 92, received orders to retreat, without clear instructions. Therefore the *Abteilungen* themselves had to see what progress they could make through forest cuttings, towards Teplitz – Schönau, with Karlsbad as their objective. When they learned of the surrender they turned off towards Aussig, until they too were caught up in a hopeless traffic jam. Some elements attempted to gain ground towards the southwest, moving cross-country over dry terrain. In the early morning of 9 May,

Soviet tanks pushed into Aussig, triggering a wild panic. Some of the vehicles headed towards Bilin on country roads where they were met by Soviet tanks. Elements of the division went into captivity on 13 May. They were loaded on trains for Dresden, and proceeded from there on foot to the Königsbrück POW camp.

XVIII

Conclusion

There then began what front line soldiers had wanted to prevent through their determined self-sacrifice, and costly commitment. They were clear that captivity in the Soviet Union meant heavy loss of life. Right at the start, it was assumed that officers would be shot immediately. All that could be hoped for was that the large numbers of prisoners would cause the Soviets to take a different course in handling them than had previously been seen. Prisoners had to expect double-dealing, deprivation, and a very low standard of living compared with that of most Soviet citizens. Above all, revenge of every sort was expected. It is very easy to be brave against a defenceless prisoner.

All the hopes that had been raised over the previous year and a half, regarding some sort of endurable cease-fire, that would end the constant killing on both sides, were thus left unfulfilled. Any possibility of such an ending foundered on the demands, made by Churchill in particular, for an unconditional surrender of the German armed forces. Prior diplomatic feelers that had been extended, between the Soviet Union and the German *Reich* via Sweden, came to a complete halt in the face of Churchill's position. That was later revealed from the files of the British Admiralty.

Since 1945, soldiers at the front have been blamed for failure to join the resistance sooner. That was a thorny point, regarding resistance directed against their own supreme command to whom they had sworn an oath of loyalty. If the resistance had been able to offer some promises of an acceptable cease-fire, on the side of the hostile powers, particularly the Western Powers, that would certainly have attracted a far greater circle of supporters. In theory, the possibility had even existed of influencing the supreme command, through a contact between the resistance and the Western Powers. Throughout, the German supreme command was informed of negotiations in Lisbon with the brother of the American foreign minister, Dulles.

As there was no spokesperson for the former *"Feldgrau"*, i.e. troops, the outcome of the war initially resulted in putting all the blame on them for all the failed military operations and losses. Indeed, they were even blamed for the concentration camps, and given the guilt of starting the war. In that respect, a soldier had no influence on the political decisions of the chief of state, over the start of a war or the like, neither on the German side, nor among the other powers. The German soldier was no more consulted regarding the declaration of war on Poland, than the British or French soldier regarding the declaration of war on Germany.

From every soldier, in every army involved in the war, independent of political decisions, total obedience was required within the framework of the disciplinary system that governed him. The German soldier cannot be reproached for the fact that, in contrast with the soldiers of the Red Army, he was not forced into whatever combat operations took place, but committed himself fully, out of total motivation to perform his duty. It must not be forgotten that after the First World War the treatment of Germany inspired the soldiers of the German armed forces to a feeling

189

of patriotic duty. Knowledge of the conduct of the war also added to the solidarity of soldiers, such as the reports of Soviet occupation of German territory, for example at Nemmersdorf, in East Prussia, and, later, in more of East Prussia, West Prussia, Silesia, etc. That was also true of the behaviour of the Western Powers who, contrary to the provisions of the Hague Convention on Land Warfare, conducted carpet-bombing attacks against the civilian population, i.e. against non-combatants. The appalling attack on Dresden did not lead to the results Harris desired, but exactly the opposite. Remembering, it is believed, that every soldier said, no matter what happens, "Now I shall remain true to the last stand and sell my life as dearly as possible".

The inner solidarity and commitment to battle were very substantially strengthened by the manner in which, particularly the Soviet Union, but also the Western Powers, conducted war contrary to the fundamental precepts of warfare. That was not only true for the combat troops, but also for the rear area services. It was astounding to discover the efforts made by retired railway personnel to resume rail traffic immediately after every air attack. It was a matter of securing the necessary supplies for the people and for the front-line. Other organisations showed the same readiness for action. The Red Cross, public welfare and others, cared for millions of wounded and refugees. Indeed, care was taken in every part of the land to which they came, whether by ship from East Prussia to Schleswig-Holstein or Pomerania, or on foot to Pomerania or Saxony. There were great movements of population, ever more demanding troop transport right across Germany, as well as the transport required for supply of ammunition and fuel. Despite all that, the traffic in supplies functioned again within a short time of an air attack. The same was true of the canal and coastal sea traffic. The troops in Mährisch-Ostrau received ammunition, made in peace-time, by horse relay traffic from the garrison locations of regiments throughout Germany. Industry worked desperately to repair damage caused by air attack, and to shift parts of their factories underground.

After the war, along with the disagreements regarding problems of the resistance and the *Nationalkomitee "Freies Deutschland"* or the *"Bundes Deutscher Offiziere"* another discussion emerged about who had rendered the greatest service to the German homeland. As far as the *"Feldgrau"* were concerned, the *Nationalkomitee* was eliminated from consideration. They had committed treason against Germany, especially as it had been committed to introduce a dictator who despised mankind to the extreme. Later it attempted to gain recognition as part of the resistance. Those people could not have cared less for the fate of the soldiers formerly entrusted to them, and placed themselves in the service of the Red Army against the interests of the German troops. The matter is very different with regard to the persons of the resistance, who became particularly evident on 20 July, after the assassination attempt against Hitler.

Unfortunately, in today's *Bundeswehr* the resistance is particularly lauded, as if offering resistance was a more valuable performance of duty than fulfilling the missions assigned to troops within the framework of the governmental system of discipline. Such a transformation in the evaluation of performance of duty would not be accepted in any military system. The Red Army was the most rigorous in its punishment of any resistance against the Red system. However, the Western Powers too, instituted disciplinary proceedings against any soldier who failed to carry out the tasks assigned to him. So it was with any front-line soldier, and also every rear area worker in the *Reichs* territory, that they had to meet absolutely the requirements of the *Reichs* government and its organisations. That was the best service for the Fatherland.

The motivation of the members of the resistance must not be impugned in any way. That too appears admirable. However, as already stated, they lacked backing by any agreement on the side of the victorious powers, who left them standing, empty handed. In addition there is the fact that the time of the assassination attempt, namely 20 July, was demonstrably unfortunately chosen, as it was at a time when the Eastern Front had been broken through on a 400-kilometre breadth. In any case, an attempt on Hitler's life, at that point, was seen by the troops as directed against them.

No matter how understandable the motivation of the people of the resistance may be, and no matter how admirable their efforts may appear, one must not fall into the error of judging that the resistance was the better and more valuable performance of duty than the service of the troops. That is something that would not be supported by the troops of any land and would exceed the requirements of a non-political soldier. Decisions, relating to declaring or ending military actions, are political decisions, beyond the sphere of the military.

After 1945, it seems understandable that the reputation of the *"Feldgrau"* would fall at a time when they were no longer needed. That happens after every war, when the previously much admired troops are no longer needed. However, the defamation of the *"Feldgrau"* after 1945 exceeds what could have been expected, and took place against the essential background of diverting attention from the war crimes of other powers. It is true however, that people still took a great deal of interest in the fate of the *"Feldgrau"*. One has only to think of the announcement in evening news broadcasts of names of prisoners of war, released by the Soviet Union, and their reception in their home communities, sometimes with the ringing of bells and the like – all forgotten today!

One must hope that the *Bundeswehr* and the troops of later generations, after self-sacrificing service in unwanted military conflicts, will not again be faced with such ingratitude.

Sources

From the time of the Second World War, presentation of events in military history has entailed considerable difficulties from the start. Either the official histories, i.e. division-, corps-, army- histories, have fallen victim to enemy attacks or they are in the hands of one of the victorious powers. The Red Army has not released any records. After a few years those records that were in the West were returned to the *Bundesarchiv* and made available, but with many gaps.

In the so-called "war-crimes" trials only incriminating material mattered, exculpating documents were lacking. Presentation of evidence was extremely one-sided. The defence had no opportunity to get at the missing documents that could have helped prove innocence.

Proceedings against the victorious powers were forbidden. The Red Army prosecuted anyone who brought accusations against them. In the West, history teachers and other people were sometimes arrested. But the primary method was the agreement, with the *Bundesrepublik Deutschland*, that contained the provision that no proceedings would be opened against members of the victorious Western Powers. The result was an extraordinarily one-sided picture of war crimes on the German side, but with no means of bringing out war crimes on their enemy's side.

There was an examination of all military operations, and consideration of them was made under the provisions of the Hague Convention Regarding the Conduct of Land Warfare. They came to the conclusion that millions of people would still be alive today, if the victorious powers of the Second World War had shown only a fraction of the self-discipline that typified German troops. War against non-combatants, as in the bombing of Hamburg, Dresden and other cities, incontrovertibly violated international law, as did the sinking of the three concentration camp ships in the Lübeck harbour.

Indeed, all the measures of expropriation, that were no longer covered by the wartime objectives of the victorious powers, were contrary to international law. Expropriation amounted to pure plundering, such as the breaking up of railways in the Soviet zone, the breaking up of factories in the Soviet and British zones, the destruction of harbour facilities on the North Sea coast, the deforestation of the Harz by the British, and the Schwarzwald by the French. In the same vein, was the limitation of nutrition of the population to a caloric intake ostensibly equal to that in the concentration camps.

Above all, after 1945 it became evident that the German side lacked a "voice". The subjective reporting in a war, that takes place on every side, ended for the Germans with the surrender of their troops. But it did not end on their enemy's side. Therefore the millions of German prisoners of war in the Soviet Union, in the Gulag, were reviled as "Fascists" and "Nazis". The British and Americans divided the prisoners of war into three groups according to teachability, or lack thereof, in the fundamentals of democracy. Thus, a clear loyalty to the Fatherland was considered "Nazi". The writing of history, especially the teaching of history in schools, took on the compulsory tendency of re-education. Any argument was considered an expression of Nazi thinking.

Only slowly, a little at a time, did the effort spread of writing about the events of the Second World War from a neutral standpoint. However, there were difficulties in so doing. As noted above, the war diaries and histories of the formations were, in part, destroyed. Some are inaccessible, or in the hands of the USSR. The literature that has appeared has presented events from an extraordinarily subjective standpoint. That is especially true of Soviet publications. According to them, only Komsomolz members performed acts of valour in the war. In fact, the motivation of the individual soldier, to go into battle to drive an enemy from his own land, served for the extension of a world view. That was shown in Stalin's negotiating technique in getting around the representatives of the Western Powers, and in the later extension of the Soviet sphere of influence over Poland and deep into Germany.

The histories put together by former members of particular formations show understandable gaps regarding historic events, as some of the official records can no longer be found. After the war, it was difficult to determine the personnel losses of individual units, the more so as not all the persons reported as missing, especially on the Eastern Front, made it into captivity. Many were shot when captured, in particular the wounded left behind in hospitals.

However, after this period of time, and the influence of subjective opinions, the endeavour to write objective history will of course return. In fact, in recent decades, publications by soldiers have gained recognition.

Bibliography

Ahlfen, *Der Kampf um Schlesien 1945* (Stuttgart, 1976)

Batow, *Von der Wolga zur Oder* (Deutscher Militärverlag, 1965)

Becker, *Die Flucht Niederschlesiens 1945* (München, 1969)

Bergner, *Schlesische Infanterie* (Bochum, Pöppinghaus, 1980)

Bergner, *Truppen und Garnisonen in Schlesien* (Friedberg/Hessen, Podzun-Pallas, 1987)

Berichte, und Meldungen der slowakischen Truppen im Feldzug gegen die Sowjetunion 1941–42 (Bundesarchiv/Militärarchiv)

Blankenhagen, *Im Zeichen des Schwertes, Erinnerungen an der Weg der 131. Inf. Division,* (Osterode am Harz, 1982)

Bohlinger, *Die deutschen Ostgebiete,* Heft 8, 3.Auflage (Verlag für ganzheitliche Forschung u. Kultur)

Bukowski, W., *Das Ende mit Schrecken – und Schrecken ohne Ende: Die letzten Tage von Gleiwitz im Januar 1945* („Kleines Tippel im Großen")

Buchner, *Ostfront 1944* (Friedberg/Hessen, 1988)

Carell, *Der Rußlandkrieg* (Berlin-Frankfurt/Main-Wien, 1967)

Creveld, Martin van, *Kampfkraft, die Leistungsfähigkeit der deutschen Streitkräfte 1914–1945* (Washington DC, 1980)

Engelmann & Scheibert, *Deutsche Artillerie (1934–1945)* (Limburg/Lahn, 1974)

Frettner-Pico, *Verlassen von des Sieges Göttern* (Wiesbaden, 1969)

Glantz (ed.), *Art of war symposium. From the Vistula to the Oder, Soviet offensive operations October 1944- March 1945* (1986)

Glantz, *Soviet War Experience: Deception Case Study* (Fort Leavenworth, 1988)

Glantz, *Soviet Use of War Experience: The Mobile Group of 5th Tank Army in the Penetration, Stalingrad November 1942* (Fort Leavenworth, 1989)

Glantz, *Soviet Use of War Experience:Tank and Mechanized Corps Exploit the Penetration* (Fort Leavenworth, 1988)

Glantz, *Soviet operational intelligence (Razvedka) in the Vistula-Oder Operation, (January 1945)* (Fort Leavenworth, n.d.)

Gleiss, *Breslauer Apokalypse 1945 Todeskampfund Untergang einer deutschen Stadt,* Band 1–6, Wedel (1987–1990)

Goßmann, *Geschichte der Rheinisch-Westfälischen 6. ID* (Bad Nauheim, 1958)

Grau, K. F., *Schlesisches Inferno – Kriegsverbrechen der Roten Armee beim Einbruch in Schlesien 1945 Eine Dokumentation,* (Informations- u. Dokumentationszentrale West Stuttgart, Seewald, 1966)

Grestschko, *Über die Karpaten* (Berlin, 1972)

Günter, G., *Letzter Lorbeer, Vorgeschichte und Geschichte der Kämpfe in Oberschlesien von Januar bis Mai 1945* (Darmstadt, Blaschke-Verlag; Augsburg, Oberschlesischer Heimatverlag 1974; Veröffentlichung der oberschlesischen Studienhilfe Neubach/Schlesien, 1978; new edition, 1990)

Hartung, *Der Himmel war unter. Untergang der Stadt Breslau* (München, 1957)

Haupt, W., *Die 8. Panzerdivision im 2. Weltkrieg* (Friedberg/Hessen)

Haupt, W., *1945 das Ende im Osten. Chronik vom Kampf in Ost- u. Mitteldeutschland Der Untergang der Divisionen in Ostpreußen, Danzig, Westpreußen, Mecklenburg, Pommern, Schlesien, Sachsen, Berlin, Brandenburg* (Dorheim, 1970)

Hillgruber, A., „Das deutsch-ungarische Verhältnis im letzten Kriegsjahr", *Wehrwissenschaftliche Rundschau* (Frankfurt/Main Nr. 10/1960)

Hillgruber, A., „Der Einbau der verbündeten Armeen in die deutsche Ostfront 1941–1944" *Wehrwissenschaftliche Rundschau* (Frankfurt/Main Nr. 12/1960)

Jüttner, *Lebe beständig, Erinnerungen eines Kommandeurs der vordersten Front* (Bramstedt, 1989)

Kosik, *Historikerstreit und Geschichtsrevision* (Grabert-Verlag, Tübingen)

Klatt, *Die 3. Gebirgsdivision 1939–1945* (Bad Nauheim, 1958)

Klose, „Festung Neisse", *Jahrbuch für die Geschichte Mittel- und Ostdeutschlands* (1981)

Kohl, „Die Geschichte der Festung Graz Kaupot/Schlesien", *Jahrbuch für die Geschichte Mittel-und Ostdeutschlands*, (1973)

Krainjukow, *Vom Dnjepr zur Weichsel*, (Berlin, 1977)

Kunkel, *Der Kampf um Steinau. Schicksal und Einsatz des Schönauer Volkssturms* (Wiesbaden, 1974)

Kurowski, *Fallschirmpanzerkorps "Hermann Göring"* (Osnabrück, 1994)

Kurzfassung, „Der Truppengeschichte 20. ID mot" im *Mitteilungsblatt der Traditionsgemeinschaft 20. Infanterie- und Panzergrenadier-Division „Mookwie!"* (Nr. 53)

Lstschenko, *Von Kampf zu Kampf*, (Berlin, 1976)

Magenheimer, H. *Abwehrschlacht an der Weichsel* (Freiburg i. Breisgau, 1976)

Mehner, *Die deutsche Wehrmacht 1944–1945 Führung und Truppe* (Rinteln, 1990)

Müller Hildebrandt, *Der Zweifrontenkrieg. Das Heer von Beginn des Feldzuges gegen die Sowjetunion bis zum Kriegsende* (Frankfurt/M., 1969)

Müller- Hildebrandt, „Die militärische Zusammenarbeit Deutschlands und seiner Verbündeten während des 2. Weltkriegs" (Manuskript aus den Jahren, 1948–50)

Pilop, *Die Befreiung der Lausitz, militärhistorischer Abriß der Kämpfe im Jahre 1945*, (Bautzen Domovina Verlag, 1986, 2. Auflage)

Ploetz, *Geschichte der Weltkriege* (Freiburg/Würzburg, 1981)

Ploetz, *Geschichte des 2. Weltkrieges* (Würzburg, 1980)

Redelis, *Partisanenkrieg* (Heidelberg, 1958)

Ryan, C., *Der letzte Kampf* (Stuttgart, 1966)

Schmidt, A., *Die 10. Infanteriedivision / 10. Panzergrenadier-division 1933–1945* (1963)

Schramm, P. E., *Die Niederlage 1945* (München, 1962)

Schwarz, W., *Flucht und Vertreibung in Oberschlesien 45–46* (Friedberg, 1965)

Seaton, *Der russisch-deutsche Krieg 1941–45* (Frankfurt/M., 1973)

Shilin, *Die wichtigsten Operationen des großen vaterländischen Krieges 1941–45* (Berlin, 1958)

Spaeter, *Die Geschichte des Panzerkorps "Grossdeutschland"* Bde II & III
    (Bielefield, 1958)
Strassner, *Europaische Freiwilliger,* (Osnabrück, 1977)
Telepuchowsky, *Die sowejetische Greschichte des groben vaterlandischen krieges
    1941–45* (Frankfurt/M.,1961)
Tessin, *Verbande und Truppen der deutschen Wehrmacht und der Waffen-SS im 2.
    Weltkrieg* (Frankfurt/M., 1970–71)
Tieke, *Das Ende zwischen Oder und Elbe – Der Kampf um Berlin 1945* (Stuttgart,
    1981)
Tippelskirch, V., *Geschichte des 2. Weltkrieges* (Bonn, 1954)
Tiso, J., *Die Wahl uber die Slowakei, Verteidigungsrede gehalten am 17. und 18.
    Marz 1947 vor dem "National"-Gericht in Bratislava* (1948)
Venohr, *Aufstand in der Tatra, der Kampf um die Slowakei 1939–44,*
    (Königstein/Ts., 1979)
Werthen, *Geschichte der 16. Panzerdivision* (Bad Nauheim, 1958)
Senger u. Etterlin, F. von, *17.Panzerdivision. Krieg in Europa* (Kapitel
    Kommandeur 17, 1916) (Literatur F. v.Senger)
Weitenhausen, Freiherr von, *Die Besetzung Schlesiens von Januar bis Mai 1945*
Wiedersehenstag der 17. Infanteriedivision (Nurnberg, 1958)

Orders of Battle

Heeresgruppe Nordukraine, 15 July 1944

1st Hungarian Army
Directly under Army command
    2 HAD, 27 HLD, 7 HID, 6 HID (en route), 19 SS PzGrD
VI Hungarian Corps
    19 HRD, 1 HMB, 2 HMB
XI *Armee-Korps*
    25 HID, 101 JD, 18 HRD, 24 HID
VII Hungarian Corps
    16 HID, 68 ID

1st *Panzer-Armee*
Directly under Army command
    20 PzGrD (en route), 14 WGD
LIX *Armee-Korps*
    1 ID, 20 HID, 208 ID
XXIV *Panzer-Korps*
    254 ID (part, remainder en route), 371 ID, 75 ID, 100 JD
XXXXVIII *Panzer-Korps*
    359 ID, 96 ID, 349 ID
III *Panzer-Korps*
    1 PzD, 8 PzD
XIII *Armee-Korps*
    KA C (DG 183, 217, 339), 361 ID, 454 SD

4th *Panzer-Armee*
Directly under Army command
    213 SD, 253 ID, 168 ID (en route)
XXXXVI *Panzer-Korps*
    340 ID, 291 ID, 17 PzD, 16 PzD
XXXXII *Armee-Korps*
    88 ID, 72 ID, 214 ID
LVI *Panzer-Korps*
    1 SJD, 342 ID, 26 ID
VIII *Armee-Korps*
    5 JD, 211 ID, 12 HRD

Heeresgruppe Nordukraine, 16 September 1944
(Elements of 8 PzD refitting)

Armeegruppe Gen.Oberst Heinrici (PzAOK 1)
1st Hungarian Army
Directly under Army command
    154 RD, 2 HMB
VI Hungarian Corps
    1 HMB, 10 HID
III Hungarian Corps
    24 HID, 16 HID
XXXXIX *Gebirgs-Korps*
    100 JD, 13 HID, 101 JD, 6 HID
1st *Panzer-Armee*
XI *Armee-Korps*
    168 ID, 254 ID, 96 ID
XXIV *Panzer-Korps*
    68 ID, 75 ID, Gr.Gen.Lt. Püchler (1 PzD, greater part of 8 PzD), 28 ID,
    357 ID

17th *Armee*
Directly under Army command
    24 PzD (en route)
XI *SS Armee-Korps*
    545 GrD, 78 GrD, 544 GrD
LIX *Armee-Korps*
    359 ID, 371 ID

4th *Panzer-Armee*
XXXXVIII *Panzer-Korps*
    304 ID, 20 PzGrD, 16 PzD, 97 JD
XXXXII *Armee-Korps*
    1 SJD, 17 PzD, 88 ID, 72 ID, 291 ID
LVI *Panzer-Korps*
    342 ID, 253 ID, 214 ID

Heeresgruppe A, 13 October 1944

Armeegruppe Gen.Oberst Heinrici (PzAOK 1)
Directly under *Armeegruppe* command
    1 HMB

1st Hungarian Army
VI Hungarian Corps
    10 HID, 24 HID, 16 HID
V Hungarian Corps
    13 HID
III Hungarian Corps
    6 HID, 2 HMB
1st *Panzer-Armee*
XXXXIX *Gebirgs-Korps*
    101 JD, 100 JD, 168 ID
XI *Armee-Korps*
    254 ID, 97 JD
XXIV *Panzer-Korps*
    68 ID, 45ID, 357 ID, 8 PzD, 1 SJD, 253 ID

17th *Armee*
XI *SS Korps*
    96 ID, 208 ID, 545 VGD, 78 VGD
LIX *Armee-Korps*
    544 VGD, 359 ID, 371 ID

4th *Panzer-Armee*
XXXXVIII *Panzer-Korps*
    304 ID, 20 PzGD, 16 PzD
LVI *Panzer-korps*
    342 ID, 214 ID

Heeresgruppe A, 26 November 1944

Directly under *Heeresgruppe* command
    DStzbV 601, 602, 603 and 608, 8 PzD, XXIV *Panzer-Korps*, 16 PzD, 17 PzD,
    20 PzGD, 19 PzD, 25 PzD

1st Panzer-Armee
Directly under Army command
    154 FAB
XXXXIX *Gebirgs-Korps*
    101 JD, 100 JD. Gr.Gen. Lt. Thielmann (254 ID, 97 JD)
XI *Armee-Korps*
    75 ID, KGr. 168 ID, 1 SJD, 253 ID

17th *Armee*
XI *SS Korps*
    96 ID, 208 ID, 545 VGD, 78 VGD
LIX *Armee-Korps*
    544 VGD, 359 ID, 371 ID

4th *Panzer-Armee*
XXXXVIII *Panzer-Korps*
　　304 ID, 68 ID
XXXXII *Armee-Korps*
　　291 ID, 88 ID, 72 ID, 342 ID
LVI *Panzer-Korps*
　　5 HRD, 214 ID, 17 ID

9th *Armee*
VIII *Armee-Korps*
　　45 VGD, 6 VGD, 251 ID
XXXXVI *Panzer-Korps*
　　337 VGD, 73 ID

Heeresgruppe A, 31 December 1944

Directly under *Heeresgruppe* command
　　DStzbV. 601, 602, 603, 608, 391 SD, 344 ID (en route), XXIV *Panzer-Korps*, 16
　　PzD, 17 PzD, 20 PzGD, KGr. 10 PzGrD, XXXX *Panzer-Korps*, 19 PzD, 25 PzD

Armeegruppe **Heinrici (Pz AOK 1)**
Directly under *Armeegruppe* command
　　154 FAB
1st Hungarian Army
XVII Corps
　　208 ID, KGr. 3 GebD, KGr. 4 GebD
V Hungarian Corps
　　24 HID, 1HMB, 16 HID
1st *Panzer-Armee*
XXXXIX *Gebirgs-Korps*
　　1 SJD,2 HRD, 97 JD, 254 ID, 101 JD
XI *Armee-Korps*
　　100 JD, 75 ID, 5 HRD, 253 ID

17th *Armee*
XI *SS-Korps*
　　320 VGD, 545 VGD, 78 VGD
LIX *Armee-Korps*
　　544 VGD, 359 ID, 371 ID

4th *Panzer-Armee*
XXXXVIII *Panzer-Korps*
　　304 ID, 68 ID, 168 ID
XXXXII *Armee-Korps*
　　291 ID, 88 ID, 72 ID, 342 ID, 70 HPB

9th *Armee*
LVI *Panzer-Korps*
   214 ID, 17 ID
VIII *Armee-Korps*
   45 VGD, 6 VGD, 251 ID
XXXXVI *Panzer-Korps*
   337 VGD, Fest.Kdt., *Warschau*, SB 1, 73 ID

Heeresgruppe A, 21 January 1945

Directly under *Heeresgruppe* command
   DStzbV 601, 602, 603, 391 SD

Armeegruppe **Heinrici (PzAOK 1)**
Directly under *Armeegruppe* command
   154 FAB
XVII *Armee-Korps*
   208 ID, KGr. 3 GebD, KGr. 4 GebD
1st Hungarian Army
V Hungarian Corps
   24 HID, 1 HMB
1st Panzer-Armee
Directly under Army command
   DStzbV 608, KGr. 253 ID, 5 HRD
XXXXIX *Gebirgs-Korps*
   16 HID, 1 SJD, 2 HRD, 254 ID

17th *Armee*
XI *SS-Korps*
   320 VGD, 545 VGD
LIX *Armee-Korps*
   78 VGD, 544 VGD, remnants 304 ID, 344 ID
XI *Armee-Korps*
   359 ID, 371 ID
XXXXVIII *Panzer-Korps*
   75 ID, 10 PzGD (part), remnants 68 ID, 712 ID (en route), 97 JD (en route)

4th *Panzer-Armee*
Directly under Army command
   100 JD (en route)
VIII *Armee-Korps*
   KGr. 168 ID, 408 ID, 269 ID (en route)

9th *Armee*
Gruppe Nehring (XXIV *Panzer-Korps*)
XXXXII *Armee-Korps*, LVII *Panzer-Korps* (individual organisation unknown):
    291 ID, 88 ID, 72 ID, 342 ID, 214 ID, 17 ID, 45 VGD, 6 VGD, 16 PzD, 17
    PzD, 20 PzGD, KGr. 10. PzGD
XXXX *Panzer-Korps*
    Panzer-Korps "GD" (en route), PzGD. "*Brandenburg*" (en route) remnants
    19 PzD, 1Fsch-Pz. "H.G." (en route), remnants 25 PzD

Heeresgruppe Mitte, 19 February 1945

Directly under *Heeresgruppe* command
    DStzbV 601, DStzbV 602, DStzbV 603, DStzbV 615, 391 SD, XXXXII
    Panzer-Korps, LVI *Panzer-Korps*, remnants 17 ID, remnants 88 ID, remnants
    214 ID, remnants 291 ID, Ers.Brig. "GD", 31 SS-Frw. Br. (en route)

1st *Panzer-Armee*
Directly under Army command
    154 FAB, 18 SS PzGrD "H.W."
XXXXIX *Gebirgs-Korps*
    KGr. 545 VGD, 3 GebD, 4 GebD, KGr. 78 VGD, KGr. 320 VGD
LIX *Armee-Korps*
    K.Gr. 359 ID, 544 ID, 253 VGD, KGr. 75 ID, KGr. 68 ID
XI *Armee-Korps*
    KGr. 1 SJD, 97 JD, KGr. 371 ID
Gr. Sieler (Stb. 314)
    KGr. 344 ID, KGr. 168 ID

17th *Armee*:
VIII *Armee-Korps*
    KGr. 20 WGD (estn. Nr.1), 45 VGD, 100 JD
XVII *Armee-Korps*
    254 ID, 20 PzD, KGr. 19 PzD
Fest. Breslau
    DStzbV 609, Fest.Kdt. *Breslau*
XXXXVIII *Panzer-Korps*
    208 ID, KGr. 10 PzGD, KGr. 269 ID
LVII *Panzer-Korps*
    408 ID, 8 PzD, Pz-Brig. 103

4th *Panzer-Armee*
Gr.Gen.Fiedrich
    KGr. 17 PzD, KGr. 6 VGD, 21 PzD
Pz-Kps. "GD" v. Saucken
    20 PzGD, 1 Fsch. "H.G.", PzGrD "*Brandenburg*"
XXIV *Panzer-Korps*
    KGr. 25 PzD, KGr. 16 PzD, KGr. 72 ID, KGr. 342 ID

XXXX *Panzer-Korps*
    DStzbV 608, Div Stb. *Matterstock*, SS-Brig. *Dirlewanger*, Br.zbV 100

Heeresgruppe Mitte, 12 April 1945

Directly under *Heeresgruppe* command
    Fest. Olmütz, DStzbV 601 & 602, Fhr. Begl. Div

1st *Panzer-Armee*
Directly under Army command
    154 FAB, 8 PzD, 75 ID (refitting), 17 PzD
XXIX *Armee-Korps*
    KGr. 153 ID, KGr. 15 ID, KGr. 8 JD, KGr. 76 ID
XXXXIX *Gebirgs-Korps*
    320 VGD, Gr. Obst. Bader, 304 ID, 16 HID, 253 ID, 3 GebD
LIX *Armee-Korps*
    4 GebD, 715 ID, 19 PzD, 16 PzD, 544 VGD
XI *Armee-Korps*
    68 ID, 371 ID, 97 JD, 1 SJD, 158 ID
XXIV *Panzer-Korps*
    10 PzGD, 78 VGD, 344 ID

17th *Armee*
Directly under Army command
    1. Fsch. PzD. "H.G.", remnants 20 WGD (estn. Nr.1), DStzbV 603, remnants 18 SS PzGrD "H.W."
XXXX *Panzer-Korps*
    168 ID, 20 PzD, 45 ID
XVII *Armee-Korps*
    KGr. 31 SS-Frw.Gr.D., KGr. 269 ID, 359 ID
Fest. Breslau (WKrs. VIII):
    DStzbV 609, FestK. Breslau
VII *Armee-Korps*
    208 ID, 100 JD, 17 ID

4th *Panzer-Armee*
LVII *Panzerkorps*
    6 ID, 72 ID
Panzer-Korps "GD"
    PzGrD "Brandenburg", DStzbV 615, KGr. 545 ID, Pz. Vbd. "Bohmen"
Kps.Gr.Gen.d. Art. Moser
    193 ID, 404 ID, 463 ID
V *Armee-Korps*
    342 ID, Kgr. 36 SS WGD (*Dirlewanger*), 214 ID, 275 ID, KGr. 35 SS Pol.Gr.D.

Heeresgruppe Mitte, 30 April 1945

Directly under *Heeresgruppe* command
    600 RID, 2 SS PzD "Das Reich"

1st *Panzer-Armee*
Directly under Army command
    304 ID
XXIV *Panzer-Korps*
    6 PzD, 8 PzD, Pz-Div. "F.H.", 1 ID + KGr. 711 ID, KGr. 182 ID, KGr. 46
    VGD, 10. FJD (en route)
XXIX *Armee-Korps*
    8 JD, 19 PzD, Sp.Vbd. Olmütz, 271 ID
LXXII *Armee-Korps*
    KGr. 76 ID, KGr. 15 ID, Sp.Vbd 601, KGr. 153 ID
XXXXIX *Gebirgs-Korps*
    320 VGD, 253 ID, 16 HID, Gr.Gen. Klatt, 3 GebD, 97 JD
LIX *Armee-Korps*
    715 ID, 544 VGr, 371 ID, 75 ID, 78 VGD, 154 ID
XI *Armee-Korps*
    4 GebD, 10 PzGrD, 16 PzD, 254 ID, 17 PzD, 158 ID

17th *Armee*
Directly under Army command
    18 SS PzGrD "H.W."
XXXX *Panzer-Korps*
    68 ID, 1 SJD, KGr. 168 ID, KGr. 45 ID
XVII *Armee-Korps*
    KGr. 31 SS Frw.Gr.D, 359 ID, 208 ID
Fest. Breslau:
VIII *Armee-Korps*
    100. JD, KGr. 20 WGD (estn. Nr.1)

4th *Panzer-Armee*
Directly under Army command
    KGr. 269 ID
LVII *Panzer-Korps*
    6 VGD, 72 ID, 17 ID
Gr.Kohlsdorfen:
    DStzbV 615, 464 ID, KGr. 546 ID
Panzer-Korps "GD"
    1. Fsch. PzD. "H.G.", PzGrD *"Brandenburg"*, 20 PzD
and
Kps. Gr. Gen. D. Art. Moser:
    193 ID, 404 ID
Fsch. Pz.Kps. "H.G."

2 Fsch. PzGrD. "H.G.", KGr. *"Frundsberg"* (remnants 10 SS PzD *"Frundsberg"* & remnants Fhr. Begl. Div.)
LXXXX *Armee-Korps*
464 ID, 469 ID, 404 ID, K.Kdt. Chemnitz
V *Armee-Korps*
K.Kdt. *Dresden*

Key (all formations German unless noted otherwise):

Br.zbV	*Brigade z.b.V.*
DG	*Division-Gruppe*
DStzbV	*Division Stab z.b.V.*
Ers.Br.	*Ersatz-Brigade*
estn.	*Estnische*
FAB	*Feldausbildung-Division*
Fest.	*Festungs*
Fest.Kdt.	*Festungs-Kommandantur*
FJD	*Fallschirmjäger-Division*
Fsch.	*Fallschirm*
GebD	*Gebirgs-Division*
Gr	*Gruppe*
GrD	*Grenadier-Division*
HAD	Hungarian Armoured Division
HID	Hungarian Infantry Division
HLD	Hungarian Light Division
HMB	Hungarian Mountain Brigade
HPB	*Heeres-Pionier-Brigade*
HRD	Hungarian Reserve Division
ID	*Infanterie-Division*
JD	*Jäger Division*
KA	*Korps-Abteilung*
KGr.	*Kampfgruppe*
Kps.Gr.	*Korps-Gruppe*
Pol.Gr.D.	*Polizei-Grenadier-Division*
Pz-Brig.	*Panzer-Brigade*
PzD	*Panzer-Division*
PzGrD	*Panzer-Grenadier-Division*
RID	White Russian Infantry Division
RD	*Reserve-Division*
SB	*Sperr-Brigade*
SD	*Sicherungs-Division*
SJD	*Ski-Jäger-Division*
Sp.Vbd.	*Sperr-Verband*
SS-Brig.	*SS Brigade*
SS-Frw.Br.	*SS Freiwilligen-Brigade*
Vbd.	*Verband*
VGD	*Volksgrenadier-Division*
WGD	*Waffen-Grenadier-Division der SS*
WKrs.	*Wehrkreis*

Afterthoughts

For many readers this presentation may raise a question. What can explain the fact that, being committed by the *Wehrmacht* in defence against the Soviet attacks, *Volkssturm* men stood their ground, and fulfilled their duty right up to the last day's capitulation. It is true that in the last days, after hard years of war, no front-line soldier intended to endanger himself too much, right at the end. Regardless of that, however, he did what he was ordered. He made the attacks deemed necessary, with proven spirit, to the day of surrender. Within the *Wehrmacht*, discipline extended so that there were no traces of breakdown of order, loss of discipline, or the like. That is something that members of the next generation often have trouble understanding.

However, it is a result of teaching history in the schools on the basis of "re-education", according to which, German history "only began" in 1933, thereby leaving out an important factor in the motivation of the front-line soldier.

It must not be forgotten that the Second World War represented the continuation of the First World War. If Germany had been treated differently after the First World War, as was done later in the western zones of Germany, after 1948, then the results would have been very different. Millions of Germans came under foreign government. That caused friction. Reparations in goods, demanded by the Treaty of Versailles, and burdensome reparation payments depressed the economy, so that unemployment rose rapidly, as did political discontent. The result was inflation caused essentially by the high reparations and other requirements of the Versailles Treaty. There was the march of the French and Belgians into the Rhineland and its seven-year occupation. In particular, there was enforced shipment to France of great quantities of coal, for which the *Reich* had to pay labour and other costs.

All the German political parties, including the German Communist Party, finally had to include the elimination of the provisions of the Treaty of Versailles in their election manifestos. After 1933, when several stipulations of the treaty had been broken, the German people had the impression that they were defenceless, with an army of only 100,000 men, in the face of the heavily armed Western Powers. As in 1923, they expected that French troops would march in. Thus, universal conscription came about, and specifically, the occupation of the Rhineland.

The fear of occupation by heavily armed neighbours, skilfully utilized by propaganda, motivated the members of the *Wehrmacht* and those who were called up for military service, to dutifully perform their assigned tasks. Thus, in a few years, a hard-hitting force was created. Without the prior feeling of powerlessness in Germany in the face of heavily armed neighbours, it is likely that, among other things, the purely physical marching performance, in great heat, in the western campaign, would have been barely conceivable. All or nothing, everything had to be placed upon a single card.

Certainly, at the start of the war, no one realised how it would be expanded by the declarations of war by Great Britain and France. However, it did give rise to a strong will for solidarity and the will to bring Germany through that situation. There was even less understanding of the later war against the Soviet Union. According to present day reports of research, one can no longer speak of Germany suddenly attacking the ostensibly unsuspecting Soviet Union, because the USSR itself had prepared to attack Germany.

During that war, too, the troops again delivered tremendous achievements, sometimes in snow and ice, achievements that are unimaginable without corresponding inner motivation. That also goes for the later great battles. As the fronts approached the territory of the *Reich*, another motive was added, namely the intention to provide the urgently necessary protection of German territory from the grasp of the Red Army, whose behaviour was already known from various occupied lands. Thus every individual felt an obligation that grew ever stronger, to continue to hold out, the closer the Red Army came to the German border.

So it is that it becomes clear that in the Silesian fighting and also later, despite substantial inferiority in strength, mighty achievements were attained in combat, as the number of tanks knocked out, alone shows. Finally, those actions served to protect German ground, above all, the German civilian population.